Fred Thompson's
SOUTHERN SIDES

250 Dishes That Really Make the Plate

Fred Thompson's
SOUTHERN SIDES

THE UNIVERSITY OF NORTH CAROLINA PRESS   CHAPEL HILL

Text and photographs © 2012 Fred Thompson

All rights reserved. Manufactured in China. Designed by Kimberly Bryant and set in Calluna types by Rebecca Evans. The paper in this book meets the guidelines for permanence and durability of the Committee on Production Guidelines for Book Longevity of the Council on Library Resources. The University of North Carolina Press has been a member of the Green Press Initiative since 2003.

Library of Congress Cataloging-in-Publication Data
Thompson, Fred, 1953–
Fred Thompson's Southern sides: 250 dishes that really make the plate / Fred Thompson.—
1 [edition].
pages cm
Includes index.
ISBN 978-0-8078-3570-8 (cloth: alk. paper) 1. Side dishes (Cooking)—Southern States.
2. Cooking, American—Southern style. I. Title. II. Title: Southern sides.
TX740.T43 2012   641.810975—dc23   2012004104

16 15 14 13 12   5 4 3 2 1

For Kyle Wilkerson

a great chef, friend, & son-in-law

Contents

DRIED & DELICIOUS 195

A Tribute to Dried Beans, the Savior during Hard Times & Good

APPEASING BEANS & PEAS 211

Shell Beans, Green Beans, May Peas, & *Petits Pois*

Acknowledgments

A porch is an important platform of southern life. On a porch, you can visit with family and friends, watch the world go by, rock until your heart is content, or just be plain lazy.

A porch is also a good place to plot the future, and that's what David Perry, editor in chief at the University of North Carolina Press, and I did ten years ago with cigars and bourbon on the front porch of Taylor's Grocery, just outside Oxford, Mississippi. We never really talked about a particular book, just some interesting generalities, but we did become friends. This book started on that porch.

So thanks, David, for believing in me and putting me together with my excellent editor, Elaine Maisner, who gently coaxed the idea of a southern sides book out of me. She has been a great editor, understanding above all else, even when both of us were under a lot of duress. Editors always make you look smarter than you are, and Elaine is a true champ. Thank you.

Kim Bryant is one of the coolest, most creative people I've ever worked with, and I think her design for this book shows it. She was also a pleasure to work with as we did the photography, and I hope you'll find that the photos make you just plain hungry.

UNC Press has a fine, fine team of dedicated professionals, and I cannot commend them enough for their efforts with this book. Gina Mahalek and her staff are top-notch when it comes to publicity. Dino Battista is truly a shrewd marketer. Thanks also to copyeditor Ellen Goldlust-Gingrich, project editor Paula Wald, who always patiently listened to me, and typesetter Rebecca Evans, who also played an integral part in the book's creation.

Many folks have influenced me and in particular this cookbook. One stands out above all others. My son-in-law, Kyle Wilkerson, sous chef at Four Square Restaurant in Durham, North Carolina, and executive chef for *Edible Piedmont* magazine, was my unwavering "coauthor" as we tested, improved, and ate every recipe. His skill, taste buds, and soul are on every page. The real treat for me was spending so much time with this creative and talented young man. Every father would be lucky and proud to have a son-in-law like Kyle. You done good, Laura.

Kyle and Belinda Ellis made up the photo shoot team, and they made my job as photographer easy. Kyle's food styling and Belinda's propping improved the photographs immeasurably. Belinda is also my expert on all things with flour and cornmeal, and I appreciate her valuable input.

Nikki Parrish has been my word-processing guru for eight cookbooks, and her dedication to those projects has taken the "pain" part of my writing on her shoulders so I could be creative. Thanks, Nikki.

Some other influences that you will feel as you read and cook through this book are my mother, Jewell Thompson; Kat Thompson; Anne Haskins; Virginia Bagby; Ben and Karen Barker; Frank Stitt; Sean Brock; Amy Tornquist; my aunt, Janice Thompson; and the legendary Jean Anderson. Thanks also go to award-winning southern writer Jim Villas, who has mentored me over the years. Pam Hoenig was the first to tell me I could write a book and got me through several. When things get crazy, Pableaux Johnson always knows when it's time to call and get me back on track.

I thank John T. Edge and the members of the Southern Foodways Alliance for making me proud to be a southern boy. Kudos go to Toni Allegra for her ongoing support and to Lynn Swann and Don and Joan Fry for their continuing efforts to make food writers better at the Greenbrier Professional Food Writers Symposium.

Without farmers and fishermen, there would be no sides—or food, for that matter. Each day I thank these folks for the sacrifices they make to fill our tables. These people have always been heroes, "rock stars," and are finally getting the respect they have long been due. A special thanks to the farmers who sell through the local farmers markets in Raleigh, Durham, and Carrboro. What you produce is outstanding, and it gives all of my recipes the extra "stuff" that takes them to the next level.

Southern cultural observer John Edgerton asked me many years ago if I was a writer who is southern or a southern writer. So, John, what do you think now?

Fred Thompson's
SOUTHERN SIDES

The Importance of Side Dishes to the American South & to Me

The crunch of a well-fried piece of chicken, the tartness of a pile of vinegar-laden barbecued pork, and the smoke-kissed beauty of a perfectly cooked rib are the images that most folks conjure up when they're asked to describe southern food. All of these dishes have been well documented—and deservedly so—in cookbooks, magazines, and newspaper articles. But what really defines southern cooking, the fabulous juxtaposition of tastes from down-home to urban, is the mouthwatering sides balanced against the fried chicken, barbecue, and ribs. Southern sides and vegetables are the apex of southern cooking. Nowhere else in the country do you find so many restaurants that are more than happy to serve you "a veg plate." In our homes, especially during the summer, a vegetable dinner once or twice a week is the norm. As much as our cooking talent is judged by our ability to fry perfect Sunday chicken dinner, the memories linger because of the collard greens slowly braised in a perfect pot likker until bitter becomes sweet and tough becomes tender. The way we wrap mayonnaise around a variety of ingredients to come up with delectable potato salad, still slightly warm, is heaven on the tongue. A simple grain, rice, transposes itself into regional variations that remove it from a bland category. Let's not forget a biscuit made with soft wheat flour, moistened with melted butter, and smeared with homemade preserves. A piece of cornbread, fresh out of a black cast-iron skillet, is dipped in buttermilk or used to soak up the pot likker from the greens. Everywhere you look in the southern culture of this country, you will find supporting players on the plate, and they deserve a spotlight of their own. Ben Barker, the chef at Durham's Magnolia Grill and winner of the James Beard Award, once told me, "Most of the time it's not the protein but what surrounds the protein that gives us our eating pleasure." I couldn't agree more. We need to celebrate those dishes that we hold so dear and that mark our culture and foodways in a unique and endearing way. The underpinning of southern cuisine

1

is the sides we choose to serve. I'm here to celebrate, glorify, and teach you the beauty of these recipes as they have been telegraphed through my life, my cooking experiences, and my joy of eating.

Southern foodways' reliance on vegetables and side dishes is important not only to southern cuisine but also to the southern lifestyle. A throwback to the Civil War and the Great Depression, when finding meat was almost an impossibility, things that could easily be grown became the centerpiece of the southern table. Side dishes reveled in their importance. Surprising to many southerners themselves as well as those from outside the region is the reality that most southern cuisine is a creole of southern cultures. The Native Americans who first inhabited, farmed, and hunted these lands pointed the early European settlers toward crops that could survive in our soils and climate. In the dark days of slavery, the African American influence made itself known as black cooks filled the bellies of white planters. Migrants from Ireland, Scotland, Italy, Lebanon, Germany, and French Canada have all contributed their piece to southern cuisine. This history and heritage continue to this day, with new arrivals from Latin America and Asia adding to the pot. This book not only celebrates and defines side dishes but also tells a tale of family, culture, and ethnicity in my beloved South through one awesome recipe after another. My southern side dishes and vegetables are more than one-dimensional. They illustrate region, style, and heritage. They demonstrate the assimilation of cultures into one mass of my fellow brethren that we call southerners today. This book leads you down a path of eating adventure. Homage must be paid to collard greens, bitter and slowly braised with ham hocks, onions, and spicy peppers until they're sweet and tender, then doused with vinegar and served at a rural farmhouse table. Sweet potato latkes take center stage on a kosher table, a remnant of the Jewish migration during Reconstruction. The Lebanese, sellers of pots and pans in the Mississippi Delta, add their mysterious spices to local produce. Garlic and ginger hold court as the Gullah way of life survives in South Carolina's lowcountry. Florida throws in a Caribbean influence, with tropical vegetables and ways of preparation. Texas gives us New World German nuances.

A southern biscuit still sets the standard and defines a great cook. A simple shell bean may be a pink-eye by name, glorified by award-winning chefs who hold true the southern delicacies yet enhanced by upscale and urban thinking. Through food, the recipes become a road map of both history and southernisms. This is my fun romp through the South. Most of the recipes have a story from family, strangers, like-minded folks, or the smells and tastes in my kitchen. While I firmly believe that there are no longer any original recipes, just riffs and takeoffs on standards or classics, I would be remiss if I didn't confess that I have been influenced by some of the best chefs and home cooks, friends, and relatives in the country, and they in turn have been influenced by me. Much of the credit for the recipes in this book should go to the community of folks who are passionate about food. I hope this book stays in your kitchen and becomes splattered with the seasonings of the South. The vegetable plate will indeed be king, and while most southern "veg" plates wouldn't pass the vegetarian test since pork fat rules as a seasoning ingredient in the preparation of many southern delights, read carefully and you may discover a few tricks to offset the fat while keeping the soul of the dish. So many outsiders make the generalization that southern sides are pork fat served with a bit of vegetable. Nothing could be further from the truth, as what follows will show. Whether you cook from these recipes or merely read them, they will bring you joy and probably some nostalgia no matter what your age.

Remember, though, that these are my sides, and while I've been influenced in some way by multiple regional cuisines and cultures, these are the ones that I put on my plate. If I skipped one of your favorites, please accept my humble apology. While I try to eat logically, locally, and sustainably, canned mushroom soup, Velveeta cheese, and Miracle Whip cannot be ignored when it comes to the great dishes of the South. Just get over it, because I guarantee that what you taste will make you forget such common ingredients. Cooking should be a joy, it certainly can be therapeutic, and the results should be damn tasty. I think you will find that the recipes in this book are all three.

Ingredients, Tools, Techniques, and Such

I wanted to let you know what types of ingredients I like the best and use in many of these recipes. I also think a few tools and techniques are important. All of these things will affect the recipes you are about to use in one way or another.

BUTTER

I use only unsalted butter. Why? Because it allows me to be in charge of seasoning my food. Each salted butter out there has a different salt content. Irish butter, for example, is saltier than Land o' Lakes. Locally produced butter is preferable, but make sure that it's unsalted. Many local dairies only make one variety.

OTHER FATS

While it has been said that all southern food is cooked in bacon fat, that's not really true. In this book, you'll see bacon drippings used frequently. You'll also see me call for canola oil, which I use because of its neutral flavor and high smoke point. When I want to add flavor with oil or cooking fat, I use olive oil, but not extra-virgin. Those are the basics. Now is probably a good time for me to tell you that I've had a heart attack, and I'm on bunches of heart medications. While I have tried in this book to give you very authentic seasoning scenarios, I'll tell you a few of my tricks to cut down on certain mischievous fats. A little bacon grease seems to go a long way. A small amount of bacon grease mixed with canola oil gives pork flavor but cuts down on the fear factor. I many times use canola or olive oil and some unsalted butter to create a flavor that I enjoy. Any recipe in this book can be made by substituting other oils for bacon grease. How you deal with it is between you and your cardiologist. I do use small amounts of bacon drippings and small amounts of butter, and my last test showed a total cholesterol of 104. You can enjoy your food and protect your health at the same time.

OTHER DAIRY PRODUCTS

I firmly believe that it's worth the effort and the expense to use local dairy products. Without question, a local dairy's buttermilks are far superior to the grocery store brand. In my area, I use Maple View Farms products because I can count on their consistency and freshness. Their cream has the most fabulous mouth feel. More than likely, there's a local dairy in your area. I have another reason for using local dairies. They usually use sustainable techniques, sell products that are free of growth hormones, and are good stewards of the land. These people make a difference.

When it comes to cheese, again, I like using local. In North Carolina, I'm blessed with a wide availability of farmstand cheeses. Every goat cheese producer in the area makes one or two superior products. I cannot tell you how thankful I am for Portia and Flo and their dairy, Chapel Hill Creamery. Their dedication to using grass-fed Jersey cows is key to their extraordinary cheeses. When I call for Asiago, mozzarella, or feta, I use Chapel Hill Creamery's cheeses. Grass-fed cheese producers are usually easy to spot. Their mozzarella cheese has a very, very faint green tinge, and that tells you that you have probably found a great artisanal cheese maker. There are fabulous and award-winning cheese makers throughout the South. Georgia has several, as does Tennessee. So never hesitate to use regional cheeses when available in conjunction with your local artisanal cheese makers. They do make a difference in the recipes' final flavor.

That being said, many of the casseroles in this book call for mixed shredded cheese. Many times you can do the shredding yourself with local cheese. But we live in a crazy world, and we all occasionally need to use a convenience product or two. If organic cheese is available, put that in your shopping cart. Also, most prepackaged shredded cheeses have cornstarch added to prevent the shreds from sticking, and it will have an impact on many dishes. While I don't talk about soups in this book, using prepackaged shredded cheese in cheese-based soups can be problematic.

SALT

I use kosher salt except in baking pies and cakes, when I use finely ground salt. Every cooking class I've ever done, I've been asked, "Why kosher salt?" To be honest, it feels good in my hands, and I can see where the grains of salt are going. I feel that I can use less but still have a big flavor impact. And, yes, kosher salt looks great from high above the pan when you're doing that chef thing. But I'm not convinced that the free-falling of kosher salt from a high distance makes it any more useful. Lately, as prices have come down, I'm using more and more gray sea salt. Some evidence seems to show that gray sea salt is better for your all-around health. I also like to use fleur de sel, not as a salting salt but as a garnish. Hawaiian pink salt also adds intrigue as a garnish.

PEPPER

I don't care where the peppercorns you buy come from. The key thing for me with pepper is that you have a pepper mill and you grind the pepper fresh every time. Pepper is more pungent when freshly ground and therefore adds more excitement to a dish's flavor profile. I make no exceptions, and I'm convinced that if you regularly grind your own pepper, you, too, will become a pepper mill freak.

MAYONNAISE

Homemade mayonnaise is obviously the best. During the peak of the summer tomato season, I make a few batches of homemade mayonnaise to slather on those delicious tomato sandwiches that I almost live on from midsummer to early fall. To me, making mayonnaise is not troublesome, but then, I do things like this for a living. I'm also lazy. I have three go-to mayonnaises. One is Duke's—truly the mayonnaise of the South. And while I like the tartness of Duke's, my favorite prepared mayonnaise is a little-known brand called JFG out of Knoxville, Tennessee. JFG's mayonnaise has a lemon note that reminds me of homemade. I also use Hellman's. As I tell my cooking classes, if you are going to make a mayonnaise-based dish—for instance, chicken salad—that your grandmother gave you the recipe for and she specifies Hellman's, you will not get the same result unless you use Hellman's. It's a major piece of the flavor profile in many recipes. It's a little sweeter, and whoever developed that recipe using Hellman's was dependent on that sweetness.

   We also need to talk about Miracle Whip. For most of my childhood years, after my father's heart attack, Miracle Whip was the

only "mayonnaise" I knew. I can remember in my late teens having some mayonnaise-based potato salad that I thought was awful.
Miracle Whip is its own entity. And for those of you who know it,
it's extremely sweet and the love runs deep. However, when you
see Miracle Whip in the ingredient list in this book, don't think
that you can substitute mayonnaise—you can't. Jean's Potato
Salad (page 132) and Rachael Thomas's Deviled Eggs (page 18)
are intensely good, yet they totally fail if made with mayonnaise.
If a recipe calls for Miracle Whip, don't substitute.

FLOUR

All the recipes that involve flour were developed and tested with
soft wheat flour. I use White Lily and Southern Biscuit Flour. Both
have a high percentage of soft wheat flour, which is necessary to
create the ultimate southern biscuit. I keep both all-purpose and
self-rising in my pantry. When it comes to making biscuits, I lean
toward the self-rising, primarily because I'm lazy and I don't have
to put in extra ingredients. Some folks believe that you must start
with all-purpose flour and add baking powder and baking soda.
It's their right to believe that, but I think there's probably only one
in ten thousand biscuit lovers who could tell you the difference.
Regardless of what some magazines and food television shows that
are not based in the South claim, you cannot make a proper biscuit
with hard wheat flour. Wondra Flour, a superfine flour, is also a
pantry staple. Wondra can be a lifesaver if you have lumpy gravy
issues.

CORNMEAL

Cornmeal is a tricky subject because of all the different grinds and
methods for grinding. I grew up in a home with relatives who insisted on water-ground cornmeal. To take it a step further, they
wanted finely ground cornmeal. Their favorite was Cattail brand
from the Atkinson Milling Company in Selma, North Carolina.
I know they liked Cattail first because it was made by the local guy
and second because none of my aunts made cornbread in a cast-
iron skillet, at least not that I remember. Their style of cornbread
is like Family Reunion Cornbread (page 261), and I do think the

fine grind is perfect for that. It also makes exceptionally tender baked cornbread. Somewhere in your community is a mill that either stone- or water-grinds cornmeal. I would encourage you to use these local mills if at all possible. Martha White, Tenda-Bake, and House Autry are larger mills whose products are both great and easy to find in supermarkets. Remember, making cornbread with just cornmeal produces a drier, less tender bread. Many cooks augment straight cornmeal with a little flour to improve the cornbread's texture and tenderness. I have found that most all the mills in the South make a very acceptable cornmeal mix, which is a pre-bagged combination of cornmeal and flour. Most folks that I know prefer cornbread made from one of the mixes. Using a mix prevents you from experimenting with the many different cornmeal grinds, from very fine to extra coarse, that are on the market. Make lots of cornbread until you find the formula that you like best—plus, the experimenting is good eating. Some good starting points are Family Reunion Cornbread (page 261), Fred's Favorite Cornbread (page 264), and Fancy Cornbread or Cornbread for Yankees (page 263).

GRITS

First rule with grits—unless you've got a kid that you have to get awake, clothed, fed, and out the door to school, forget that there's such a thing as instant grits. Even with the kid, they're a bad idea. I keep a wide variety of different types of grits in my pantry. Some days I'm in the mood for white, some days I'm in the mood for yellow. And there are times that I even want an artisanal ground bag of grits like Anson Mills in South Carolina produces. Delta Grind out of Water Valley, Mississippi, just south of Memphis, makes some of the finest grits that I've ever cooked with, as does the Old Mill of Guilford near Greensboro, North Carolina. For the most part, however, I can find happiness, and I think you can, too, by purchasing locally ground grits. Yes, they take longer to cook. Yes, you have to keep an eye on them. But in terms of flavor and the acceptance of other flavors that you might want to incorporate into your grits, locally produced are far superior to national brands. Interestingly, Muddy Dog Coffee Roasting Company in Morrisville, North Carolina, just outside of Raleigh, roasts corn like coffee and then grinds it. The result is an extremely intense corn flavor with a slight woodiness that is very ethereal on the tongue. They do mail order, and you can contact them at (919) 371-2818.

The Main Ingredients

In my perfect world, I would buy all of my vegetables from a farmer at the peak of the season. To extend that season, I would freeze or can for later use. But as we all know, good intentions pave the road to hell. So here's my pecking order for ingredients: farmer first; your own frozen or canned second; and the freezer case at your grocery store third. The only commercially canned products that I tend to use are tomatoes and pork and beans. I wish that I had time to can enough tomatoes every summer to last me until the following tomato season. The problem is that I use a heck of a lot of tomatoes. My experiments over the last couple of years have taught me that freezing tomatoes is not a bad alternative, but they do get a bit waterlogged, and you need to cook the water out of them. In the grand scheme of things, for me anyway, freezing is a better way to extend a vegetable's season than canning. Don't get me wrong—I enjoy the process of canning. Heck, I do ketchup and jams and jellies and pickles. But I do these things for fun, unlike my grandmother, who canned to survive. After two or three years of attempts to can items, my respect has grown a hundredfold for the members of my grandmother's generation and their efforts to preserve food. My kitchen has air-conditioning; my grandmother's didn't. My kitchen has a very precise stovetop; my grandmother's didn't. Every time I can, I do it in honor of the people who brought great food to our tables two generations ago. And I think we all honor them by realizing that some old ways are better than new ones when it comes to food.

What's in My Toolbox

You can probably cook every recipe in this book with what is already in your kitchen. But I have a few specific suggestions. Tongs of different sizes are really useful in the kitchen. I get mine from a restaurant-supply company, where the tongs are normally sturdier and cheaper. Have at least one pair of tongs that you can use on a nonstick surface. I don't mean ice tongs or salad tongs, but metal, chef-worthy utensils.

I'm always preaching the value of fish spatulas, which are long and narrow and slotted with a diagonal tip that is slightly upturned. They come in right-handed and left-handed models. They are absolutely essential when cooking fish, and because of their unique design, you can use them on a whole bunch of other things. It will be the best seventeen dollars you'll spend for the kitchen.

I'm a big fan of wooden spoons. This may sound quirky, but the only thing I'll use to stir grits is a wooden spoon. I can't give you a reason; I'm just telling you what I do.

Slotted spoons are also kitchen essentials. One thing that you may not have considered are tasting spoons. I buy the cheapest ones I can find, usually between fifty cents and a dollar. You should get in the habit of tasting your food while it's cooking. It helps you stay on top of seasoning and doneness.

I call for three different sizes of casseroles or baking dishes: 7×11, 9×13, and 11×17 inches. I also like having $1\frac{1}{2}$-quart and $2\frac{1}{2}$-quart round soufflé baking dishes. Every kitchen should have at least one of each size.

If you don't have a cast-iron skillet, call your mother and demand hers. If you can't do that, buy a 10-inch seasoned cast-iron skillet from Lodge Manufacturing. Their heat retention is second to none, and they are great for getting a good, crisp sear on meats and vegetables.

I call for the use of sauté pans throughout the book. A sauté pan is basically a skillet with sides, usually $2\frac{1}{2}$–3 inches high. Many recipes in the book call for adding a lot of ingredients at different times, and sauté pans are perfect for this. They don't have to be expensive, but they should have heavy bottoms. If you can only afford one, get a 12-inch sauté pan.

Mixing bowls—glass or metal? I don't know. Most of mine are metal. They can certainly take more abuse than their glass counterparts. At some point, you might want to buy a dough bowl, which is a superlarge metal mixing bowl. That size comes in real handy when you're making stuffing or puréeing things to can or freeze.

Both a food mill and a potato ricer are inexpensive yet extremely useful. Food mills can do many things a food processor can't do, like remove tomato skins while puréeing tomatoes. If you want the smoothest and creamiest mashed potatoes, running cooked potatoes through a potato ricer will do the trick.

Parchment paper or Silpats (nonstick baking mats) will make your baking much easier. Nothing sucks worse than biscuits stuck to the baking pan.

One of the most important kitchen utensils is a coffee can for accumulating bacon grease. Okay, maybe that's a little nostalgic, but you'll need a heatproof jar with a lid. I use a widemouthed Mason jar for this purpose. Yes, I know, Granny kept her coffee can up on the stove, but you'll need to keep yours in the refrigerator. Why? Because Granny went through her bacon grease a lot faster than you're going to.

Some of these items may seem like luxuries, but having them will make for a smoother, more efficient, and more fun kitchen experience.

A LITTLE SOMETHING
TO GET THE HOSPITALITY STARTED

There's a reason why folks around the country and around the world talk about southern hospitality. That's because hospitality is a mainstay of the southern mind-set. Hospitality can take many shapes, including just being a gracious and attentive listener, being an impeccable conversationalist, and putting food in someone's mouth shortly after he or she walks through the door. Southern hospitality is never just reserved for a dinner or cocktail party. It's also evident when your neighbor pops over to say hi and how are you getting along, when friends pile a table with food for someone saddened by a loved one's passing, and even when we're practicing the art of tailgating.

Much of this well-known warmth comes from the speed with which we can get something to eat in front of our guests. It can be as simple as always having homemade cookies and a fresh pot of coffee. One of my uncles was generous with his moonshine and always had pickled eggs. For some people, it's a glass of sweet tea or lemonade on a scorching hot summer day. In my house, I try to have things that I can bring together at a moment's notice. I believe in a mixture of classic and new southern cuisine. Some things you just can't do without: deviled eggs, pimento cheese, cheese straws, and pickled shrimp. So when company comes to my house, they will be offered a glass of iced tea or lemonade, some good sipping bourbon on the rocks, or a Jack Daniels with Blenheim

ginger ale. I try to always have a jar of pickled shrimp in the refrigerator. And in the freezer, I'll have some Apple-Walnut Pâté (page 22), some cheese straws ready to be baked, probably a Shrimp Ball (page 25), and an artichoke dip that's quickly baked. While some may call me old-fashioned, I keep a block of cream cheese around as well as local farmer cheese. To go with that, there's always a jar of hot pepper jelly (sometimes homemade, occasionally from Braswell's) or some of Sarah Foster's awesome Seven Pepper Jelly. Add an assortment of crackers, and you have a truly southern hors d'oeuvre.

I also like to throw a few new twists into the mix. Sweet Potato Guacamole (page 13) is a culture clash between a North Carolina bumper crop and the flavors of a Latino table. The result will have your friends demanding the recipe and confused about what's in the mixture. My advice—keep them guessing for a while. Hummus has been a major part of Middle Eastern cuisine for centuries, but did you know that it's also pretty doggone good when you make it with butterbeans? Or how about new-wave kale chips? They're interesting and delicious and show everyone that you are contemporary.

The recipes in this chapter only scratch the surface, but they will delight your company and can be slid on a plate just like a side dish of field peas. Just remember—hospitality is part of the underpinning of our famous generosity, so be very good at it. We're being watched.

Sweet Potato Guacamole

This very southern twist on guacamole came from my son-in-law, Kyle Wilkerson, a chef at Four Square Restaurant in Durham, North Carolina, and my biggest playmate with food. Daughter, you really did right with Kyle. You will be totally surprised how well this guacamole fits with standard Mexican fare. Nibbling on corn chips with some Sweet Potato Guacamole, some regular guacamole, and some salsa is a great way to spend an afternoon with friends, a football game, and a couple of beers. Put this guacamole alongside some fish tacos, and it's oooh so good.

Serves 4–6

1 Using a spoon, scrape the cooked sweet potato from the peel into a medium mixing bowl. Add all the remaining ingredients except salt and lime juice. Mash with the back of a fork and stir together. Season with salt and lime juice. Serve the same day, with blue corn tortilla chips.

1 large cooked sweet potato

1 tomato, peeled and chopped

½ cup chopped onions

1 garlic clove, minced

2 poblano chilis, roasted, peeled, and chopped

Kosher salt

Fresh lime juice

Lighter-Than-Air Cheese Straws

Makes 2 dozen

Many businesses in the South are devoted to selling cheese straws, but none will come close to your homemade ones in taste and visual appeal. (Yes, we do eat with our eyes first.) Easy, easy, easy to make, and they freeze great for emergency drop-ins. Award-winning pastry chef Karen Barker taught me a trick that really makes these straws exceptional: Roll the cheese into the pastry instead of sprinkling the cheese over the top, as many recipes suggest. The result is a very intense, cheesy straw.

1 box frozen puff pastry, preferably Dufour, thawed in the refrigerator overnight

All-purpose flour

1 large egg, beaten

1 teaspoon water

2 cups grated hard cheese (I like a combination of Parmesan, Pecorino, and Asiago)

½ teaspoon cayenne pepper

½ teaspoon dried thyme

1 Remove the puff pastry from the refrigerator and unfold. Flour the counter or a cutting board and a rolling pin. Roll each sheet into a rectangle about 9 × 14 inches.

2 Beat the egg with the water and brush the mixture over both sheets. Sprinkle each piece of dough with about half the cheese and then all the cayenne pepper. Reflour the rolling pin and lightly roll over the dough to push in the cheese. Lightly flour the top of each sheet and flip it over. Brush the dough again with the egg wash and sprinkle with the remaining cheese and then the thyme. Run the rolling pin over the dough to push in the cheese.

3 Square up the dough by trimming the edges with a pizza wheel or knife. Cut the dough in half lengthwise and then crosswise into about 1-inch sticks. Line a couple of baking sheets with parchment paper and sprinkle with a small amount of flour. Hold each stick of dough between your thumb and forefinger. With the thumb and forefinger of your other hand, twist the dough. Place each twisted piece of dough on a baking sheet, leaving at least ½ inch between pieces. Chill in the refrigerator or freezer until very firm. (You can freeze them at this point to bake later.)

4 Preheat your oven to 425 degrees.

5 Bake the cheese straws for 12–14 minutes, then reduce heat to 325 degrees for an additional 15 minutes or until the cheese straws begin to brown. Remove from the oven and allow to cool. The cheese straws are best served within 30 minutes to 1 hour. If you bake them in advance, reheat them in a 425 degree oven for about 5 minutes to get them crispy again.

Cheddar Cheese Straws

Makes about 8 dozen

No self-respecting southern host or hostess would ever be caught without cheese crackers or cheese straws. They are almost as important as biscuits and cornbread. Sure, you can buy them, but homemade cheese straws are infinitely better. I wouldn't think of having a party without them.

1½ cups all-purpose soft wheat flour

¼ teaspoon cayenne pepper

2 cups shredded sharp cheddar cheese

8 tablespoons unsalted butter

Pepper jelly

Cream cheese

1 Preheat your oven to 375 degrees.

2 Combine the flour and cayenne pepper in a bowl.

3 Place the cheese and butter in a food processor and pulse until smooth. Add the flour and pulse until well combined. (You can also do this with an electric hand mixer using softened butter.)

4 If you have a cookie press, fit it with the star attachment and press out the straws. Otherwise, roll the dough ⅛ inch thick. Use a pizza cutter or knife to cut it into 1 × 2-inch strips. Transfer the straws to baking sheets lined with parchment paper. If you've rolled your dough, twist each strip to give it some visual interest.

5 Bake for 8–10 minutes or until lightly browned. Serve immediately, or cool completely and store in an airtight container for up to 3 weeks. Serve with pepper jelly and cream cheese.

Au Courant Kale Chips

The latest craze in culinary snacking is the kale chip. Not one to be out of fashion, I played with several different ways of creating the chips. My first efforts were fried kale chips with the leaves coated like fried green tomatoes. And gosh darn, they were really good. But, you know, kale is one of those "good for us" vegetables, and by frying it, I was negating much of that benefit. So I played around with the idea of baking the chips. It's a fairly simple process, and the results are outstanding. What separates these kale chips from others is the addition of a little vinegar, which I put on braised kale since it helps mellow out the bitterness of dark greens. Make a batch of these and see how fast they get gone.

Serves 2–3

1 bunch regular kale or
  3 bunches Tuscan kale

2 tablespoons extra-virgin
  olive oil

1 tablespoon sherry, white
  balsamic, or apple cider
  vinegar

Sea salt or seasoned salt

1 Preheat your oven to 350 degrees.

2 Remove the tough stems that run through the kale leaves. Tear the leaves so they are all about the same size. Remember, we're making chips, so think about the size of a potato chip. Throw the torn kale into a colander and rinse. Then either toss the leaves in a salad spinner or lay them between two kitchen towels until the kale is perfectly dry.

3 Place the dry kale pieces in a large bowl. Add the olive oil, 1 tablespoon at a time, and toss the chips with your hands until the leaves are evenly coated. Add the vinegar and toss again. Spread the chips evenly on a baking sheet lined with parchment paper.

4 Roast the chips until they are crisp and slightly browned on the edges, usually about 35 minutes (but begin checking at 25 minutes). Remove from the oven and give them a generous pinch of salt. Serve immediately.

Rachael Thomas's Deviled Eggs

Makes 12

You know that these unassuming small packages of taste have come into their own now that restaurants are calling them appetizers and charging an arm and a leg for them. That's not the way deviled eggs should be consumed. They should be on a deviled egg platter, and there should be lots of them.

I used to think that I made some first-rate deviled eggs. That was before my neighbor, Rachael Thomas, shared her recipe. No one else has the audacity to bring deviled eggs to our neighborhood parties—that's Rachael's domain.

6 large hard-boiled eggs, still warm

¼ cup sweet pickle juice, preferably bread-and-butter pickle juice

¼ cup Miracle Whip, not mayonnaise

½ teaspoon prepared yellow mustard

1 While the eggs are still warm, peel and slice them in half lengthwise. Pop the yolks out into a medium bowl and set the whites on a plate. Warm egg yolks will absorb more flavor. Add the pickle juice a little at the time, Miracle Whip, and mustard. Beat with a fork or hand mixer until smooth. You are better off with the filling being a little thick then adding more juice, Miracle Whip, and mustard as necessary. Pipe or spoon the filling into the egg whites and serve immediately, or cover with plastic wrap and refrigerate for up to 4 hours.

PIPING PLEASURE Need to fill those deviled eggs quickly? Or stuff some celery? Or put some frosting trim on a cake? Zip-top plastic bags, especially the sandwich and quart size, make perfect piping solutions. Fill the bag and force the mixture toward one bottom corner. Snip off the corner to the size that you need, and pipe to your heart's content.

Butterbean Hummus

Makes 2 cups

This hummus is always a surprise at cocktail parties or as a predinner finger food. Folks take a while before they're truly convinced that the base of it is butterbeans. It's very simple to make and is nice served with toasted baguette slices. But don't stop there. A dollop atop any whitefish, especially grouper, is a nice addition. And it truly becomes a side with grilled lamb chops. Try it—you'll find ways to use it.

3 garlic cloves

4 sprigs oregano, tied

4 cups homemade or low-sodium chicken broth

4 cups fresh butterbeans

1 tablespoon fresh lemon juice

1 tablespoon chopped basil

Hot pepper sauce

Kosher salt and freshly ground black pepper

1 Bring the garlic, oregano, and chicken broth to a boil in a 3-quart saucepan. Add the butterbeans, reduce heat to medium, and simmer for 35–40 minutes or until tender. Drain the beans, reserving 1 cup of the cooking liquid.

2 Remove the oregano and discard. Pour the beans into a food processor or blender. Add the lemon juice, basil, and a dash of hot sauce plus a little salt and pepper and ½ cup of the bean-cooking liquid. Process on high until smooth. If the hummus is too thick, thin with small additions of the remaining cooking liquid. You want the texture to be spreadable but not juicy. Serve immediately with toasted baguettes or other crackers, or place in an airtight container and refrigerate for up to 2 days.

Sharon's Awesome Artichoke Dip

Many of you know the magic that Allan Benton can work with a country ham. But when it comes to serious good eats, Allan's wife, Sharon, is a true star. This is one of my starter recipes.

Serves 10–12

1 Preheat your oven to 325 degrees.

2 Combine the artichokes, the mayonnaise, the chilis, the Monterey Jack, and ½ cup of the Parmesan in a medium bowl. Stir in a couple of dashes of hot sauce and the cayenne pepper.

3 Spread the mixture in a shallow 1½ quart baking dish. Sprinkle a nice coating of Parmesan cheese evenly over the top. (You can prepare this dish up to this point 1 day ahead. If you do, cover and refrigerate it.)

4 Bake uncovered for 30 minutes, then serve hot with crackers, grilled bread, or raw vegetables.

1 14-ounce can artichoke hearts, drained and chopped

1½ cups mayonnaise

2 4½-ounce cans green chilis, drained and diced

1 cup shredded Monterey Jack cheese

½ cup grated Parmesan cheese, plus more to sprinkle over the top

Hot pepper sauce

⅛ teaspoon cayenne pepper

Crackers

Grilled bread

Raw vegetables

Apple-Walnut Pâté

Serves 15–20

Even if you don't like chicken livers or pâtés, you still owe it to yourself to give this a try. Mine is patterned after a spread sold by a famous gourmet store, and I quite frankly think mine is better. I like to make a batch and divide it among 8-ounce containers, using whatever I need now and freezing some for surprises later on. It thaws nicely on the defrost setting of your microwave. It will keep in the freezer for about 6 months, but I doubt you'll leave it alone that long.

8 tablespoons unsalted butter, divided

3 large shallots, minced

3 garlic cloves, minced

1 cup finely chopped onions

2 apples, peeled, cored, and chopped

1 pound chicken livers

8 ounces hot country sausage

¼ cup apple brandy

1 8-ounce package cream cheese, at room temperature

½ teaspoon kosher salt

1 teaspoon dried tarragon

½ teaspoon dried thyme

¼ teaspoon allspice

1 cup walnut pieces, roughly chopped

Toast points

Crackers

1 Melt 3 tablespoons of the butter in a large sauté pan. When the butter foams, add the shallots, garlic, and onions. Sauté for about 3 minutes, then add the apples and cook until they are soft, usually 4–5 minutes longer. Remove the mixture from the pan.

2 Place the pan back over medium heat and melt the remaining butter. Add the chicken livers and sausage, and cook until thoroughly done, 8–10 minutes.

3 Now, I don't want to get phone calls about kitchen fires, so if you really want to skip the flames, you can. However, this is the way to do it. Remove the pan from heat. Pour in the apple brandy and light the pan. It should burn down relatively quickly. If that's too exciting for you, add the brandy and let it cook off for a few minutes.

4 Combine the onion/apple mixture with the meat mixture, then purée everything in batches in a food processor. Add the cream cheese, salt, and spices and pulse to combine completely. Add the walnuts and pulse. Serve with toast points or crackers.

Fred's Opinion on Pimento Cheese

To include a pimento cheese, one has to be ready for abuse. Everyone has an opinion about pimento cheese. This is one recipe that I use. I'm going to include another one. Between one or the other, you should find a recipe that works for your taste buds. Please don't laugh at the ingredients.

Depending on your upbringing, you should be able to get 4 generous sandwiches or feed 20 people at a cocktail party

1 Put the cheeses in a large mixing bowl and add ½ cup of the Miracle Whip. Combine with a fork. If you want a creamier pimento cheese, add more Miracle Whip. Fold in the remaining ingredients. Serve immediately, or refrigerate in an airtight container for up to a week—though I doubt you'll be able to make it last that long.

2 cups shredded sharp or extra-sharp orange cheddar cheese

2 cups shredded Velveeta

½–1 cup Miracle Whip

1 2-ounce jar chopped pimentos, drained

2 teaspoons prepared horseradish, drained

1 teaspoon Worcestershire sauce

¼ teaspoon onion powder

Lots of freshly ground black pepper

A Classic or "Company's Coming" Pimento Cheese

Makes about 1 pint

If you're trying to impress somebody or having a fancy cocktail party, then this is the pimento cheese for you. Of course, the pimento cheese will be better if you use homemade mayonnaise, but Duke's or JFG works just fine without missing a beat. I tend to use white cheddar for visual appeal as well as taste.

3–4 cups grated white sharp cheddar cheese

1 4-ounce jar whole pimentos, drained

Mayonnaise

⅛ teaspoon onion powder

⅛ teaspoon ground red pepper

Dash or two of Worcestershire sauce

2 tablespoons granulated sugar

1 If you have a food processor, this comes together quick and easy, otherwise mix by hand or with an electric mixer. Using a metal blade in a food processor, pulse together the cheese and pimentos. Add about ½ cup of mayonnaise and pulse again. For a creamier pimento cheese, add some more mayo. Add the remaining ingredients and pulse until well blended. Serve immediately or refrigerate in an airtight container for up to 2 weeks.

Shrimp Ball

Bon Air Seafood just outside of Richmond, Virginia, has been famous for their shrimp balls for decades. Since I live several hours away, I had to come up with my own recipe to satisfy my cravings.

Makes 2 balls, which serve about 20 people

1 Divide the shrimp in half. Roughly chop one group.

2 Heat the oil in a sauté pan over medium heat. When the oil shimmers, throw in the leek and cook slowly until lightly caramelized, about 5–6 minutes. Add the garlic and cook for an additional minute. Remove from heat.

3 In a food processor, pulse the unchopped shrimp into small pieces. Add the lemon zest, cream cheese, and seafood seasoning. Purée until smooth, and place the mixture in a large bowl.

4 Fold in the chopped shrimp and the vegetables. Season with salt and pepper. Cover the mixture and refrigerate for 1 hour.

5 Place 2 12 × 12-inch pieces of plastic wrap on your counter. Divide the parsley between the two. Remove the shrimp mixture from the refrigerator and divide in half. Roll each half around on the parsley and then use the plastic wrap to help you form a ball. Chill in the refrigerator for at least 4 hours. Remove about 15 minutes before serving. Place on a platter and surround with crackers.

1½ pounds 31–40 count peeled and deveined shrimp, cooked

1 tablespoon olive oil

1 medium leek, roughly chopped

3 garlic cloves, roughly chopped

Grated zest of ½ lemon

2 8-ounce packages cream cheese, at room temperature

2 teaspoons Chesapeake Bay–style seafood seasoning

Kosher salt and freshly ground black pepper

½ cup finely chopped parsley

Assorted crackers

Oysters with Pancetta and Garlic Butter

My friend Gene Mattiuzzo used this recipe to get his wife to eat oysters. Now, there is nothing southern about Gene. He is proud of his Italian heritage, and though he lives in Fort Bragg, it's California, not North Carolina. He has given me more information on Pacific Coast fishing than I could ever digest. I've used at least one of Gene's recipes in the last eight cookbooks I've written: The man can cook. He uses these oysters both as an appetizer and as a side dish. I've found them to be extremely good party food, but I've also served them beside an Easter lamb. Be prepared to fight for your share.

Serves 4

1 Over a fine mesh strainer, shuck the oysters, discarding the top shell and loosening the meat from the bottom. Pour most of the liquid through the strainer and reserve. Fill a shallow baking pan with about ½ inch of rock salt. Nestle each oyster and shell in the rock salt so it will be stable and not tip and spill out the cooking liquid. It may take several pans.

2 Melt the butter in a small saucepan over medium heat. Add the lemon juice and garlic and cook for 2 minutes. Add any strained oyster liquid and cook for 2 minutes more. Add the parsley, the oregano, and 6–8 dashes of hot sauce. Stir and heat for another 2 minutes. Remove from heat.

3 Mix the bread crumbs and the Pecorino Romano in a medium bowl. Add 1 teaspoon of the garlic butter and just enough of the vermouth to dampen the mixture. When pinched, the crumbs should barely stick together. Using a teaspoon, divide the garlic butter among the oysters. Add a few pieces of pancetta to each oyster. Then cover with the crumb mixture.

4 Preheat your grill to high or your oven to 400 degrees. Place the baking pans on the grill and close the lid, or place the pans in the oven. Cook for about 7 minutes or until the oysters start to bubble and the crumbs slightly brown. Serve immediately (although they're not bad at room temperature either).

12 oysters, approximately 3½ inches in size

Rock salt

4 tablespoons unsalted butter, melted

2 tablespoons fresh lemon juice

3 garlic cloves, finely chopped

1 tablespoon finely chopped parsley

1 tablespoon finely chopped oregano

Hot pepper sauce

½ cup seasoned bread crumbs

½ cup Pecorino Romano

2 ounces pancetta, chopped and cooked

Extra-dry vermouth or Pernod

Fred's Pickled Shrimp

Serves 6–8

Southern novelist Pat Conroy has written that he uses pickled shrimp as "funeral food." That may be, but they're way too good to save for such occasions. I keep a jar of pickled shrimp in the refrigerator throughout the summer and early fall. They have a multitude of uses—a nibble for unexpected company, a topping for a salad, scattered around a platter of fish, or a really cool martini garnish.

1 cup thinly sliced yellow
   or sweet onions

1 cup white vinegar

½ cup olive oil

1 lemon, thinly sliced

¼ cup fresh lemon juice

1 2-ounce jar brined capers,
   drained and coarsely
   chopped

4 bay leaves, crushed

2 small garlic cloves, minced

1 teaspoon kosher or sea salt

1 teaspoon celery seeds

1 teaspoon crushed red
   pepper flakes

Water

2 pounds 24-count wild-
   caught shrimp, peeled
   and deveined

1 Mix the onions, vinegar, oil, lemon, lemon juice, capers, bay leaves, garlic, salt, celery seeds, and pepper flakes in a large (at least 2 quarts) heatproof glass or ceramic bowl.

2 Place a 6- to 8-quart stockpot over high heat and fill ⅔ full of water. Bring to a boil and add the shrimp. Immediately remove from heat and let the shrimp steep for 4 minutes. Drain and immediately pour the shrimp into the marinade. If the shrimp are a little undercooked, don't be concerned. They will continue to cook in the marinade.

3 Place the shrimp and the marinade in an airtight container. Refrigerate at least overnight; 3 days will give you a better flavor. The shrimp will keep in the refrigerator for 2 weeks. Serve at room temperature.

WE CHILL, CONGEAL, & PICKLE THINGS DOWN HERE The Legacy of Jiggly & Cool Sides

How many of you have never eaten a congealed salad? Raise your hands so I can see you. By the end of this chapter, a congealed salad will be part of your southern foodways repertoire, along with our many other chilled side dishes.

It makes perfect sense to me that we southerners are masters of the cold side dish. At the beginning of August, when it's 90 degrees and the humidity is 80 percent, nothing sounds or tastes better than something cool. At such times, I want to keep the heat out of the kitchen and out of my house, so side dishes that I can prep in the cool of the evening for the next day's feasting are perfect. Most of these recipes will find their way onto a plate that also features something from the grill. But an even bigger enjoyment will be eating them for lunch the next day. Again, in this chapter we'll find the confusion that is Fred Thompson. I love both old and classic and contemporary and current. Ambrosia is a no-brainer at most potlucks. But I also might take along a South Asian sweet-and-sour slaw. I love making tomato jam at the height of tomato season and spooning it over all manner of things throughout the year. Try it on collard greens on New Year's Day for a flavor jolt. And slaw is an important side dish because cabbage grows well in the South. But be sure to use the right slaw for the right main dish. Southerners can't do without their pickles, and I've included a few of the important ones for you to make.

By now you should be over your laughter at congealed salads. The ones here have withstood the test of time and can be extremely helpful for dinner parties or holiday gatherings. They are the ultimate make-ahead side dish. Mrs. Haskins's Grapefruit Salad (page 36) is marvelous for any holiday. Michael Rider's Asparagus Salad (page 37) welcomes the spring. And the rest of these recipes are just plain fun eating during the hot summer. A generation or two has bypassed the use of congealed salads, which is a shame. Why don't you help me bring the good ones back to our tables?

Ambrosia

This is a classic, and I would be remiss if I didn't have a bowl of ambrosia at every holiday event. It is a good potluck dish and bereavement recipe. But I must confess that when I make it, I never give it away. I just sit down with the bowl and a big spoon and eat about half of it myself.

Serves 8

1 Combine all of the ingredients in a large glass bowl. Stir gently, cover, and refrigerate for at least 8 hours; overnight is better. Remove from the refrigerator, stir once, and serve nicely chilled.

9 oranges, peeled, seeded, and sectioned

2 20-ounce cans crushed pineapple, drained, or 1 pineapple, peeled, cored, and crushed in your food processor

1 cup honey

2 teaspoons almond extract

1 cup sweetened flaked coconut

Sawdust Salad

Serves 8–10

Laugh at me if you want, but every time I take this salad to a family reunion or a potluck, it disappears within the first 10 minutes. Yeah, it may be old-fashioned, but that doesn't mean it isn't good. On a warm summer day, this is a refreshing side dish.

1 3-ounce box lemon Jell-O

1 3-ounce box orange Jell-O

1½ cups boiling water

1½ cups cold water

1 20-ounce can crushed pineapple, drained, juice reserved

1 package mini marshmallows

1 tablespoon flour

1 cup granulated sugar

1 large egg, beaten

1 8-ounce package cream cheese, at room temperature

1 pint whipping cream

2 cups shredded cheddar cheese

1 Dissolve both Jell-Os in the boiling water in a medium pan. When completely dissolved, add the cold water. Fold in the pineapple and marshmallows. Pour into a 9 × 13-inch dish. Place in the refrigerator until the Jell-O is set.

2 Pour 1¼ cups of the reserved pineapple juice into a small saucepan. Add the flour and sugar and cook over low heat until the sugar is dissolved. Whisking rapidly, slowly add the egg. Cook for another minute or two, then remove from heat and let cool.

3 Pour the pineapple juice mixture over the top of the set Jell-O and return it to the refrigerator.

4 Using a hand mixer or stand mixer, whip the cream cheese and whipping cream in a bowl until spreadable. Spread this mixture over the Jell-O. Evenly sprinkle the cheddar cheese over the top. Cover with plastic wrap and chill until ready to serve.

Frozen Cranberry-Banana Salad

If you've never had something similar to this at Thanksgiving, then I might suspect your southern heritage. There are probably a hundred variations of frozen cranberry salad, but this is my favorite. (Don't tell my mother.) Since you're using canned cranberry sauce, you can make this any time of the year. It's really good nestled up to some fried chicken.

Serves 6

1 Thoroughly combine all the ingredients in a large bowl. Place 6 muffin cups into a muffin pan and ladle the mixture into the cups. Freeze overnight and serve directly from the freezer.

1 20-ounce can crushed pineapple, drained

2 cups sour cream

1 8-ounce container Cool Whip

4 bananas, peeled and mashed

½ cup granulated sugar

½ cup pecans, chopped

2 14-ounce cans whole cranberry sauce

Cherry Salad with Southern Cola

Since the South is the birthplace of both Pepsi and Coke, seems natural to use their products in all manner of ways from glazing hams to making this surprising and eloquent salad.

Serves 6–8

1 Combine the pineapple and cherry juice and pour about 1½ cups of the liquid into a large mixing bowl. Add the Jell-O and stir to dissolve. Pour in the pineapple, cherries, cola, and pecans. Transfer the mixture to a 9 × 13-inch dish or a mold. Chill until firm. During the first 30 minutes, stir occasionally so that all the pineapple, cherries, and nuts don't sink to the bottom. Serve over lettuce leaves and topped with a dollop of mayonnaise.

1 20-ounce can crushed pineapple, drained, juice reserved

1 15-ounce can cherries, not pie filling, juice reserved, cherries cut into quarters

2 3-ounce boxes cherry Jell-O

16 ounces Pepsi or Coke

1 cup toasted pecans, chopped

Lettuce leaves

Mayonnaise

Mrs. Haskins's Grapefruit Salad

Serves 8–10

There are a lot of times that I blame Anne Haskins, who became my mother-in-law, for my current occupation. She came from a large family, and all of her brothers were either Baptist ministers or lawyers. When I was at the Haskinses' for some family event, I had two choices: to play one-upmanship with my uncles-in-law or hide out in the kitchen. Guess which one I chose. And that was part of the beginning of my appreciation of a completely different idea of food than what I had grown up with. This grapefruit salad was one of Anne Haskins's centerpiece dishes. It completely changed my mind about grapefruit and gave me a poppy seed dressing recipe that's also unbelievable on a spinach salad. When I serve this dish, it throws people for a loop until they taste it; then they always want the recipe.

4 envelopes unflavored gelatin

1 cup cold water

4 grapefruit, peeled and cut into sections, or 1 20-ounce jar of refrigerated grapefruit sections, drained

1 15-ounce can crushed pineapple, drained

1 cup toasted pecans, chopped

1½ cups granulated sugar, divided

1 cup boiling water

1 teaspoon kosher salt

1 teaspoon Dijon mustard

1 tablespoon poppy seeds

1 tablespoon finely grated onions

⅓ cup apple cider vinegar

1 cup canola oil

Lettuce leaves (butter lettuce works really well)

1 Pour the gelatin into a medium bowl, add the cold water, and stir to dissolve.

2 In another medium bowl, toss the grapefruit, the pineapple, the pecans, and 1 cup of the sugar until well combined.

3 Add the gelatin mixture to the fruit and pour in the boiling water. Fold to combine. Pour into a 9 × 13-inch baking dish or individual molds or a decorative mold. (I tend to stick with the 9 × 13.) Chill for at least 12 hours.

4 To make the dressing, whisk together the remaining sugar, salt, mustard, poppy seeds, onions, and vinegar in a small bowl until well blended. Whisk in the canola oil and then pour the mixture into a jar with a lid. Refrigerate until needed.

5 Line several salad plates with lettuce. Run a knife under warm water and then cut all the way around the mold. Cut the salad into 3 × 4-inch rectangles. Place one rectangle on each lettuce leaf. Vigorously shake the dressing to recombine and then pour a tablespoon or so over each slice. Best if served while still cold or at least cool.

Michael Rider's Asparagus Salad

Serves 10

Michael Rider, a friend of mine who lives in Richmond, Virginia, is an excellent cook and entertainer and has won many blue ribbons at the Virginia State Fair. Twenty-five years ago, I needed a really good congealed salad to serve for my in-laws' fiftieth wedding anniversary. Michael came through with this recipe. I had never made a congealed salad before, and there were a few tricks that I didn't quite understand, like stirring the mixture so that all the ingredients were balanced. So when I unmolded this dish, I had the most beautifully layered salad you've ever seen, and my sister-in-law wanted to know how I had performed this magic. I looked her right square in the eye and told her it was my secret. Twenty years later, I finally fessed up that it was totally by accident. Michael's recipe calls for canned asparagus, but I have also made this recipe with a pound of fresh asparagus boiled for four or five minutes until it's tender. The choice is yours, but in honor of Michael, I'm giving you the recipe as he wrote it.

---

1 Dissolve the gelatin in the cold water.

2 Bring the remaining water, vinegar, sugar, and salt to a boil in a small saucepan over medium-high heat, stirring to dissolve the sugar and salt. Remove from heat and stir in the dissolved gelatin mixture.

3 In another bowl, toss the asparagus, pimentos, lemon juice, pecans, onions, and celery. Pour the hot liquid mixture over the asparagus and stir. Pour the mixture into a lightly greased circular mold or individual molds. Refrigerate until set. Serve with a dollop of mayonnaise.

2 envelopes unflavored gelatin

½ cup cold water

1 cup water

½ cup distilled white vinegar

¾ cup granulated sugar

½ teaspoon kosher salt

1 10½-ounce can chopped green asparagus, undrained

2 2-ounce jars chopped pimento

2 tablespoons fresh lemon juice

½ cup broken pecan pieces

¼ cup finely chopped onions

½ cup finely chopped celery

Good-quality mayonnaise

Twisted Tomato Aspic

Serves 8

I didn't become acquainted with tomato aspic until I was twenty, when this salad was placed in front of me at my future mother-in-law's table. I had never seen anything like it. To me, Jell-O was supposed to be sweet. At the time, it really wasn't my favorite, and fortunately my soon-to-be brother-in-law, Jack Bagby, just about hurled every time he had to eat tomato aspic. My reaction wasn't that extreme, though it wasn't my favorite dish either. I like the notion of tomato aspic, so I started experimenting, and Martha Pearl Villas, mother of my mentor, food writer Jim Villas, helped me get the idea to use V-8 juice. This brightened the aspic considerably—almost like a gelatin bloody Mary. I have added sliced, stuffed green olives or chopped cooked shrimp with great success. It's a throwback to the Old South, but it's a show-stopper, and we need to treasure and remember it. I've almost gotten Jack to admit that he likes this one.

4 cups V-8 juice

3 envelopes unflavored gelatin

1 tablespoon Worcestershire sauce

1 tablespoon sherry vinegar

2 tablespoons fresh lemon juice

1 tablespoon minced onions, rinsed under cold water and drained

1/4 teaspoon kosher salt

1/2 cup finely chopped celery

1/2 cup sliced green olives or chopped cooked shrimp

Lettuce leaves

Good-quality mayonnaise

1 In a large bowl, combine 1/2 cup of the V-8 juice with the gelatin and let stand to soften.

2 Pour the remaining V-8 juice into a 3-quart saucepan over medium heat. Just before it comes to a boil, pour the juice into the bowl with the gelatin mixture. Stir in the Worcestershire sauce, vinegar, lemon juice, onions, and salt. Refrigerate until slightly thickened, usually about 20 minutes.

3 Stir in the celery and the olives or shrimp. Pour the mixture into a shallow baking dish or individual molds. Cover and chill until firm. Serve on lettuce leaves with a dollop of mayonnaise.

Pretzel Salad

I'm fairly certain that a transplanted Pennsylvanian brought this salad south. I first had it at a potluck and think it's just a hoot. You have to try this textural mismatch.

Serves 8–10

1 Preheat your oven to 400 degrees.

2 Combine the pretzels, the butter, and 3 tablespoons of the sugar in a large bowl. Pour the mixture into a 9 × 13-inch baking dish and bake for 10 minutes.

3 Blend the cream cheese, whipped cream, and remaining sugar. Put the Jell-O in a small mixing bowl and pour in the boiling water. Stir in the strawberries.

4 Spread the cream cheese mixture over the pretzels. Pour the strawberry mixture over the cream cheese. Cover and refrigerate until set.

2 cups crushed hard pretzels

¾ cup unsalted butter, melted

1 cup plus 3 tablespoons granulated sugar

1 8-ounce package cream cheese, at room temperature

2 cups whipped cream

1 6-ounce package strawberry Jell-O

2 cups boiling water

2 cups fresh strawberries, hulled and quartered

Sun Gold Pasta Salad

Serves 10–12

I love the screaming-out-loud flavor of little Sun Gold tomatoes. A farmer once told me that they were nature's Cheetos, and I definitely agree that they are addictive. I like this recipe for summer picnics and potlucks. It will keep nicely for a couple of days. Go ahead and make the whole recipe. You'll thank me for the urging later.

¼ cup of your favorite Italian dressing (I use Good Seasons)

2 tablespoons good-quality mayonnaise

1 pound elbow pasta, prepared as directed, rinsed to chill

1 cup (or more) halved Sun Gold tomatoes

6 large basil leaves

4 sprigs thyme, leaves stripped

2 sprigs oregano, leaves stripped and chopped

Kosher salt and freshly ground black pepper

A few lemon wedges

Croutons (optional)

1 In a large mixing bowl, stir together the dressing and the mayonnaise. Pour in the pasta and the tomatoes. Stir. Stack the basil leaves and roll them like you would a cigar. Cut across the cigar in very narrow strips. This is called a chiffonade. Add the basil, thyme, and oregano to the mixing bowl with a good pinch or two of salt and several grindings of pepper. Toss all the ingredients to combine. Season with lemon juice as necessary. Serve immediately with croutons, if desired. The dish can be refrigerated, but let it come back to room temperature before serving.

Red-Skinned Potato Salad

This is another version of a southern standard. Using red-skinned potatoes gives the dish a little different texture, and lots of mustard gives it a sharper flavor and makes it perfect with cold fried chicken.

Serves 8–10

1 Place the potatoes in a large saucepan and add enough water to cover them by about 1 inch. Bring to a boil over high heat, then lower heat and simmer vigorously for 18–20 minutes. The potatoes should give easily when pierced with a knife but should not be mushy. Remove from heat and drain.

2 In a large bowl, combine the eggs, mayonnaise, relish, mustard, milk, and vinegar. If you would like to add onion, place the onion in a colander and run under hot water for about 2 minutes. This helps keep the onion from overpowering the other ingredients. Drain and dry well before adding to the mix. If you want to include dill, add it to the mixing bowl.

3 Add the warm potatoes and stir to coat. Season with salt and pepper. I like to serve this while it's still a bit warm, but room temperature and even straight out of the refrigerator are also fine.

2 pounds red-skinned potatoes, unpeeled and cubed

Water

6 hard-boiled eggs, coarsely chopped

½ cup good-quality mayonnaise

2 tablespoons (or more) sweet pickle relish, drained

3 teaspoons prepared yellow mustard

1 tablespoon whole milk

1 tablespoon apple cider vinegar

½ cup diced onion and/or ½ cup chopped dill (optional)

Kosher salt and freshly ground black pepper

Quick, Easy, Convenient Pasta Salad

Serves 6

This pasta salad is always a star wherever I take it. It belies the use of a few convenience products that help elevate it to that status.

8 ounces prepared cheese tortellini, cooked, rinsed with cold water

Canola oil

½ cup mango chutney, large pieces chopped

⅓–½ cup prepared red wine vinegar and oil salad dressing (I use Wishbone)

6 slices thick-cut bacon, cut into narrow strips

1 small red onion, peeled and thinly sliced

1 10-ounce bag spinach or about 1 pound baby spinach, trimmed

Kosher salt and freshly ground black pepper

1 Toss the tortellini with oil in a bowl and set aside.

2 In a small mixing bowl, whisk together the chutney and dressing.

3 Cook the bacon in a sauté pan over medium heat until nicely browned and crisp, about 8 minutes. Drain on paper towels, then crumble.

4 If you're transporting the salad, here's what I suggest. Once you've rinsed the tortellini and tossed them with oil, put them in a zip-top bag. Pour the dressing in a container that you can shake. Place the bacon in a zip-top bag, the onions in another, and the spinach and a paper towel in another.

5 To assemble the salad, toss the tortellini, onions, and spinach in a bowl. Add the dressing and toss until everything is well coated. Season with salt and pepper. Sprinkle the bacon on top and serve immediately.

Mrs. Gibbs's Hearts of Palm Salad

Betsy Gibbs had a place in the Florida Keys for many years—local lore even claims that Jimmy Buffett used to perform there in his early years—so how did I come across this recipe? My father-in-law found it and had a chef at a very swanky hotel make it for an office Christmas dinner. It may be the funkiest recipe in this book, but it's delicious, different, and wonderful on a hot summer day.

Serves 4

1 In a bowl, mix together the ice cream, mayonnaise, peanut butter, and pineapple juice. Pour the mixture into a freezer-proof container and freeze until the mixture can be scooped like ice cream, usually an hour or two.

2 In a large mixing bowl, gently stir together the hearts of palm, pineapple, dates, ginger, and celery.

3 Divide the shredded lettuce among 4 chilled salad bowls. Divide the hearts of palm mixture among the 4 servings and top with an ice cream scoop of the dressing. Serve immediately.

4½ cups softened vanilla ice cream

2 tablespoons good-quality mayonnaise

2 tablespoons peanut butter

1 tablespoon pineapple juice

1 14-ounce can hearts of palm, drained and sliced

½ cup pineapple chunks

2 tablespoons chopped dates

1 tablespoon finely chopped crystallized ginger

½ cup chopped celery

About ½ head iceberg lettuce, shredded

Lexington-Style Red Slaw (front); Alabama Sweet-and-Sour Slaw (page 47) (rear left); and Perfect-for-Barbecue Slaw (page 46) (rear right)

Lexington-Style Red Slaw

There's no red cabbage in this recipe. This slaw is typically served with North Carolina's Lexington-style barbecue, and it pairs extremely well with hickory and oak flavors. If you're doing anything with a tomato-based sauce—cooking shoulders or ribs or barbecuing some pork chops—you should really give this a try. It's also great on a hot dog North Carolina–style—that would be a slaw dog in any other state.

Serves 8

1 Mix the vinegar, ketchup, sugar, and salt in a large bowl. Stir until the sugar dissolves. Add the cabbage and toss until nicely combined. Add the pepper, stir, and taste for spiciness. Add more pepper or the hot sauce, if desired. The slaw will keep for about 2 days refrigerated. Stir before serving.

½ cup apple cider vinegar

½ cup ketchup

¼ cup granulated sugar

½ teaspoon kosher salt

5–6 cups finely chopped green cabbage, pieces about the size of BBs (a food processor is a helpful tool here)

1 teaspoon (or more) freshly ground black pepper

1 teaspoon hot pepper sauce (optional)

Perfect-for-Barbecue Slaw

Serves 8

I have a law about slaws. They should be more than just plate-fillers. They should answer other flavors on the plate. While this recipe is loosely based on the slaws at Wilbur's Barbecue in Goldsboro, North Carolina, and Holt Lake Barbecue in Smithfield, North Carolina, it is perfect for any vinegar-based-sauce barbecue—Memphis-style ribs, Texas brisket, South Carolina mustard-style, or eastern North Carolina–style. And don't limit this to just barbecue. It's great with fried chicken and perfect on a hot dog. However, don't even *think* about making this slaw with mayonnaise.

½ cup (or more) Miracle Whip

¼ cup sweet pickle relish, with juice

2 tablespoons prepared yellow mustard

1 tablespoon granulated sugar

1 teaspoon kosher salt

¼ teaspoon celery seeds

Freshly ground black pepper

6 cups finely chopped green cabbage

2 carrots, peeled and finely grated

1 In a large bowl, combine the Miracle Whip, relish, mustard, sugar, salt, and celery seeds and at least 5 or 6 grindings of pepper. Add the cabbage and carrots and fold to blend. The slaw can be prepared several hours in advance and refrigerated, covered. Best when served cool.

Alabama Sweet-and-Sour Slaw

Every southern region has its own particular slaw, and they all seem to be based on how well they go with that area's barbecue. This sweet-and-sour slaw brings out the smoky flavor of northern Alabama's coarsely chopped pork barbecue and white-sauce barbecue chicken. In your kitchen, this slaw will pair well with barbecued ribs or fried fish or shellfish.

Serves 6–8

1 Put the shredded cabbage in a large bowl.

2 Heat the vinegar in a small saucepan over medium heat. Stir in the sugar and heat until the sugar has dissolved, stirring occasionally.

3 Pour the mixture over the cabbage. Add the oil, dry mustard, and celery seeds and toss until everything is combined.

4 Let the slaw marinate for at least 1 hour, tossing occasionally. Serve immediately or refrigerate for up to 1 week.

8 cups shredded cabbage

1 cup apple cider vinegar

¾ cup granulated sugar

½ cup canola or other vegetable oil

1 teaspoon dry mustard

½ teaspoon celery seeds

LAW OF SLAW Slaw is not a plate-filler. Slaw should be made with care and served in the appropriate setting. This book has recipes for four different slaws, and they're not really very interchangeable, although they all work beautifully on hot dogs. To accompany fried fish or fried chicken, try Mom's North Carolina Fish House Slaw (page 48). If you're doing Lexington-style barbecue heavily infused with hickory and oak smoke, then the perfect solution is Lexington-Style Red Slaw (page 45). Alabama Sweet-and-Sour Slaw (above) cozies up to white-sauce barbecue chicken or chunky and smoky pulled pork. Having ribs or Texas-style brisket? Go for the Perfect-for-Barbecue Slaw (page 46). Perfect-for-Barbecue Slaw is also good with eastern North Carolina barbecue or any heavily vinegared sauce. Shrimp and seafood go well with Alabama Sweet-and-Sour Slaw or Mom's North Carolina Fish House Slaw. But no slaw should be a second-class citizen on any plate of food. Nuances of the slaw-making world mean that certain slaws join with certain foods. Pick a slaw that will complement the seasonings of what's in the center of the plate.

Mom's North Carolina Fish House Slaw

Serves 4–6

Continuing on my law of slaw, fried seafood needs a special blend. Fried fish and other seafood are heavenly with this tangy and sweet slaw. This was Mom's version, and I see no reason to change it. Every time I serve this slaw at a seafood feast, alongside a pot of chowder, or at an oyster roast, it gets rave reviews.

6 tablespoons good-quality mayonnaise

2 tablespoons distilled white vinegar

1 tablespoon granulated sugar

1 teaspoon freshly ground black pepper

4 cups finely shredded cabbage

Kosher salt

1 In a medium bowl, stir together the mayonnaise, vinegar, sugar, and pepper. Add the cabbage and toss to coat. You might think that you don't have enough dressing. Be patient—you do. Place the slaw in the refrigerator for a couple of hours. Remove, toss again, and add salt to taste. Transfer to a serving bowl, head to the table, and dish up with your favorite fried foods.

Seared Green Bean Salad

A cross between a European-style potato salad and a southern green bean salad, this is a wonderful potluck or outdoor entertaining recipe. I've thrown in an Asian hint or two to completely confuse you. Just know that this is one good salad.

Serves 8–10

1 Cut the potatoes into quarters and place them in a 3-quart saucepan. Cover with cold water and bring them to a boil over high heat. Parboil for 4 minutes. Drain and place cut side up on a paper towel to dry.

2 Heat a thin layer of the olive oil in a large skillet over medium-high heat. When the oil begins to shimmer, add enough of the beans to cover the bottom of the pan. Sear them on one side for 3 minutes. Transfer the beans to a bowl. Repeat with the remaining green beans. Cover the bowl with foil.

3 Add ¼ inch of the olive oil to the skillet. Fry the potatoes cut side down over medium to medium-low heat for 20 minutes until they are crisp and the bottoms are browned. Remove.

4 In a bowl, stir together the shallots, lemon juice, sesame oil, sesame seeds, and 2 tablespoons of the olive oil. Pour this mixture over the green beans and toss. Add the potatoes and toss again. Season with salt and pepper. Serve at room temperature or slightly chilled.

1 pound small Yukon Gold potatoes or fingerlings

½ cup extra-virgin olive oil, divided

2 pounds green beans, trimmed

1 large shallot, sliced paper-thin

2 tablespoons fresh lemon juice

2 teaspoons toasted sesame oil

2 tablespoons toasted sesame seeds

Kosher salt and freshly ground black pepper

Cucumbers, Onions, and Sour Cream

Serves 4

Every now and then, I get a hankering for this old-time cucumber salad. I have a feeling it was the star of many a book club luncheon in days gone by. For the best flavor, make this in midsummer, when the cucumbers are at their peak and very fresh. You'll be well rewarded.

4 cups cucumbers (preferably Kirbys), cut into ¼-inch rounds

2 cups sliced red onions

¼ cup sour cream

1 tablespoon mayonnaise

2 teaspoons chopped thyme

Kosher salt and freshly ground black pepper

5 or 6 torn basil leaves

1 Toss together the cucumbers and onions in a large bowl.

2 Mix the sour cream, mayonnaise, and thyme in a small bowl. Add a generous pinch of salt and several grindings of pepper. Stir to combine. Pour the mixture over the cucumbers and onions and toss until they're nicely coated. Serve immediately or chilled, adding the basil leaves right before serving.

Spicy Tomato Jam

Verla, my neighbor in New York, thought of herself as a gourmet cook. She was thrilled when I moved into the building because she had someone to share her favorite recipes with. This is a riff on her tomato jam. When I first made it, I asked her if she had any southern blood. Her answer: "Yes, I'm from southern Canada." She passed away a few years ago, but I keep her memory alive with the recipes she shared. This stuff is great on a cheese plate or with homemade cheese crackers or as a topping for a burger or grilled fish. I've even spread the jam on garlic bread, with great success. But be warned: It's pretty intense.

Makes 4 8-ounce jars

1 Bring all of the ingredients to a boil in a 4-quart saucepan over medium-high heat. Reduce heat and simmer until the mixture thickens and most of the liquid has evaporated, 35–40 minutes. Skim off any foam that develops on the surface and stir frequently, especially during the last 15 minutes of cooking. Transfer the jam to hot sterilized jars, filling to within ½ inch of the top. Wipe the rims of the jars with a clean damp cloth, place the lids on the jars, then hand-tighten the rings.

2 You have two choices at this point. One is allow the jars to cool and then store in the refrigerator for up to 4 months. Or you can put them through a hot-water-bath canning process, which will give you about a year's shelf life outside the refrigerator. Check out Ball's website, http://www.freshpreserving.com, for exact instructions. Serve the jam at room temperature so that all of the flavors will be evident.

6 cups peeled, seeded, and chopped ripe heirloom tomatoes, the more varieties the better

4 lemons, peeled, seeded, and finely chopped

3 cups granulated sugar

4 tablespoons fresh ginger, peeled and minced

1 teaspoon crushed red pepper flakes

3 generous pinches of salt

Crunchy Pickled Okra

Makes about 6 pints

No southerner in his or her right mind would be caught dead without a jar of pickled okra. Store-bought is okay but will never measure up to your own okra pickles. My friend Rick Ellis and I started using pickled okra as a garnish for martinis many years ago, and it's an excellent southern twist on a serious cocktail. Ben Barker at Magnolia Grill in Durham, North Carolina, likes to split open the pickled okra, stuff them with homemade pimento cheese, and serve them as a predinner cocktail food, or as he calls them, "southern tapas." They are an absolute must on any dinner table pickle tray.

12 small red chili peppers

12 sprigs dill

12 garlic cloves

1 carrot, peeled, quartered, and cut into very small wedges

1 tablespoon dill seeds

4½ pounds small, young okra

Pickle Crisp (optional)

6 cups distilled white vinegar

3 cups water

½ cup kosher salt

1 There are two ways to go about pickling okra. The refrigerator method is simple and allows you to keep pickled okra for up to 1 month. The hot-water-bath method will allow you to keep pickled okra up to 6 months. Whichever method you choose, you need to sterilize 6 1-pint canning jars.

2 In each jar, place 2 chili peppers, 2 dill sprigs, 2 garlic cloves, 2 carrot wedges, and ½ teaspoon dill seeds. Tightly pack the okra into the jars, leaving about ½ inch at the top. Add the Pickle Crisp to each jar, if desired, according to the directions on the label. Combine the vinegar, water, and salt in a 3-quart saucepan and bring to a boil over high heat, stirring to dissolve the salt. Ladle the hot liquid into the jars. (A canning funnel will help a lot here.)

3 Wipe the rims of the jars with a clean damp cloth, place the lids on the jars, then hand-tighten the rings. Refrigerate for up to 2 weeks before eating to allow the flavors to develop. To process these using the hot-water-bath method, see Ball's website, http://www.freshpreserving.com, for exact instructions.

Cranberry Conserve (page 60) (far left); Crunchy Pickled Okra (center top); Southern Dill Pickles (page 56) (center bottom); Quick-and-Easy Green Tomato Pickles (page 54) (front); Spicy Tomato Jam (page 51) (right top); Watermelon Rind Pickles (page 58) (right bottom); Fred's Bread-and-Butter Pickles (page 55) (far right)

Quick-and-Easy Green Tomato Pickles

Makes 2 quarts or 4 pints

You've got to have green tomato pickles. This recipe is a refrigerator-style pickle and will last 4–6 months refrigerated. They get better with age, but I'll bet you eat them too fast to find out.

2½ pounds green tomatoes, sliced about ¼ inch thick

1½ pounds thinly sliced yellow onions

1½ teaspoons whole yellow mustard seeds

2 tablespoons pickling salt

½ cup granulated sugar

2 cups apple cider vinegar

1 Combine the tomatoes, onions, and mustard seeds in a large bowl. Add the salt and mix gently with your hands. Leave the tomatoes at room temperature for 12 hours or overnight.

2 Drain any liquid from the vegetables and pack them into 2 hot sterilized quart jars, alternating the tomatoes and onions. Combine the sugar and vinegar and stir until the sugar is dissolved. Pour this mixture equally into the 2 jars. Wipe the rims of the jars with a clean damp cloth, place the lids on the jars, then hand-tighten the rings and let stand at room temperature for 24 hours before refrigerating. While the pickles are ready to eat at this point, I always like to give them 3 or 4 more days before jumping in. You can also process these, making them shelf stable. Check out Ball's website, http://www.freshpreserving.com, for exact instructions.

Fred's Bread-and-Butter Pickles

Makes about 5 pints

To me, bread-and-butter pickles are a little bit like candy. I serve these pickles at all cookouts and use the pickling juice to help season my deviled eggs. The trick to making any good pickle is to use a cucumber that's designed for pickling, like a Kirby or a gherkin, and to use the freshest and firmest cukes you can find. But even after you find the correct cucumber, buy from a vendor whose farmstand sells a lot of cucumbers. Old cucumbers do not make good pickles.

10 cups pickling cucumbers, cut into ¼-inch rounds, blossom end piece discarded

4 medium onions, thinly sliced

½ cup pickling salt

Cold water

3 cups distilled white vinegar

2 cups granulated sugar

2 tablespoons mustard seeds

1 teaspoon celery seeds

1 teaspoon turmeric

Pickle Crisp (optional)

1 Mix the cucumbers, onions, and salt in a bowl. Cover with cold water and let stand at room temperature for 2 hours.

2 Transfer the cucumbers to a colander in the sink and rinse with cool water. Drain thoroughly.

3 In a 3-quart saucepan, preferably stainless steel but definitely not aluminum, combine the vinegar, sugar, mustard and celery seeds, and turmeric. Bring to a boil over medium-high heat, stirring to dissolve the sugar. Stir in the vegetables and return to a boil.

4 Pack the vegetables into hot sterilized jars, leaving at least ½ inch at the top. Add ¾ teaspoon Pickle Crisp to each jar, if desired. Ladle the pickling juice using a canning funnel into the jars, covering the vegetables but leaving the ½-inch space at the top. Using a chopstick or a knife, remove any air bubbles, and if need be, add more of the pickling liquid. Wipe the rims of the jars with a clean damp cloth, place the lids on the jars, then hand-tighten the rings. Cool and place in the refrigerator for a couple of months. I tend to make several batches of these pickles, so I also process some. See Ball's website, http://www.freshpreserving.com, for exact instructions.

VARIATION Want to surprise the daylights out of folks? To make zesty bread-and-butter pickles, substitute 2 tablespoons of prepared horseradish that has been well drained for the celery seeds and 2 tablespoons of grated ginger for the turmeric. The sweet heat on this variation is uncommonly good.

Southern Dill Pickles

Makes 6 pints

Traveling around the country, I've discovered that there are a lot of definitions for dill pickles. But I grew up on this classic and still enjoy it today. This version is garlicky and reminds me a bit of the pickles I encountered in the great delis of Manhattan. I always have this pickle for cookouts.

3 cups distilled white vinegar

3 cups water

6 tablespoons pickling salt

12 sprigs dill

12 garlic cloves, cut in half

3 tablespoons mustard seeds

Pickle Crisp (optional)

30 4-inch Kirby cucumbers, trimmed

1 Bring the vinegar, water, and pickling salt to a boil in a 3-quart saucepan over medium-high heat, stirring to dissolve the salt.

2 In each hot sterilized jar, place 1 sprig of dill, 4 pieces of garlic, ¾ teaspoon of mustard seeds, and Pickle Crisp, according to package directions. Pack the jars half full with cucumbers. Divide the remaining dill and mustard seeds among the jars. Pack the remainder of the cucumbers into the jars as tightly as possible. Cover the cucumbers with the vinegar solution, leaving ½ inch at the top. (A canning funnel will help here.) Remove any air bubbles, wipe the rims of the jars with a clean damp cloth, place the lids on the jars, then hand-tighten the rings. Let them sit in the refrigerator for a week, for the flavors to meld, and use within 4 months. I like these better as a refrigerator pickle because they stay brighter in flavor, but if you want to process them, check out Ball's website, http://www.freshpreserving.com, for exact instructions.

SOME THOUGHTS ON PRESERVING FOOD Canning and preserving food have become chic. Unlike my grandmother, who sweated through canning season in a house with no air-conditioning preserving food for survival, we preserve food because we are beginning to learn what a boon to our pantries home canning and freezing can be. Give it a try.

Pickled Ramps

Ramps are wild leeks that make their presence known in April in the Appalachian Mountains. They have a wonderful, tasty, stinky, garlicky-oniony flavor that inspires an almost cultlike following. Pickling is the best way to make them available for longer. Use them like you would any pickle, but they are best alongside roasted meats and fish.

Makes 2–4 pints, depending on the size of the ramps

1 Bring the vinegar, sugar, water, and salt to a boil in a 4-quart or larger pot over high heat, stirring to dissolve the sugar and salt. Throw in the mustard seeds, coriander, fennel, peppercorns, and bay leaf. Cook for about another minute.

2 Pack the ramps into hot sterilized mason jars. (I like to use pint jars.) Pour the hot vinegar mixture over the ramps using a canning funnel. Let cool, seal tightly, and place in the refrigerator for up to 2 months. Or use traditional canning methods and store for up to 6 months (check out Ball's website, http://www .freshpreserving.com, for exact instructions). But it's really not worth the trouble since you'll eat them much faster than that.

1 cup white wine vinegar

1 cup granulated sugar

1 cup water

1 tablespoon kosher salt

1 teaspoon yellow mustard seeds

1 teaspoon coriander seeds

1 teaspoon fennel seeds

1 teaspoon whole black peppercorns

1 bay leaf

2 pounds ramps, cleaned and with root ends and leaves trimmed, leaving about 1/4-inch of green, blanched for about 30 seconds (see page 230) and dried almost completely

Watermelon Rind Pickles

Makes about 6–8 pints

Watermelon rind pickles seem to be as southern as grits. In a lot of other regions of the country, they sound foul until that dude from Ohio actually tries one. Then he's hooked. I'd love to know who first decided that watermelon rinds could be pickled. This recipe can be canned with about a 10-minute hot bath, but I like to keep them as a refrigerator pickle, making a new batch every so often. I do not usually serve these past Thanksgiving, but that's just the weirdness that lurks in me.

6 cups cold water

⅓ cup pickling salt

2 medium watermelons, rinds removed and reserved—the remnants of your last picnic or just enjoy the watermelon flesh as you make the pickles

2 cups ice (from your freezer's icemaker is fine)

4½ cups granulated sugar

2 cups distilled white vinegar

2 cups water

4 cinnamon sticks about 3 inches long

2 bay leaves

1 tablespoon whole yellow mustard seeds

1 tablespoon coriander seeds

1 tablespoon whole juniper berries

½ tablespoon whole allspice berries

½ teaspoon whole cloves

1   Make the brine by combining the water and the pickling salt in a very large bowl. Cut the rinds into 1-inch pieces. Add them to the brine and pour the ice over the top. Allow to brine for at least 6 hours, but overnight in the refrigerator is better.

2   Bring the sugar, vinegar, water, and spices to a boil in a large pot over high heat. Reduce heat and simmer for 10 minutes. Drain and rinse the rinds and add them to the pot. Cook for 1 hour or until translucent. Pack into hot sterilized jars and either continue the canning process (see Ball's website, http://www.freshpreserving.com, for exact instructions) or store in the refrigerator for up to 4 months. Either way, serve cold.

Holiday Chutney

When you need something different for your holiday ham or crowned pork roast, give this chutney a try. It hits all the right notes for pork as well as for quail and duck.

Makes about 2 pints

1 Cook the pineapple, vinegar, brown sugar, and salt in a 3-quart saucepan over low heat for 30 minutes, stirring occasionally. Add the ginger, garlic, almonds, raisins, and peppers. Simmer, stirring frequently, until thickened, 15–20 minutes. Spoon into airtight containers and store in the refrigerator for up to 1 month.

2 16-ounce cans crushed pineapple, undrained

1 cup apple cider vinegar

1 cup light brown sugar, packed

½ teaspoon kosher salt

½ teaspoon ground ginger

1 garlic clove, minced

¼ cup toasted sliced almonds

½ cup golden raisins

½ cup finely chopped green bell peppers

Cranberry Conserve

Makes 2 pints

I can't imagine having a holiday bird without cranberries. I grew up on canned, jellied sauce and thought that was the best stuff until I had my first Thanksgiving at my in-laws. Their cranberry sauce was chunky, like chutney, and ten times better than what I was used to. I begged for the recipe. My mother-in-law looked at me and laughed: "It's on the back of the bag of cranberries." I always like to change things up a bit, but even after all my experiments, this isn't really much more than the recipe on the back of the bag. The acidity of the orange and the sweetness of the raisins complement the cranberries, and the chopped pecans add a cool texture (though they're not necessary). Don't you just love the word "conserve"? It makes anything sound old-moneyed southern.

4 cups fresh or frozen cranberries

⅔ cup cold water

1 small thin-skinned orange, unpeeled and thinly sliced (usually juice oranges)

1 cup golden raisins, roughly chopped

¼ cup currants

3 cups granulated sugar

1 cup toasted chopped pecans (optional)

1 Cook the cranberries and the water in a 3-quart saucepan over medium heat until the cranberry skins burst, usually 15–20 minutes, stirring occasionally. Add the orange slices, raisins, currants, and sugar and simmer, stirring occasionally, until thickened, about 20 minutes. Add the nuts, if desired, and cool before serving. Refrigerate any leftovers in an airtight container for up to 4 weeks.

NIGHTSHADES OF SUMMER

Tomatoes, Peppers, & Eggplants

Nightshades. What an intriguing and mysterious word for a group of fruits and vegetables. Nightshades include tomatoes, peppers, eggplants, and potatoes. Here, let's focus on the three princes of summer. (Potatoes get their own chapter.) Tomatoes, peppers, and eggplants provide very different but universal tastes of the season. They play well with each other as well as with summer's other garden gifts. They also stand heroically on their own. Each one has its own value in the way it's treated. An eggplant must always be cooked. Tomatoes and peppers, however, shine both raw and cooked.

For me, the best use of a tomato is sliced and tucked between two pieces of Wonder Bread slathered with mayonnaise. The tomato must be ripe enough to turn the bread slightly pink. I have just described my lunch every day from mid-June to mid-September. How crazy am I about tomatoes? There are ten different varieties of tomatoes growing in my garden and a total of thirty-four plants. The diversity of tomato types and their subtleties in taste create a nirvana. Tomatoes have led the way in our understanding and desire for heirloom and heritage products. When I was growing up, Dad grew a combination of German Johnsons (an heirloom variety that he grew up with in the '30s) and a few new hybrids, such as Better Boys or Beefmasters. The German Johnsons set the standard for what I think a tomato should taste like. But over the next few

decades, hybrid tomatoes bred to be uniform in size and to travel well overtook other types of tomato. I, too, was part of this problem. As a food stylist, my job included locating and nurturing perfectly round, perfectly red tomatoes for photography; on the vine was preferable, but they at least had to have some green stem. This is what food editors at the major magazines demanded. The only problem was that the tomatoes had become as tasteless as the paper the photos were printed on. My first experience with heirloom tomatoes was a salad at Magnolia Grill in Durham, North Carolina. The tomatoes had been grown by a young rebel farmer, Alex Hitt, at his Peregrine Farms. At that time, most all heirloom tomatoes produced in the Carolinas were being sold directly to restaurants. During my time in Manhattan, I learned to love the Union Square farmers' market and stayed completely irritated that in my hometown, the capital of an agricultural state, no such market existed. In New York, I discovered heirloom tomatoes that I could buy and prepare. At the same time, the farmers' market in Carrboro, North Carolina, was beginning to come into its own, finally giving me a local source.

The number and types of heirloom tomatoes planted and the amount of their fruit purchased have grown phenomenally in the last two and a half decades. The heirloom tomato has changed our opinions about how foods should taste.

We now challenge farmers to bring us flavor first, whether in a tomato, a pound of hamburger, an egg, or a pork chop.

Peppers and eggplants are two of my favorite vegetables to just simply grill, and this chapter offers you some interesting ideas for doing just that. Peppers—bell, jalapeño, and poblano—have always been a mainstay for me. Their flavors invigorate food no matter how they are prepared.

I came to liking eggplant later in life; my time in New York really turned that tide, too. Eggplant Parmesan made by a true Italian is a taste explosion, but what really got me curious about eggplants was the caponata that I had at Cafe Fiorello, across from Lincoln Center. I spent more than five years trying to duplicate that flavor—and eating a lot of eggplant. I've finally gotten the recipe fairly close (page 79), but it took a hint (brown sugar!) from my culinary buddy Sheri Castle.

These three veggies have become important to me—and I think to most southerners—as an integral part of the summer palate.

Roasted Tomatoes

Roasting tomatoes simplifies their sweet acidity. From this recipe, you can get many things—a wonderful side dish right out of the oven, the base for homemade marinara sauce, or the beginnings of a bruschetta. These tomatoes are definitely worth the time it takes to cook them, and the actual preparation is quick and easy.

Serves 6

1 Preheat your oven to 325 degrees.

2 Arrange the tomatoes on a rimmed baking sheet and sprinkle the onions across the top. Drizzle the olive oil over this mixture and then evenly sprinkle on the seasonings.

3 Bake for 2 hours, stirring after 1 hour. Increase the oven temperature to 400 degrees and bake for another 30 minutes or until the tomatoes have taken on a little color. Remove from the oven and stir, then transfer to a serving dish. Serve hot or at room temperature.

8 large tomatoes or 12 Roma or plum tomatoes, sliced in half

1 cup chopped onions

2 tablespoons olive oil

1 teaspoon dried thyme

1 teaspoon dried oregano

1 teaspoon dried basil

¼ teaspoon kosher salt

¼ teaspoon freshly ground black pepper

Virginia Bagby's Tomato Pie

Another wonderful taste of summer is tomato pie, and Virginia Bagby's is worth baking. I get the impression that this pie originated with her grandmother's cook back in the early 1900s. I've tinkered with it a little by suggesting that heirloom tomatoes be used, but they're certainly not necessary. Please be sure to allow the pie to cool before you try to slice it.

Serves 6–8

1 **Preheat your oven to 350 degrees.**

2 **Spread the red onions around the bottom of the pie shell. Place the tomatoes in a fan pattern over the onions.**

3 **Combine the mayonnaise, Swiss cheese, and basil in a bowl. Pour into the pie shell and spread evenly.**

4 **Top the pie with the mozzarella. Bake in the oven for about 45 minutes or until hot and bubbly. Remove from the oven and let cool for at least 30 minutes before slicing. Of course, if you don't mind a messy presentation, go ahead and eat it while it's hot.**

1 small red onion, thinly sliced

1 9-inch unbaked pie shell

About 14 ½-inch tomato slices, preferably heirlooms

1 cup good-quality mayonnaise

¼ cup shredded Swiss cheese

6 basil leaves, cut into thin strips

8 ¼-inch slices fresh mozzarella cheese, preferably farmstand

Nick's Stewed Tomatoes

Serves 6–8

One of the best places to eat along the ocean in Virginia Beach is Nick's Seafood, on Laskin Road. It's a total dive, but all good seafood places should be. And when the chairman of one of the country's largest law firms—a man who can afford to eat seafood anywhere—gives you the tip, you go. One of Nick's best side dishes is his stewed tomatoes. Don't even think about confusing these tomatoes with what you can buy in a can. The two tastes are entirely different. This is an old recipe that came from when times were tough and every dish had to be stretched. In this case, stretching the dish turned out delightful. This is a must-try recipe.

4 tablespoons unsalted butter, divided

1 medium onion, peeled and sliced

1 tablespoon light brown sugar

1 tablespoon canola oil

8 cups tomatoes, cut into chunks (canned whole tomatoes are fine; homemade canned tomatoes are great, too)

¼ cup granulated sugar

2 slices white bread

Kosher salt and freshly ground black pepper

1 tablespoon chopped basil

1 Melt 2 tablespoons of the butter over medium heat in a large saucepan. Add the onions and brown sugar, stir, and reduce heat to low. Cook until the onions are nicely browned, 15–20 minutes, stirring occasionally.

2 Melt the remaining butter and the canola oil in another saucepan over medium heat. When the butter is foaming, add the tomatoes and bring to a boil. Reduce heat and simmer briskly for 45 minutes.

3 Stir in the onions and the white sugar and cook for 15 minutes longer. Add the bread and cook until soft, 3–5 minutes. Season with salt and pepper and stir in the basil. Serve warm or at room temperature.

Baked Sun Gold Tomatoes with Herbs

Serves 4

Sun Gold tomatoes have an intense flavor right off the vine. When I bake them for almost 2 hours, the flavor becomes brighter and even more intense. You can use these tomatoes as an hors d'oeuvre or piled up next to a beautiful grouper fillet. Be careful when you taste these. Try to remember you've prepared these for a meal and not for your personal snack. It will be tempting, however.

4 tablespoons extra-virgin olive oil, divided

1 pint Sun Gold tomatoes, stems removed and sliced in half

2 garlic cloves, minced

1 tablespoon finely chopped thyme and oregano

2 tablespoons grated Parmesan cheese

Sea salt

1 Preheat your oven to 300 degrees.

2 Brush a baking sheet with 1 tablespoon of the olive oil. Arrange the tomatoes cut side up on the pan.

3 In a small bowl, combine the remaining olive oil with the garlic, herbs, and cheese. Use a spoon to drizzle a little of this mixture on each of the tomatoes. Sprinkle on a generous pinch of sea salt and bake for 2 hours. The tomatoes will be shriveled and a little caramelized. Transfer them into a serving bowl and top with any accumulated liquid from the baking sheet. Serve warm or at room temperature.

Tomatoes with Simple Balsamic Vinaigrette

Serves 4

At the height of tomato season, when my vines are laden and farm-stands have nothing but dead-ripe tomatoes, I hesitate to use them any way but raw. I know that in the fall and winter I'll be longing for this flavor, so I might as well get my fill at the moment of perfection.

2 tablespoons fruity extra-virgin olive oil

2 tablespoons balsamic vinegar

1 tablespoon minced shallots

2 Brandywine tomatoes or other heirloom reds, cored and cut into ¼-inch slices

1 Cherokee purple tomato, cored and cut into ¼-inch slices

Sea salt and freshly ground black pepper

1 In a small bowl, whisk together the olive oil, vinegar, and shallots. Arrange the tomatoes in an overlapping pattern on a serving platter. Whisk the dressing again and drizzle it over the tomatoes. Sprinkle with a generous pinch of sea salt and several grindings of pepper. Let sit at room temperature for 30 minutes before serving.

Tomatoes and Onions

If my parents had neglected to include a bowl of tomatoes and onions at the dinner table at the height of tomato season, I think I would have worried that they were ill. No matter what kind of meal we had, from about mid-June and through early September, this vinegary mixture was an everyday part of my youth. Today I maintain that tradition. I've goosed it up a little bit—Mom and Dad wouldn't have known olive oil or balsamic vinegar if it slapped them in the face. But the memories are still there, the tastes are still there, and to me, this is summer.

Serves 8

1 Whisk together the olive oil, vinegar, salt, sugar, and pepper. If you're using slices, arrange the tomatoes and onions in alternating rows on a serving dish. Sprinkle with the basil and thyme. Spoon the dressing evenly over the tomatoes. If you're using wedges, combine all the ingredients in a bowl. Either way, cover with plastic wrap and let stand at room temperature for at least 2 hours (4 is better). Serve with a slotted spoon.

¼ cup fruity extra-virgin olive oil

1½ tablespoons balsamic vinegar

½ teaspoon kosher salt

½ teaspoon granulated sugar

¼ teaspoon freshly ground black pepper

4 large meaty tomatoes, thinly sliced or cut into wedges

1 medium sweet onion, thinly sliced

¼ cup chopped basil

1 teaspoon thyme leaves

Heirloom Tomato and Mozzarella Salad

As soon as heirloom tomatoes hit the farmers' market stands, this salad becomes a three-times-a-week indulgence for me. I love the brilliant colors of heirloom tomatoes, from the pinks to the bright reds, the yellow stripes, and even the greens. But even better is the unique taste of each tomato variety. When plated with mozzarella, these tomatoes make one of the most appealing salads you'll ever see. But as important as the tomato is, so is the mozzarella. Try to seek out mozzarella that's been made with milk from grass-fed cows. You'll know it because the mozzarella is slightly off-white, or as my mother would say, antique white. My go-to mozzarella comes from Chapel Hill Creamery, but with a little perseverance, I'm sure you can find excellent, locally made cheese.

Serves 6, but can be scaled up to serve as many folks as you want

1 I tend to make this salad on a large oval platter. Arrange the tomato slices, the cherry tomatoes, and the mozzarella in an appealing pattern. Drizzle the olive oil over the tomatoes and cheese and follow with the balsamic glaze. Scatter the herbs atop the tomatoes and sprinkle with salt and pepper. I like to make this salad an hour or so ahead and serve it at room temperature.

5 or 6 different heirloom tomatoes, sliced

Handful of heirloom cherry tomatoes, like Sun Golds, cut in half

About 1 pound mozzarella cheese, sliced

¼ cup of the finest and fruitiest olive oil you can find and afford

2 tablespoons balsamic vinegar glaze (white is most beautiful)

4 or 5 basil leaves, torn

2 teaspoons thyme leaves

Sea salt and freshly ground black pepper

A Salad of Remembrance

Serves 6

When a member of my mother's or my father's family died, this salad was a standard among the bereavement foods brought to the house. Some of the best food that I've ever eaten has been because somebody passed on. Food and fellowship at my aunt's table helped to make grieving for Dad more tolerable. I try to remember that feeling when I take food to others in grief. I guess bereavement food brings out the best in every cook.

3 large tomatoes, seeded
   and chopped

1 small green bell pepper,
   chopped

1 celery stalk, thinly sliced

½ cup chopped red onions

2 tablespoons apple cider
   vinegar

1 tablespoon (or more)
   granulated sugar

½ teaspoon kosher salt

Freshly ground black pepper

2 tablespoons olive oil

1 In a large bowl, toss together the tomatoes, green peppers, celery, and onions. In a small bowl, whisk together the vinegar, sugar, salt, and several grindings of pepper. Pour the dressing over the tomatoes and toss to combine. Drizzle in the olive oil and toss again. Cover and let sit at room temperature for an hour before serving. You can serve this with a slotted spoon, but you really want to get some of that liquid with every bite, so I use a regular spoon.

Tomatoes and Eggs

Most every southern kitchen has hard-boiled eggs at the ready. You never know when you might need deviled eggs. This recipe makes more cream cheese mixture than you need, so use the extra on your toast or bagel the next morning. For a really incredible experience, you can use the mixture instead of butter and sour cream on your baked potato.

Serves 8

1 Use a fork or an electric hand mixer set on medium speed to blend together the cheese, horseradish, onions, and herbs in a large bowl.

2 Place 3 tomato slices on each plate. Add a tablespoon of the cream cheese mixture in the center of the tomato slices. Press 3 egg slices over the cream cheese and tomatoes. Sprinkle with cracked pepper and serve immediately.

- 1 8-ounce package cream cheese, at room temperature
- 1 tablespoon prepared horseradish, drained
- ¼ cup finely grated onions
- 2 tablespoons chopped flat-leaf parsley
- 2 tablespoons chopped dill
- 24 ¼-inch tomato slices
- 24 hard-boiled egg slices
- Freshly cracked black pepper

APPLE OF LOVE? In the early 1800s, the tomato was known in Europe and France as the apple of love. You gave it as a token of affection, but it was not eaten. Some say that Sir Walter Raleigh presented one to Queen Elizabeth. In this country, it was considered an ornamental plant, and many physicians warned against eating it because it was poisonous (or so they thought). I sure am glad we got all that stuff straightened out, although a tomato is a whole lot cheaper than a dozen roses.

Sort-of-Atlanta's Famous Tomato Casserole

Serves 8–10

Mary Mac's Tea Room in Atlanta is famous for its down-home cooking and great hospitality. Everybody loves Mary Mac's "tomato pie," though it's really more like a casserole. When you're itching for rich tomato flavor but tomatoes aren't quite in season yet, this recipe will satisfy you. The bacon addition is all mine.

Vegetable cooking spray

4 sleeves Ritz crackers

2 28-ounce cans diced tomatoes (fire-roasted are particularly good)

2 tablespoons olive oil

3 cups chopped onions

Kosher salt and freshly ground black pepper

2 cups good-quality mayonnaise

6 slices thick-cut bacon, cooked and crumbled (optional)

1½ cups shredded white cheddar cheese

1 cup grated Parmigiano-Reggiano cheese

4 tablespoons chopped basil

1 tablespoon chopped thyme

1 Preheat your oven to 350 degrees.

2 Spray a 9 × 13-inch baking dish with vegetable spray and set aside.

3 Roughly crush 2 sleeves of the crackers and layer into the bottom of the prepared dish. Pour 1 can of the tomatoes, juice and all, over the crackers.

4 Heat the olive oil in a large sauté pan over medium heat. When the oil begins to shimmer, throw in the onions and cook for 5–6 minutes or until translucent. Give them a generous pinch of salt and several grindings of pepper. Place half the onions over the tomatoes in the dish. Crush 1 sleeve of the crackers and layer them over the onions. Pour the second can of tomatoes evenly over the crackers and spread the remaining onions on top.

5 Fold together the mayonnaise, bacon, cheese, basil, and thyme in a medium mixing bowl. Drop the mixture by spoonfuls over the casserole and then spread the mixture evenly across the top. Crush the last sleeve of crackers and top the mayonnaise mixture with the crumbs. Bake for 40–45 minutes or until golden brown and set. Let cool for at least 10 minutes before serving. Serve hot or at room temperature.

Good Fried Green Tomatoes

Southern writer Fannie Flagg gave up a huge southern secret with her tales of the Whistle Stop Cafe and fried green tomatoes. They're probably the most well-known southern dish after grits. Fried green tomatoes are for breakfast, dinner, and supper, and many people use them as an appetizer. You can do a lot of things with them, and one of my favorites is to put a tablespoon of pimento cheese atop a slice and then cover it with a second slice, making a fried green tomato and pimento cheese sandwich. I also really like fried green tomatoes with breakfast foods like eggs, sausage, grits, and gravy, but at my house, breakfast can come at any time of the day. For the best green tomatoes, wait until the end of the season and buy them from farmstands. They just have better flavor and haven't traveled a long distance. If you don't keep your bacon drippings, then I highly recommend you fry some bacon just for the fat—it's an important taste element of this dish.

Serves 8

1 Place a cooling rack over a baking sheet.

2 In a shallow dish, beat the eggs with the buttermilk or half-and-half. Place the cornmeal in another shallow dish (pie plates work great). Mix a generous pinch of salt and several grindings of pepper into the cornmeal. Dip the tomato slices in the egg mixture and then dredge them through the cornmeal, shaking until the excess falls back into the plate. Place each coated slice on the rack. When all are done, place them in the refrigerator for 30 minutes to 1 hour. Don't skip this step. Chilling helps everything adhere better to the tomato slices.

3 Preheat your oven to 200 degrees.

4 Place a skillet (I like cast-iron) over medium-high heat and pour in oil to a depth of about ½ inch. Stir in the bacon fat. Heat the oil until cornmeal tossed into the fat sputters (or, more scientifically, to 365 degrees). Fry a few tomatoes at a time until golden, about 1 minute per side. Drain on paper towels. Keep warm on a platter in the oven until ready to serve. They ain't good any way but hot.

2 large eggs

½ cup full-fat buttermilk or half-and-half

1½ cups stone-ground yellow or white cornmeal

Kosher salt and freshly ground black pepper

5 medium green tomatoes, cored and cut into ¼-inch slices

Canola oil for frying

2 tablespoons bacon fat

Eggplant Caponata

Some of you may think of caponata as a relish, but I want a mess of it on my plate, making it a side dish especially with grilled fish. Use canned tomatoes to make caponata year-round, but during the summer, shift over to garden or farmstand tomatoes and eggplant.

Serves 4

1 Heat the bacon fat and butter in a 12-inch sauté pan over medium heat. As they start to melt, add the eggplant, tossing to coat the cubes. Add the garlic, capers, thyme, and oregano. Cook, stirring, for about 5 minutes. Add the mustard, lemon zest, olives, raisins, and diced tomatoes. Stir in the brown sugar and simmer for about 20 minutes, until the caponata has tightened up and the eggplant is very tender. Remove from heat and stir in the vinegar. Season with salt and pepper. Stir in the parsley, cherry tomatoes, and pine nuts. Serve warm, at room temperature, or cold. Can be refrigerated for at least a week.

2 tablespoons bacon fat

1 tablespoon unsalted butter

2 medium eggplants, peeled and cut into 1-inch cubes

2 garlic cloves, minced

1 tablespoon salt-packed capers, rinsed

2 sprigs thyme, leaves stripped and finely chopped

2 sprigs oregano, leaves stripped and minced

1 tablespoon coarse-grained mustard

Grated zest of ½ lemon

½ cup kalamata olives, pitted and roughly chopped

½ cup pitted green olives, roughly chopped

¼ cup golden raisins

1 15½-ounce can diced tomatoes

2 tablespoons light brown sugar

2 tablespoons apple cider vinegar

Kosher salt and freshly ground black pepper

2 tablespoons finely chopped flat-leaf parsley

½ cup cherry tomatoes, quartered

1 tablespoon toasted pine nuts

Eggplant, Zucchini, and Tomato Bake

Serves 6

This pleasing combination of all things summer has a Mediterranean twist—feta cheese. However, I play with this recipe a lot, sometimes using blue cheese or Swiss and sometimes substituting yellow squash for the zucchini or using zucchini and yellow squash but no eggplant. Don't be afraid to deviate from the plan.

1½ pounds zucchini, sliced lengthwise ¼-inch thick

1½ pounds eggplant, peeled and sliced lengthwise ¼-inch thick (try to pick eggplants that are long and narrow)

Vegetable cooking spray

3 tablespoons olive oil, divided

¼ cup finely chopped shallots

1 pound plum or Roma tomatoes, cubed

¾ cup crumbled feta cheese

¼ cup chopped basil

2 tablespoons chopped thyme

1 tablespoon chopped oregano

½ cup panko or dried bread crumbs

Kosher salt and freshly ground black pepper

1 Preheat your grill to medium.

2 Place the zucchini and eggplant slices on rimmed baking sheets. Spray with vegetable spray. Grill each slice of zucchini for about 2 minutes on each side and each slice of eggplant for 3–4 minutes on each side. You want the vegetables to be tender and to take on a little color.

3 Heat 2 tablespoons of the oil in a large skillet over medium heat. When the oil shimmers, toss in the shallots and cook until softened, 3–4 minutes. Remove from heat and add the tomatoes. Let the heat from the pan soften the tomatoes slightly.

4 Spray a 10 × 15-inch baking dish with vegetable spray. Lay half of the eggplant in the bottom of the dish and scatter on top about ¼ of the tomatoes along with half of the feta, basil, thyme, and oregano. Layer on half of the zucchini, followed by another ¼ of the tomatoes, the remaining herbs, the rest of the eggplant and zucchini, and the remaining tomato and feta. Mix the bread crumbs with the remaining oil and sprinkle over the top. Add a good pinch of salt and a few grindings of pepper. Let stand for 15 minutes at room temperature.

5 Preheat your oven to 425 degrees.

6 Bake the vegetables for about 20 minutes or until they bubble and the bread crumbs are golden brown. Let stand for 5–10 minutes before serving. Good hot or warm.

Quick Italian Eggplant

Southerners like to introduce themselves with food, and I'm no different. Whether it's a new neighbor or a new baby, food is always appreciated during the first weeks of adjusting to a new routine. I routinely use this recipe in those settings, but I also love this eggplant with grilled lamb or pork.

Serves 6–8

1 Place the eggplant in a large roasting pan. Cover barely with water and sprinkle in the salt. Soak for 30 minutes, then rinse and pat dry.

2 Heat the oil in a large sauté pan over medium heat. When the oil begins to shimmer, add the eggplant. Cook for 2–3 minutes per side until the eggplant takes on some color.

3 Put the tomatoes and garlic in a 2-quart saucepan over medium heat. Bring to a boil, then reduce heat and simmer for about 10 minutes until a saucelike consistency develops.

4 Spray a 9 × 13-inch casserole dish with vegetable spray. Layer half the eggplant in the bottom, followed by half of the tomato sauce, half of the mozzarella, half of the salami, and half of the Parmesan. Repeat.

5 Preheat your oven to 350 degrees.

6 Bake for 15 minutes until hot and bubbly. Serve hot or at room temperature. Leftovers can be served straight out of the refrigerator.

1½ pounds eggplant, peeled and sliced lengthwise ¼ inch thick

Water

1 tablespoon salt

2 tablespoons olive oil

2 15½-ounce cans Italian-style diced tomatoes

1 garlic clove, finely chopped

Vegetable cooking spray

8 ounces fresh mozzarella cheese, sliced

½ pound sliced salami, coarsely chopped

2 cups shredded Parmesan cheese

Stuffed Peppers

Serves 4

I don't know why stuffed peppers seem so relevant to the South. I do know that they're easy to make and extremely tasty, but is that the real reason? In any case, they look darned good sitting on a plate, and southerners (this one in particular) like to feast with our eyes as well as our mouths. This recipe calls for yellow peppers, but orange, red, or green can be used. Many times, I use a mix of colors.

¾ cup uncooked long-grain rice

Homemade or low-sodium beef broth

3 tablespoons dried currants

¼ cup fresh orange juice

2 tablespoons olive oil

2 cups chopped sweet onions

2 garlic cloves, finely chopped

1 tablespoon oil-packed sun-dried tomatoes, drained and chopped

1 teaspoon ground coriander

1 tablespoon chopped flat-leaf parsley

1 tablespoon chopped basil

Kosher salt and freshly ground black pepper

4 large yellow bell peppers

1 Cook the rice according to the package directions, substituting beef broth for water.

2 Soak the currants in the orange juice for at least 10 minutes. Drain and reserve.

3 Heat the oil in a large sauté pan over medium heat. When the oil shimmers, throw in the onions and cook, stirring occasionally, until they begin to take on color, about 10 minutes. Add the garlic and cook for 1 minute more. Toss in the rice, currants, tomatoes, coriander, parsley, and basil. Add a generous pinch of salt and several grindings of pepper. Stir the ingredients and remove from heat.

4 Cut the tops off the peppers. Reserve the tops but clean out and discard seeds and membranes from the body of the pepper. If the peppers won't stand up on their own, use a paring knife to shave little bits off the knobs on the bottom of the pepper. Fill each pepper with the rice mixture and replace the top. Place the peppers snugly in a 2½-quart round soufflé dish.

5 Preheat your oven to 350 degrees.

6 Cover the peppers with aluminum foil and bake for 35 minutes, until tender. Remove the foil and bake for an additional 15 minutes or until the tops are light brown. Remove from the baking dish and let stand for 5 minutes. Serve warm or at room temperature.

Fried Eggplant with "Étouffée" Sauce

My son-in-law, Kyle, and I in a moment of insanity came up with this little twist from New Orleans to goose up fried eggplant. The combination is awesome. The étouffée sauce takes a little while to make, but it will keep for a week and is good over fish, shrimp, and even pork chops. Without the sauce, the fried eggplant can stand on its own.

Serves 4–6

1. Combine the egg and the half-and-half in a 9-inch pie plate. Add the eggplant and toss to coat. Your hands are your best tool for this. Let the eggplant soak for at least 5 minutes.
2. Combine the flour, cornmeal, and spices in another pie plate.
3. Place a cooling rack over a baking sheet.
4. Dredge each eggplant slice through the flour mixture. Shake off any excess and lay all the slices on the rack.
5. Fill a large cast-iron skillet with 2½- to 3-inch sides half full with canola oil. Bring the oil to 350 degrees and then add a few of the eggplant slices. Cook for 4–5 minutes per side or until golden brown. Drain on paper towels. When all the eggplant is cooked, serve immediately as is or with the "Étouffée" Sauce.

1 large egg

½ cup half-and-half

4 medium eggplants, cut into 1-inch slices

¼ cup all-purpose flour

3 tablespoons cornmeal

⅛ teaspoon smoked paprika

⅛ teaspoon ground ancho chili or chili powder

⅛ teaspoon dried thyme

⅛ teaspoon kosher salt

⅛ teaspoon freshly ground black pepper

Canola oil

"Étouffée" Sauce (page 319)

Eggplant with Shiitake Mushrooms and Peppers

Serves 6

This dish not only has Asian twists and turns but also is visually beautiful and somewhat beefy. When you get right down to it, I don't know why this works, but it does.

2 tablespoons dry vermouth

1 tablespoon low-sodium soy sauce

1 tablespoon red wine vinegar

2 teaspoons chili paste, such as Sambal

1 medium eggplant, peeled and cut into 1-inch cubes

2 teaspoons kosher salt

6 tablespoons canola oil

4 shallots, thinly sliced

4 garlic cloves, minced

1 red bell pepper, cut into 1-inch pieces

1 yellow bell pepper, cut into 1-inch pieces

12 large fresh shiitake mushrooms, quartered

1 Using a fork, combine the vermouth, soy sauce, vinegar, and chili paste in a small bowl.

2 Place the eggplant in a large bowl and sprinkle with the salt. Let stand for 30 minutes, drain, and pat dry.

3 Heat the oil in a large sauté pan over medium-high heat. When the oil begins to shimmer, throw in the eggplant and cook until golden brown, 5–10 minutes. Remove the eggplant with a slotted spoon. Stir-fry the shallots, garlic, and peppers in the oil until tender, 3–5 minutes. Add the mushrooms and cook for another minute.

4 Return the eggplant to the pan and pour the vermouth mixture over the vegetables. Toss to uniformly coat and cook until just heated, 2–3 minutes. Serve hot or at room temperature.

Portabella "Pizzas"

Looking for something interesting to serve with grilled fish and baked chicken? Try these portabella mushroom caps all dressed up. The flavors blend into an earthy but bright and creamy amalgamation. If you need something for a vegetarian, this isn't a bad choice. Like everything else, the quality of the ingredients makes a huge difference. Using home-made tomato sauce (or even better, homemade sauce from heirloom tomatoes) and mozzarella cheese from a local producer elevates these mushrooms even further.

Serves 4

1 Place the mushrooms, gill side up, in a baking dish, and pour the olive oil and vinegar over them. Add a generous sprinkling of salt and several grindings of pepper. Let sit at room temperature for about 30 minutes.

2 Place 2 tablespoons of marinara sauce in each cap. Equally divide the thyme among the 4 caps. Place 2 slices of cheese on each mushroom.

3 Grill on medium high for 6–8 minutes or until the mushrooms feel tender when you touch them. Pour any juice left in the baking dish over the mushrooms and cook for another minute. Remove from the grill and serve immediately.

4 medium-sized portabella mushroom caps, gills scraped out

¼ cup extra-virgin olive oil

2 tablespoons sherry or balsamic vinegar

Kosher salt and freshly ground black pepper

8 tablespoons marinara sauce (not canned tomato sauce)

1 tablespoon thyme leaves

8 slices fresh mozzarella cheese (about 6 ounces)

MIDSUMMER NIGHT'S VEGGIE DREAMS

Corn, Okra, & Squash

Daddy used to say to me, "Your eyes are bigger than your stomach." If he could see my stomach now, his opinion might be different, but I still have that same lack of impulse control, especially in midsummer at the farmers' market. Sweet corn, fresh okra, and squash are just too tempting to pass up. With some tomatoes and field peas, I have no trouble buying enough vegetables to fill the backseat of my car.

A farmers' market in midsummer is full of all kinds of vibes. The farmers themselves, proud of what they've grown, create one sensation. The smells of just-picked ripe fruits and vegetables call to us. The community of buyers and their interactions with each other as well as with the farmers give us a sense of nostalgia and belonging and create a setting that almost resembles a family reunion. Farmers' markets have now become the new town center or village green. And in high summer, there's no place I'd rather be.

I'd love to follow every tomato I eat with a fresh lightly cooked ear of corn. I have yet to find a way to cook corn that I don't like (unless it's overcooked). Corn has always been a staple in the South, and I early on learned the difference between "roast'n ears" and feed corn. When we visited my grandmother and uncles, Daddy always made sure that we got some of those tender kernel ears of corn. Lately I've been per-turbed by what seems like an obsession with the Silver Queen variety, and I've cajoled farmers to look for sweet yellow corn varieties. They have accepted the challenge, and now we have mul-tiple varieties of sweet corn.

Growing up, I wouldn't have given you a plug nickel for okra or squash. It's funny how our taste buds change as we age. Southern-fried okra has become one of my favorite things. It has a brini-ness to go with its sweetness, bathing my taste buds almost like an oyster. The heritage of this West African vegetable is colored with both sor-row and joy. I hate the way it got here, but I'm glad it did.

For some reason, my mother's pan-fried squash and onions never appealed to me, and I was nervous when I was served a squash casse-role at my future mother-in-law's table. I couldn't just look at her and say, "Eww—I can't eat that." I'm glad I gave it a try, because it was a turning point for me. Summer squash and zucchini are now two of my mainstays. I think nothing of slicing them up, grilling them, and serving them alongside a steak; puréeing some to use as a soup base; or letting them be the "noodles" in a summer pasta. The recipes that follow are my ab-solute favorites. But don't forget that simplicity with perfectly ripe seasonal vegetables is always a good thing.

Fried Corn

I learned about fried corn, a very close cousin to cream-style corn, from folks who live in the upcountry region of South Carolina, where they love this stuff. It's a little fancy but a good platform for showing off the corn's magnificent flavor.

Serves 4–6

1 Heat the oil in a large sauté pan over medium heat. When the oil begins to shimmer, throw in the shallots, peppers, and garlic and cook for about 5 minutes. Add the corn and cook for an additional 5–8 minutes or until tender, stirring often.

2 Add the butter, the heavy cream, the thyme, and a dash or two of hot sauce to the corn mixture. Cook for another few minutes or until the cream has thickened. Season with salt, pepper, and lemon juice and serve immediately.

2 tablespoons olive oil

⅓ cup finely chopped shallots

½ cup finely chopped green bell peppers

1 garlic clove, finely chopped

6 ears corn, kernels cut off the cob

2 tablespoons unsalted butter

⅓ cup heavy cream

4 sprigs thyme

Hot pepper sauce

Kosher salt and freshly ground black pepper

Squirt of fresh lemon juice

REMOVING KERNELS FROM A CORNCOB Removing kernels from a corncob can be a messy and exasperating job. Here's a trick to make it much easier. Take a tube pan or a Bundt pan, open side up, and place an ear of corn into the center hole. Use a knife to cut down along the kernels, turning the ear as you go. The pan collects the kernels, and the hole gives you the stability to hold the ear without cutting yourself. Don't forget to run the back of your knife along the cob once you've removed the kernels to collect the sweet milk, too.

Nikki's Corn Pudding

Serves 6–8 easily

An Alabama native who now lives in Richmond, Virginia, Nikki Parrish uses this recipe for potlucks and holiday entertaining. I think you'll find it just as useful.

Vegetable cooking spray

2 16-ounce cans creamed corn

1½ cups granulated sugar

4 eggs, beaten

8 tablespoons unsalted butter, melted

½ cup all-purpose flour

2 teaspoons vanilla

2 cups evaporated milk

1 Preheat your oven to 350 degrees.

2 Spray a 9 × 13-inch baking pan with vegetable spray.

3 Combine all ingredients and pour into the prepared pan. Bake uncovered for 1 hour or until firm.

NOTE This recipe may be halved and baked in a 1½-quart casserole.

Bourbon Creamed Corn

I know—you think I've lost my mind. But the key to any great bourbon or Tennessee sipping whiskey is the corn within the mash bill, so adding a little bourbon to a corn dish seems perfectly normal to me.

Serves 6–8

1 Melt the butter in a large skillet over medium-high heat. Add the shallots and garlic and sauté for 2 minutes. Add the corn and continue cooking until almost tender, about 2 minutes. Add ⅓ cup of the cream and the bourbon. Simmer until the sauce thickens and coats the corn, 2–3 minutes. Add the remaining cream and 1 cup of the green onions. Simmer until the sauce thickens enough to coat the corn thinly, about 2 minutes longer. Season with salt and pepper. Serve immediately, topped with the remaining green onions.

¼ cup unsalted butter

1 cup chopped shallots

3 garlic cloves, finely chopped

3 cups corn kernels

⅔ cup heavy cream, divided

¼ cup bourbon

1¼ cups chopped green onions, divided

Kosher salt and freshly ground black pepper

Grilled Corn on the Cob with Avocado Butter

Serves 8

After I've gotten my fill of fresh corn when the season begins around the Fourth of July, I start playing with corn on the cob because I enjoy seeing what flavors give an added boost to freshly picked corn. This avocado butter was a surprising experiment, and I make it often. Any leftover butter can be used on grilled fish or shrimp.

1 small ripe avocado, seeded, peeled, and chopped

½ cup butter, softened

1 tablespoon fresh lime juice

¼ teaspoon chili powder

Kosher salt

8 ears corn, husks on

2 tablespoons olive oil or a homemade vinaigrette

Additional kosher salt and freshly ground black pepper

1 Mash the avocado in a small bowl with a fork. Stir in the butter, lime juice, chili powder, and a generous pinch of salt. Cover and chill this mixture for at least 1 hour.

2 Peel back but do not remove the corn husks. Remove the silks and place the corn and husks in cold water for 30 minutes. Drain and then pat dry.

3 Brush the corn with the oil or vinaigrette. Sprinkle lightly with additional salt and a grinding or two of pepper on each cob. Fold the husks back around the corn and tie once with kitchen twine.

4 Preheat your grill to medium.

5 Place the corn on the grill and cover. Grill for 20–25 minutes, turning the ears every 5 minutes. Pull the corn off the grill and remove the husks. Serve immediately, slathering the corn with the butter.

CORN ON THE COB ETIQUETTE "Corn may be eaten from the cob. Etiquette permits this method, but does not allow one to butter the entire length of an ear of corn and then gnaw it from end to end. To hold an ear of corn if it may be a short one, by the end, with the right hand and bite from the ear is good form. A little doily, or very small napkin, is sometimes served with corn to fold about the end of a cob that is to be grasped by the hand, but this arrangement is as inconvenient as it is unnecessary." From *Good Form: Dinners Ceremonious and Unceremonious*, 1890.

Give me a break! I'll eat corn on the cob any way I please.

Charred Corn Salad with Mustard Vinaigrette

Serves 6

This is my favorite side dish with crab cakes or soft-shell crabs. If fresh corn is not available, frozen corn works almost as well—just brown the corn in a sauté pan. The nice bite of this dish makes it a wonderful contrast to sweet crab or fish.

---

4 ears corn

3 tablespoons Dijon mustard

3 tablespoons apple cider vinegar

1 tablespoon fresh lemon juice

1 teaspoon finely chopped garlic

1 teaspoon finely chopped shallots

½ teaspoon granulated sugar

¼ teaspoon cracked mustard seeds

½ cup extra-virgin olive oil

1 Preheat your grill to medium.

2 Grill the corn, turning frequently so it doesn't burn and gets an equal amount of char on all sides, usually 5–7 minutes. Remove and let cool. Cut the kernels off the cob.

3 Combine the mustard, vinegar, lemon juice, garlic, shallots, sugar, and mustard seeds in a blender or food processor. With the motor running, slowly add the oil. Spoon some dressing over the corn and toss to combine. Serve immediately.

Maque Choux

Maque choux (pronounced mack shoe) is one of those venerable dishes from South Louisiana. It's a joyful combination of some of summer's best bounty. But why did they have to give it such a crazy name? Legend and lore claim that the recipe is Arcadian French (Cajun) and Native American with a French interpretation of the native word for the dish. Whatever it's called, it's good eating with any Cajun fare.

Serves 6

1 Heat the oil in a large skillet over medium-high heat. Throw in the onions and green peppers and cook for 8 minutes or until the onions are translucent. Add the corn, milk from the corncobs, tomatoes, and milk. Reduce heat to medium low and cook for about 20 minutes. Stir frequently to prevent the mixture from sticking to the bottom of the pan, and do not let it boil. Season with a generous pinch of salt and a tiny pinch of cayenne pepper. Reduce heat, cover, and cook for about 5 minutes. Stir in the green onions and bacon. Serve immediately.

2 tablespoons canola oil

1 large onion, thinly sliced

1 cup chopped green bell peppers

6 ears corn, kernels cut off the cob and milk reserved

1 large tomato, seeded and chopped

¼ cup milk

Kosher salt

Cayenne pepper

¼ cup chopped green onions

8 strips thick-cut bacon, cooked until crisp, then crumbled

Fred's Southern-Fried Okra

Fried okra is one of my favorite vegetables—I think because it faintly reminds me of fried oysters. I hate when the coating falls off the okra and makes a greasy mess. This recipe has a simple trick that I guarantee will make the coating stick and yield a nice crunchy result.

Serves 4–6

1 Place the okra in a large mixing bowl and sprinkle with the flour, tossing to coat evenly. Transfer the okra to a strainer to knock off any excess. This coating should be very light. Return to the mixing bowl and add the egg, making certain that each piece of okra is coated. Pour the cornmeal into another mixing bowl. Add the salt and pepper. Place a handful of the okra in the cornmeal and toss with your hands until each piece is coated. Place on a wire baking rack while you coat the remainder of the okra.

2 At this point I will tell you that I prefer to use lard and a little bacon fat to fry these okra. If this is new to you, I suggest you use the canola oil. Pour about ½ inch of the oil into a large cast-iron skillet or sauté pan with 3-inch sides and place over medium heat. When the oil is between 375 and 400 degrees, add the coated okra a handful or so at a time and fry until the pieces are golden, 3–5 minutes. Remove with a slotted spoon and drain on paper towels. When all the okra is fried, get it to the table as fast as you can.

1 quart fresh okra, cut into ½-inch rounds or sliced lengthwise

3 tablespoons all-purpose flour

1 large egg, beaten

1½ cups yellow cornmeal (not cornmeal mix), preferably stone-ground

1 teaspoon kosher salt

½ teaspoon freshly ground black pepper

Lard, bacon fat, or canola oil for frying

Okra Fritters

Serves 6

These fritters are sort of like your standard okra and tomato dish but neatly fried. You can use them as a bread or put them alongside some fried catfish or croakers. They're also fun when used at cocktail parties as hors d'oeuvres.

2 pounds fresh okra, cut into ⅛-inch rounds

1 large tomato, peeled, seeded, and diced

½ cup diced onions

2 cups all-purpose flour

2 large eggs, beaten

Kosher salt and freshly ground black pepper

Canola oil for frying

1 Combine the okra, tomato, and onions in a large mixing bowl. Add the flour, the eggs, a good pinch of salt, and a few grindings of pepper. Mix with your hands.

2 Place about ¼ inch of oil in a large cast-iron skillet over medium-high heat. Form the okra mixture into patties about 2 inches in diameter and about ¼ inch thick. When the oil is shimmering, cook a fritter or two at a time for about 5 minutes, then turn and cook for an additional 5 minutes. The fritters should be golden. Remove with a slotted spoon and drain on paper towels. Serve immediately.

Mother's Favorite "Stewed" Okra

My mother's love of okra has always surprised me. We used to have it often at home, but it wasn't quite this fancy. Now that Mother has given me the reins to do most of the cooking for holidays and family gatherings, I've added a few tricks to her simple okra. She loves it, and that's all that counts.

Serves 4–6

---

1 Heat the butter and olive oil in a large skillet over medium heat. When the butter stops foaming, add the onions and garlic, and cook for about 5 minutes. Reduce heat to medium low and add the okra, cooking for around 15 minutes and then adding a generous pinch of salt and a few grindings of pepper. Taste and add 3 or 4 dashes of hot sauce, if desired. Serve immediately.

1 tablespoon unsalted butter

2 tablespoons olive oil

½ cup finely chopped onions

1 garlic clove, minced

1 pound okra

Kosher salt and freshly
   ground black pepper

Hot pepper sauce

Grilled Okra

This recipe may have surprised me more than any other I've worked on. I'm pretty much a fried okra kind of guy, but this recipe, well, let's just say I love these little grilled pods. This was a total lark. They are fabulous with a steak and make great munchies with cocktails or beer.

1 pound medium-size okra

2 tablespoons canola oil

Kosher salt and freshly ground black pepper

Wooden or metal skewers (if wooden, soak in water for at least 45 minutes)

2 tablespoons balsamic vinegar

1 Preheat your grill to medium.

2 Toss the okra with the oil in a large bowl and then add a large pinch of salt and several grindings of pepper. Skewer the okra, leaving plenty of space between pieces. Grill the okra for 4–5 minutes per side until it's firmed up and taken on a grilled, caramelized color. Pull the pieces off the skewers and toss with the vinegar. Serve immediately.

Limpin' Susan

Serves 4–6

I guess if you've got hoppin' John, you need to be politically correct and have a female version. Actually, limpin' Susan has been around low-country Georgia, South Carolina, and North Carolina for a long time. I cook this dish in the summer, when the okra is at its absolute freshest, because I think it goes wonderfully with almost all grilled foods.

1 Place a 3- to 4-quart saucepan over medium heat. Throw the bacon in the pan, reduce to low, and cook for 7–8 minutes or until the bacon has given up its fat and the pieces are crispy. Remove the bacon from the pan, leaving the fat, and drain the bacon on paper towels. Add the okra, onions, and garlic to the pan and cook for about 5 minutes or until the onions have softened. Stir in the herbs and then the rice and cook for about 1 minute. Pour in the chicken broth, tomatoes, and hot sauce. Add a generous pinch of salt and several grindings of pepper. Cover and cook over low heat until the rice is done, about 20 minutes. You may need to adjust your temperature to medium low. When done, fluff the mixture with a fork. Transfer to a bowl and serve immediately.

4 slices thick-cut bacon, diced

½ pound fresh okra, cut into rounds

1 cup chopped onions

3 garlic cloves, minced

1 tablespoon chopped basil

1 teaspoon thyme leaves

1 cup long-grain rice, like Carolina Gold

2 cups homemade or low-sodium chicken broth

2 tomatoes, cored and finely chopped (almost crushed)

⅛ teaspoon hot pepper sauce

Kosher salt and freshly ground black pepper

Old-Fashioned Squash and Onions

Serves 4–6

Growing up, I thought my parents could eat this dish every day during the summer, and I hated it. About when I turned twenty, though, I changed my mind. It's a simple country farmhouse kind of recipe, and it's a classic.

2 tablespoons unsalted butter

2 tablespoons bacon fat

2 sweet onions, thinly sliced

5 large yellow squash, thinly sliced

Kosher salt and freshly ground black pepper

¼ teaspoon granulated sugar

Hot pepper sauce and cider or sherry vinegar (optional)

1 Melt the butter and bacon fat in a large cast-iron skillet over medium heat. Throw in the onions, stir, and cook for 10–15 minutes, until they have a tiny bit of color. Add the squash and stir. Cook for an additional 20 minutes or until the squash becomes tender. Add a generous pinch of salt and several grindings of pepper. Sprinkle on the sugar and stir to combine everything. Serve immediately with hot sauce and vinegar on the side.

Nick's Squash Casserole

Serves 6–8

Another great way to prepare zucchini and yellow squash when they take over your garden. I'm sorry, but there's just no way to make a good southern casserole without a can of soup, so swallow your pride and eat well.

4 zucchini, cut into ¼-inch rounds

4 yellow squash, cut into ¼-inch rounds

2 10¾-ounce cans condensed cream of mushroom soup

1¼ cups milk

1 cup thinly sliced sweet onions

1½ cups shredded cheddar cheese

Kosher salt and freshly ground black pepper

1 cup crushed saltine crackers

2 tablespoons unsalted butter, melted

1 Preheat your oven to 375 degrees.

2 Toss together the zucchini, squash, soup, milk, and onions in a large bowl. Pour this mixture into a 9 × 13-inch baking dish. Sprinkle the cheese evenly over the top, followed by a generous pinch of salt and several grindings of pepper. Toss the crushed crackers with the butter and sprinkle them evenly over the top of the casserole. Bake uncovered for 35–40 minutes or until bubbly and a little firm. Cool for about 10 minutes and then serve.

THE THREE SISTERS Native Americans were extremely frugal with their land and very efficient with their food production. One ancient tradition was planting corn, beans, and squash together on the same bit of land. The combination replenished the soil nutrients and made each of the plants more productive. Corn demands nitrogen, but beans replace it. Beans climb on the cornstalks. The large squash leaves shade the land, helping to retain moisture and blocking weeds. Sounds like smart gardening to me.

Mixed-Vegetable Grill

During the summer, I grill vegetables a lot. It seems to intensify their flavor. I often grill a few extra and purée them to use as a base for a pasta sauce later on.

Serves 6–8

1 Combine the oil, wine, garlic, herbs, salt, and pepper in a large bowl. Cover and let the flavors develop for at least 2 hours.

2 Add the vegetables and toss to coat. Let sit at room temperature for another hour. Remove the vegetables from the marinade and place in a single layer on a medium-hot grill. Cook until each is well marked and tender. The asparagus and squash will take about 5 minutes, the peppers and eggplants about 10 minutes. Serve immediately.

1 cup extra-virgin olive oil

¼ cup dry white wine

2 tablespoons minced garlic

1 cup chopped basil

¼ cup chopped rosemary

1 teaspoon kosher salt

1 teaspoon freshly ground black pepper

1 pound fresh asparagus, woody ends removed

4 medium zucchini, sliced lengthwise ¼-inch thick

4 yellow squash, sliced lengthwise ¼-inch thick

4 red bell peppers, cut in half, seeds and membranes removed

4 small eggplants, cut into ¼-inch rounds

Grilled Zucchini and Summer Squash Salad

Serves 6

Considering how many vegetables squash plants produce, it's good to have a variety of recipes for zucchini and yellow squash. This easy salad is great with just about any grilled food.

4 large zucchini, cut in half lengthwise

4 medium to large yellow squash, cut in half lengthwise

5 tablespoons olive oil, divided

Kosher salt and freshly ground black pepper

½ cup chopped basil

⅓ cup grated Parmesan cheese

2 tablespoons balsamic vinegar

1 tablespoon toasted sesame seeds

1 Place the zucchini and squash on a large baking sheet and brush all sides with 3 tablespoons of the oil. Sprinkle with salt and pepper. Place the vegetables on a medium-hot grill and cook until tender and brown, about 10 minutes, turning often. Remove the squash to a cutting board and cut on the diagonal into 1-inch pieces. Place in a large bowl and add the basil, cheese, vinegar, and remaining oil. Toss to blend. Sprinkle with the toasted sesame seeds and serve immediately.

Zucchini with Bacon Stuffing

People will eat anything if you put enough bacon on it. Zucchini is in such abundance during the summer, it's a shame to ignore it, but many of us do. When I want to be a little fancy or I'm having company over for a cookout, I goose the zucchini up with this bacon mixture.

Serves 6–8

1 Blend the lemon juice, the oil, the garlic, a good sprinkling of salt, and several grindings of pepper in a small bowl. Brush the zucchini with this mixture and pour any leftover mixture into the zucchini shell. Let sit at room temperature for 30 minutes.

2 Combine the bacon, cheese, basil, pepperoncini, lemon zest, garlic, and 3–4 grindings of pepper in a medium bowl.

3 Preheat your grill to medium.

4 Grill the zucchini cut sides down for 5–7 minutes or until it starts to brown. Turn over the zucchini and grill for 1–2 minutes longer. Remove the zucchini to a sheet pan. Spoon the bacon mixture into the shell, pressing down to compact it and mounding it slightly. Return the zucchini to the grill and cook for 2–4 minutes longer with the lid down or until the cheese starts to melt. Serve immediately.

2 tablespoons fresh lemon juice

1 tablespoon olive oil

3 garlic cloves, minced

Kosher salt and freshly ground black pepper

4 medium to large zucchini, cut in half lengthwise and seeds removed

16 slices bacon, cooked until crisp, then crumbled

1 cup finely shredded Parmesan cheese

¼ cup chopped basil

¼ cup chopped pepperoncini

1 tablespoon grated lemon zest

2 garlic cloves, minced

Freshly ground black pepper

Grilled Romaine

Grilled romaine may be overdone these days, but I still think it's incredibly tasty and I eat this salad quite a bit over the summer. You can swap out the romaine for radicchio or iceberg or substitute a local goat or farmer cheese for the Parmesan.

4 hearts of romaine,
    cut in half lengthwise

¼ cup sherry or balsamic
    vinegar

Extra-virgin olive oil

Kosher salt and freshly
    ground black pepper

About 1 cup freshly
    shaved Parmesan cheese
    (a vegetable peeler will
    do the trick)

1 Splash the romaine with the vinegar and place it, cut side down, on a grill at medium heat. Cook for about 4 minutes until you get a small amount of wilting and some char. Transfer to individual salad plates. Drizzle liberally with oil and sprinkle with salt and pepper. Sprinkle the cheese evenly over the romaine and serve immediately.

WHITE & ORANGE, OUR FAVORITE POTATOES

Potatoes in most any form are the heroes of side dishes. I mean, think about it, have you ever heard anyone say, "I'm allergic to potatoes," or "I don't like potatoes," or "Potatoes taste yucky?" No, and you probably never will.

Potatoes are the base of many a plate. We think of potatoes as the ideal comfort food. You have to admit, there aren't many things better than some creamy, rich mashed potatoes. Well, duck-fat home fries are pretty good, too. And hash brown casseroles. And oh my goodness, how can you not just love french fries? So I guess the list is a little bit longer than just mashed potatoes. But we grew up with mashed potatoes as a side dish several nights a week. Potatoes give us hugs when we're down in the dumps and make us happy.

As a child, I wouldn't get near a sweet potato unless it was in a casserole topped with marshmallows. Daddy, on the other hand, regularly ate sweet potatoes cold. To him, sweet potatoes were upscale. White potatoes (or Irish potatoes, as my relatives called them) were easy to grow in the fields of Johnston County. So were sweet potatoes. During the Depression, my parents were thankful that both types of potatoes were plentiful.

Mama tried to give us a balanced plate at every meal, but she didn't wear out us out on potatoes. Every Saturday night was steak night, complete with a baked potato with sour cream and butter, like the great steakhouses of the day served; bacon bits sometimes would share in this glory. After Mother, like many housewives in the 1960s, switched to instant mashed potatoes, which are only good smothered in gravy so you can't taste the artificial stuff in them, that baked potato became even more important to me. I still treat myself to one weekly. I no longer endure instant potatoes, and no one else should either. Perfect Mashed Potatoes (page 110) are so easy to make.

While I've always been a white potato freak, in the past ten years, I have come to love one of North Carolina's biggest crops, sweet potatoes. I'm constantly playing with sweet potatoes, trying to balance their natural sweetness with tart or sharp flavors. Those trials have resulted in some great recipes. Almost anything a white potato can do, a sweet potato can do, too.

There are now many, many types of white potatoes on the market. Yukon Golds were a gourmet potato just twenty years ago, and now they are super easy to get. Farmers are harvesting potatoes much earlier, creating "baby" new potatoes that are really sweet, and, well, they taste like dirt with cream, but that's some highfalutin dirt. Fingerling potatoes, which are perfect for roasting, can be found at farmers' markets and larger grocery stores. The number of varieties of sweet potatoes has also exploded, and in addition to orange ones, you can find red, blue, and white ones. Heirloom potatoes are ugly, yet their veins and knolls are signs of sugar and exploding flavors. Try different potatoes in these recipe, though you should stay with russets for baking and russets and Yukon Golds for mashing and french frying. Do not, do not, *do not* use a food processor to cream potatoes. And yes, duck fat is a perfect medium for frying potatoes, white or orange.

You'll find potato salads in this chapter, too, because they are best when served slightly warmed. Yet when you're taking leftovers out of the fridge, you'll find that potato salads are pretty doggoned good cold, too. Jean's Potato Salad (page 132) is a true southern classic.

Yes, I know, potatoes are nightshades. But how do you put potatoes and tomatoes in the same chapter?

Fred's French Fries

Good french fries are very important to me. I love them with hanger steak, beside a hamburger, alongside fried shrimp, or by themselves with my homemade ketchup. Follow this method and you'll have perfect fries every time.

Serves 4–6

4 large long russet potatoes, sliced lengthwise into ¼-inch sticks

Water

Canola oil for frying

Coarse sea salt or truffled sea salt

1 Place the cut potatoes in a bowl, cover with water, and refrigerate for 8 hours or overnight.

2 Drain the potato sticks and lay them out on dish or paper towels to dry. Be sure they are completely dry before frying.

3 In a deep-fryer or Dutch oven, heat 2 inches of oil to 300 degrees. Add the potatoes a handful at a time and cook until they're slightly limp, about 2 minutes. You don't want to brown them at this point. Remove the fries from the oil with a spider or slotted spoon. Transfer the potatoes to a rack set over a baking sheet and separate the sticks. Repeat with the remaining potatoes.

4 Increase the oil temperature to 375 degrees. Again, add the potatoes in batches and fry until they are browned on the edges and crisp, around 5 minutes. Drain and transfer them to a bowl lined with paper towels. Season the fries with salt while they are still hot and serve immediately.

NOTE I have cooked fries at 375 degrees for the first fry and then 385 degrees for the second. This produces more European-style frites.

Perfect Mashed Potatoes

Serves 4–6

The importance of good—no, great—mashed potatoes should never be overlooked. Lately, we've somehow seemed willing to accept just so-so mashed potatoes, and we shouldn't. It really doesn't take very long to do homemade mashed potatoes. Five ingredients and you're good to go. Mashed potatoes are an emulsion of the potatoes and the butter. A major key to making outstanding mashed potatoes is to make sure you stir in the butter so that it's completely incorporated.

4 large russet potatoes, peeled and cut into chunks

Water

½ cup whole milk

10 tablespoons unsalted butter, cut into small bits

Kosher salt and freshly ground black pepper

1 Place the potatoes in a large saucepan with enough water to cover them. Bring to a boil over high heat, then reduce heat and simmer for about 20 minutes or until the potatoes are easily pierced with a knife.

2 Slowly warm the milk.

3 Drain the potatoes and return them to the pan. Place the pan back over the heat and shake for about 1 minute to dry out the potatoes.

4 Mash the potatoes and then start adding the butter, a little at a time, stirring to incorporate. When all the butter has been used, start adding the warm milk, stirring until the potatoes become creamy. You may not need all of the milk. Season with salt and pepper. Serve immediately.

Mashed Potatoes with Caramelized Onions and Fennel

Since I love potatoes, onions, and fennel, it was only a matter of time before they all wound up together in a dish. I particularly like these potatoes in the fall and winter and usually include them in holiday buffets. I really love them on New Year's Day, even though I'm having hoppin' John as well. Who said it was against the law to have two starches?

Serves 6–8

1 Place the potatoes in a 4-quart saucepan and cover with water. Bring to a boil over high heat, then reduce heat and simmer until the potatoes are easy to pierce with the tip of a knife, about 20 minutes. Drain the potatoes and return them to the pan. Place the pan back over the heat and shake for 3–4 minutes to dry out the potatoes. Carefully remove the skin. Mash the potatoes with a ricer or a potato masher. (The ricer will give you a much smoother and more elegant result.) Reserve the potatoes.

2 Melt the butter in a large sauté pan over medium heat. When the butter foams, add the onions, fennel, sugar, salt, and pepper and a few grindings of nutmeg. Cook the onions until they are tender and caramelized, about 15 minutes. Transfer the onion mixture to a food processor. Purée until smooth.

3 Pour the milk into a small saucepan over medium-high heat and bring just to a boil. In large bowl, combine the potatoes, onion mixture, and sour cream. Slowly whisk in the milk until the mixture is silky smooth. Serve immediately (although these potatoes aren't bad at room temperature either).

3 pounds Yukon Gold potatoes

Water

2 tablespoons unsalted butter

1 cup coarsely chopped sweet or yellow onions

1 fennel bulb, fronds and core removed, coarsely chopped

2 teaspoons granulated sugar

1 teaspoon kosher salt

1/4 teaspoon freshly ground black pepper

Fresh nutmeg

1 cup whole milk, buttermilk, or half-and-half

1/2 cup sour cream

Duck-Fat Home Fries

Serves 4

Nothing will make a potato more proud than if you somehow involve duck fat in the cooking process. This recipe is pretty direct, and these home fries not only are excellent for brunch but can hold their own with a juicy T-bone steak. Aren't you glad that fat isn't fatal any more?

3 tablespoons rendered duck fat

4 large Yukon Gold potatoes, cut into ½-inch cubes

2 teaspoons southwest or creole seasoning blend

½ cup thinly sliced green onions, white and green parts

1 tablespoon unsalted butter

1 Melt the duck fat in a 3-quart sauté pan or 12-inch cast-iron skillet over medium heat. Add the potatoes to the pan in an even layer. Cook for about 4 minutes or until they start to brown. Turn the potatoes with a spatula and cook for another 4 minutes.

2 Sprinkle the seasoning over the potatoes and shake the pan to keep the potatoes loose. Cook for another 2 or 3 minutes. Add the green onions and toss. Cook for 3 more minutes or until the potatoes are golden brown and tender. Throw in the butter, swirling it to coat the potatoes. Remove from heat and serve immediately. These potatoes can also be reheated in duck fat or canola oil.

Duck-Fat Home Fries and Fred's Simple Grilled Asparagus (page 296)

Breakfast Potato Cakes

Serves 2

A Yankee or midwesterner would call these hash browns because the potato is grated and cooked like a large cake. When I make this recipe, I tend to fry a couple of eggs sunny side up or over easy and plop them atop the potato cake. Cutting into the eggs and letting the runny yolk mingle with the potatoes is wonderful in the morning and great for a Sunday supper.

3 medium to large Yukon Gold potatoes, skin on and shredded

3 tablespoons unsalted butter, divided

Kosher salt and freshly ground black pepper

1 Squeeze as much liquid as you can from the potatoes. Melt 1 tablespoon of the butter in a 10-inch skillet over medium heat. When the butter stops foaming, put in the potatoes and use a spatula to work them into a pancake shape.

2 Cut the remaining butter into small chunks. As the potato cake browns, add little chunks of butter to the outside edges. Cook for 5–6 minutes before turning the potatoes with a spatula (or if you are really good, flip them). Don't be overly concerned when the cake falls apart. Season with a generous pinch of salt and a few grindings of pepper. Press down on the potatoes to reshape them. Cook for another 5–10 minutes or until the potatoes are golden brown. Serve immediately.

Oven-Roasted Steakhouse Hash Browns

If you're looking for a change of pace from the obligatory baked potato alongside a steak, give this recipe a try. I like this method when I have lots of people over since it cooks in the oven. The first time I was served hash browns with a steak was at the Palm Restaurant in New York. They were so good that I quickly got over the notion that hash browns were only for breakfast.

Serves 6–8

1 Preheat your oven to 400 degrees.

2 In a large mixing bowl, combine the potatoes, oil, paprika, garlic, onion, and cayenne pepper. Toss until the potatoes are well coated. Add a generous pinch of salt and a few grindings of pepper and toss again.

3 Pour the potatoes onto a baking sheet in a single layer. Bake for 40–45 minutes, turning halfway through. When they're done, a knife will easily pierce the potato. Serve immediately or at room temperature.

4 large russet potatoes, cut into 6 wedges each (or cut into chunks if you want)

3 tablespoons olive oil

¼ teaspoon smoked paprika

⅛ teaspoon granulated garlic

⅛ teaspoon granulated onion

⅛ teaspoon cayenne pepper

Kosher salt and freshly ground black pepper

Barbecued Potatoes

Serves 6–8

In eastern North Carolina, no self-respecting barbecue joint would leave barbecued potatoes off the menu. There's a good reason. These potatoes are perfect with eastern-style barbecue, that luscious chopped pork doused with vinegar and peppers. When I have a gang over for barbecue, I always have a gigantic pot of these potatoes, and they're also good with grilled chicken, pork chops, and shrimp.

2½ pounds potatoes, peeled and cut into large chunks

Water

Kosher salt and freshly ground black pepper

1 cup coarsely chopped onions

2 tablespoons bacon fat

1 10-ounce bottle ketchup

2 tablespoons Texas Pete or other hot pepper sauce

2 tablespoons granulated sugar

1 Place the potatoes in a 4-quart or larger saucepan and cover with water. Place the pot over high heat and bring to a boil. Reduce heat and simmer for 30–40 minutes until the potatoes are tender and easily pierced with a knife. Drain the potatoes and add a generous pinch of salt and several grindings of pepper. Combine all the remaining ingredients in a large mixing bowl and gently fold in the potatoes. Try to avoid breaking up the potatoes too much. Serve immediately or at room temperature.

Grilled Potato Slices Fancied Up

Grilled potato slices on their own are a very good thing, but the addition of some sharp and tart flavors really brings them alive. I usually use a mixture of sweet potatoes, russet potatoes, and Yukon Golds, but you can use any potatoes you want.

Serves 4–6

---

1 Brush both sides of each potato slice with the olive oil and sprinkle with a little salt and pepper.

2 Preheat your grill to medium.

3 Grill the potato slices for 10–15 minutes until they're tender and brown. Turn each slice several times while grilling. Remove the potato slices from the grill and sprinkle with the tomatoes and capers. Stir the chives into the sour cream for the topping. Serve immediately or at room temperature.

$1\frac{1}{2}$ **pounds mixed potatoes, cut into $\frac{1}{2}$-inch slices**

2 tablespoons olive oil

Kosher salt and freshly ground black pepper

$\frac{1}{4}$ **cup oil-packed sun-dried tomatoes, drained and chopped**

2 tablespoons capers, drained and mashed slightly with the back of a knife (if salt-packed capers are available to you, then use them since they have a much brighter and truer flavor; just rinse off the salt before adding)

2 tablespoons chopped chives

$\frac{1}{2}$ **cup sour cream**

Mustard Potatoes

Serves 6

I'm always looking for new ways to deal with potatoes. Infusing the potatoes with mustard as they cook is simple and makes for a wonderful side dish with corned beef, pot roast, barbecued chicken, or duck. At a farmstand if you see "iced or Irish taters," buy them. These potatoes are usually freshly dug and have the perfume of dirt, but they have a flavor that's hard to beat. This simple, quick, and easy recipe delivers some intense flavors.

6 cups water

½ teaspoon kosher salt

½ cup prepared yellow mustard

¼ cup coarse-grained mustard

6 boiling potatoes, preferably Yukon Golds or "iced" taters, peeled and halved

1 Whisk together the water, salt, and mustards in a 3- to 4-quart saucepan and bring to a boil over medium heat. Add the potatoes, reduce heat to medium low, and simmer until the potatoes are tender, 20–25 minutes. Drain the potatoes and serve hot or at room temperature.

These-Sound-Disgusting-but-They're-Wonderful Potatoes

Only a lunatic would think of mixing pimento cheese into mashed potatoes, but my Jeep's license plate says "IMCRAZY," so go figure. If you love pimento cheese, you'll go gaga for these mashers. Serve them with seafood, poultry, or pork or just take a spoon to the pot.

Serves 6–8

1 Place the potatoes in a 4-quart or larger saucepan and cover with water. Bring to a boil over medium-high heat, reduce heat, and simmer for 20–30 minutes or until the potatoes are easily pierced with a knife.

2 Drain the potatoes and return to the pan. Place the pan back over the heat and shake the pan for 1 minute.

3 Mash the potatoes with a potato masher or ricer. (I use a ricer with this recipe because of the chunkiness of the pimento cheese.) Return to the pan and stir in the butter. Then stir in the buttermilk and the pimento cheese until well blended. Season with salt and pepper. Serve immediately.

NOTE Every time I'm near Lexington, North Carolina, I buy some of Conrad and Hinkle's fabulous pimento cheese. When Carolina Creamery has pimento cheese, it is awesome in a totally different way. I'm sure there is a purveyor of excellent pimento cheese somewhere in your area.

2½ pounds medium russet potatoes, peeled and cut into chunks

Water

8 tablespoons unsalted butter

1 cup buttermilk

¾ cup pimento cheese, preferably homemade

Kosher salt and freshly ground black pepper

The Hash Brown Casserole

This recipe should convince you that I am not a food snob but a lover of everything that tastes good. This casserole has several variations, but none very far from its roots. I serve it for breakfast, I serve it for lunch, I serve it for dinner, I take it to potlucks. It's one of the most versatile dishes you can imagine. Laugh at the ingredients. Then go make it.

2 pounds frozen cubed hash browns

½ cup unsalted butter, melted

1 10¼-ounce can cream of chicken soup

2 cups sour cream

2 cups shredded cheese

½ cup chopped onions

Kosher salt and freshly ground black pepper

Bread crumbs (I like panko crumbs) to sprinkle over the top

1 Preheat your oven to 350 degrees.

2 In a large bowl, mix together the hash browns, butter, soup, sour cream, cheese, and onions. Add a generous pinch of salt and several grindings of pepper. Pour into a large baking dish and sprinkle the top evenly but lightly with the bread crumbs. Bake for 45 minutes or until the casserole is hot and bubbly. Serve hot, at room temperature, or cold.

Smashed Sweet Potatoes

The older I get, the more sweet potatoes I eat. It's kind of odd, since while I was growing up I wouldn't touch them, much to the dismay of my parents, who loved them. Sweet potatoes are one of those colorful vegetables that we now know to be important to our diet. More important, they just taste plain good.

Serves 4–6

1 Place the sweet potatoes in a 3-quart saucepan and cover with water. Cook over medium-high heat for 15–20 minutes until the potatoes are easily pierced with a knife. Drain and return the potatoes to the pan and place back over the heat for 1 minute, shaking the pan.

2 Mash the potatoes and add the butter. Then pour in the milk, brown sugar, and bacon fat. Stir to combine, remembering that you want a chunky mashed potato. Season with salt and pepper. Remove to a serving dish. Drizzle with maple syrup and serve immediately.

2 pounds sweet potatoes, preferably Beauregards, peeled and chopped

Water

6 tablespoons unsalted butter

2 tablespoons milk

1 tablespoon light brown sugar

1 tablespoon bacon fat (optional)

Kosher salt and freshly ground black pepper

Pure maple syrup, preferably Grade B, for drizzling

Grilled Sweet Potato Salad with Orange Dressing

Serves 6

Since sweet potatoes store very well, they're easy to find at any time of the year. This is a great salad for the summer, especially with smoked pork or ribs. The sweetness is sublime, and the earthiness pairs well with smoke. I'm fairly certain that Baton Rouge food writer Susan Dey coached me on this one.

2 large sweet potatoes

Water

2 teaspoons canola oil

Kosher salt and freshly
 ground black pepper

½ cup fresh orange juice

¼ cup rice vinegar

1 tablespoon maple syrup

¼ cup minced green bell
 peppers

¼ cup minced red bell
 peppers

1 tablespoon finely chopped
 jalapeños

2 green onions, thinly sliced

1 teaspoon fresh ginger,
 peeled and finely chopped

¾ cup extra-virgin olive oil

Additional salt and pepper

3 or 4 cups mixed salad
 greens

1 Place the sweet potatoes in a large pot and cover with water. Simmer over medium heat for 15 minutes or until a knife can easily pierce a ¼ inch of the potato but the center is still firm. Drain the potatoes and let cool completely. Peel and cut into ¾-inch slices. Brush with the olive oil and add a generous pinch of salt and several grindings of pepper.

2 Grill the slices over medium heat for 3–5 minutes per side. They should soften but still be firm.

3 In a mixing bowl, whisk together the remaining ingredients except the salad greens. Divide the greens among salad plates and arrange the sweet potato slices on top of the greens. Drizzle the vinaigrette over the salad and serve immediately.

Sweet Potato Steak Fries

I occasionally like steak fries when I'm grilling a New York strip, so I thought I would move from a white potato to one that's bright orange.

Serves 6

1 Preheat your oven to 375 degrees.

2 Place the potatoes in a large mixing bowl with the olive oil and maple syrup. Toss until well coated.

3 In a small bowl, mix together the spices plus a generous pinch of salt and several grindings of pepper.

4 Scatter the potatoes on a baking sheet lined with parchment paper or a Silpat. Sprinkle the spice mixture evenly over the potatoes and roast in the oven for 30 minutes or until they can easily be pierced with a knife. Serve hot or at room temperature.

3 sweet potatoes, peeled, cut into eighths lengthwise, and then halved

2 tablespoons olive oil

1 tablespoon maple syrup

½ teaspoon ground ginger

½ teaspoon ground cinnamon

Several grindings of fresh nutmeg

Kosher salt and freshly ground black pepper

Sausage and Sweet Potato Hash

Serves 4

This dish was inspired by Ben Barker at Magnolia Grill. Many years ago, he served his sweet potato hash with poblano chilis and tarragon. Now neither Ben nor I can completely remember the recipe. With that dish in mind, I've come up with this recipe, which I love to serve with duck, short ribs, or nearly any hearty protein. For a fabulous breakfast, serve several sunny-side-up eggs on top of the hash. The sausage is totally my addition.

2 cups peeled and cubed sweet potatoes

Water

1 tablespoon canola oil

2 andouille sausages, cut into medium chunks

1 tablespoon unsalted butter

2 garlic cloves, finely chopped

1 shallot, finely chopped

2 celery stalks, diced as small as possible

3 sprigs tarragon, leaves stripped and coarsely chopped

1/4 cup thinly sliced chives

1 tablespoon whole-grained mustard

Kosher salt and freshly ground black pepper

1 Place the sweet potatoes in a 3-quart saucepan and cover with water. Boil over medium-high heat for 5 minutes. Strain the potatoes and run cold water over them.

2 Heat the oil in a large skillet over medium heat. When the oil shimmers, add the potatoes and the sausage. Cook for about 5 minutes until both have taken on some color. Add the butter, garlic, shallots, celery, and herbs. Continue cooking for another 5 minutes. Remove from heat and stir in the mustard. Season with salt and pepper. Serve hot or at room temperature.

Twice-Baked Sweet Potatoes with Sage, Sorghum, and Black Walnuts

Serves 8

It's too easy to always do sweet potatoes with cinnamon, nutmeg, maple syrup, and pecans. I wanted a different twist on my twice-baked sweet potatoes. So I looked at flavors that are very much a part of the Appalachian culture. Granted, ricotta cheese is not, but it helps to pull all the flavors together and gives the potatoes texture and balance. Another great fall dish that serves up well on the holiday table.

8 sweet potatoes, uniform in size

1 tablespoon unsalted butter

1 cup finely chopped shallots

1 tablespoon chopped sage

2 tablespoons sorghum molasses

$1\frac{1}{4}$ cups ricotta cheese

1 teaspoon kosher salt

$\frac{1}{4}$ teaspoon freshly ground black pepper

$\frac{1}{4}$ cup coarsely chopped black walnuts

1 Preheat your oven to 400 degrees.

2 Use a fork to poke holes in the sweet potatoes. Place on a baking sheet and bake for 45 minutes or until tender and a knife slides easily to the center. Remove from the oven and allow to cool for 5–10 minutes. Reduce temperature to 375 degrees.

3 Cut the sweet potatoes in half. Using a spoon, scoop out the insides from all of the potatoes into a large bowl. Discard half the skins.

4 Melt the butter in a medium sauté pan over medium heat. When the butter foams, throw in the shallots and cook until limp, about 6 minutes. Add the sage and cook for 1 minute longer. Pour this mixture into a food processor and add the molasses, ricotta, salt, and pepper. Pulse until the mixture is smooth. Transfer this mixture to the bowl with the sweet potatoes and mash with a hand masher until smooth. Divide the mixture equally among the skins. Sprinkle the tops evenly with the black walnuts and place on a baking sheet. Bake until the potatoes are hot and the walnuts are toasted, about 20 minutes. Serve hot, warm, or at room temperature.

Matt's Mom's Baked Potatoes

I think we all know how to bake a potato, but here's a little twist. Matt Hunt is my son-in-law's best friend, and he shared his mom's recipe. I'm going to throw in a few variations.

Serves 4

1 Preheat your oven to 400 degrees.

2 Generously rub Crisco all over the potatoes. Place in a glass baking dish and season liberally with salt and pepper. Bake for 1 hour or until the potatoes yield easily when pierced with a knife. Remove from the baking dish to individual plates. Break the potatoes open and serve with Potato @#$%*.

VARIATIONS Instead of using shortening, you can rub the potatoes with bacon fat or lard, but you should lower the oven temperature to 375 degrees. Or rub the potatoes with olive oil and sprinkle with sea salt and bake at 400 degrees.

Crisco shortening, usually less than ¼ cup

4 russet potatoes

Kosher salt and freshly ground black pepper

Potato @#$%* (page 320) (optional)

Classic Twice-Baked Potatoes

Serves 4

Every now and again I like a good twice-baked potato, but I don't like one that has so much junk in it that you can't taste the potato. Here's my version. After you've followed the recipe once and enjoyed the renewed flavor of the potato, feel free to add any ingredients you want.

2 baked potatoes, sliced in half lengthwise

1 tablespoon unsalted butter

¼ cup whole milk or buttermilk

3 slices bacon, cooked and finely chopped

½ cup grated Asiago cheese, divided

1 tablespoon chopped chives

Kosher salt and freshly ground black pepper

1 Preheat your oven to 400 degrees.

2 Scoop out the flesh from the potatoes and place it in a medium mixing bowl. Add the butter, the milk, the bacon, ¼ cup of the cheese, and the chives. Mix like mashed potatoes. Season with salt and pepper.

3 Divide the mashed potato mixture equally among the 4 skins. Liberally sprinkle the remaining cheese on each half. Place on a baking sheet and bake for 5–8 minutes or until the cheese is gooey. Serve immediately.

Sour Cream and Horseradish Red Potatoes

I think sour cream and horseradish go on anything. Stir the mixture into earthy new red potatoes and the alchemy of taste comes alive.

Serves 4–6

1 Place the potatoes in a 3–4 quart saucepan and cover with water. Bring to a boil over high heat, then reduce heat and simmer for 20–30 minutes or until the potatoes yield easily when pierced with a knife.

2 Drain the potatoes and return to the pan. Lightly mash the potatoes but still keep them fairly chunky. Stir in the horseradish, sour cream, butter, and milk and add a squeeze of lemon. Season with salt and pepper. Spoon into a serving bowl and sprinkle with the chives. Serve immediately or at room temperature.

2 pounds red-skinned potatoes

Water

2 tablespoons prepared horseradish, drained

¼ cup sour cream

4 tablespoons unsalted butter

½ cup milk

1 lemon wedge

Kosher salt and freshly ground black pepper

3 tablespoons chopped chives

Mediterranean-Influenced Potato Salad

Why, you may ask, do I have so many potato salad recipes in this book? The answer is simple—tailgating. The average college or university plays six home games. Therefore, multiple potato salads. We wouldn't want to get bored, would we? This salad has no mayonnaise, which makes it nice for hot afternoons. If you don't want to heat up your kitchen, you can boil the potatoes instead of roasting them.

Serves 6–8

1 Preheat your oven to 375 degrees.

2 Toss the potatoes with the canola oil. Sprinkle with salt and pepper and spread on a baking sheet. Bake for 30–35 minutes, turning halfway through. The potatoes should yield easily when pierced with a knife.

3 Whisk together the olive oil, vinegars, garlic, capers, anchovies, and mustard. Stir in the red peppers, olives, and parsley.

4 As soon as the potatoes are done, place them immediately into the dressing, stirring to coat. Let the potatoes sit in the dressing for at least 15 minutes, stirring often. Serve warm or at room temperature.

$1\frac{1}{2}$ pounds baby yellow potatoes, cut in half lengthwise

$\frac{1}{4}$ cup canola oil

Kosher salt and freshly ground black pepper

$\frac{1}{4}$ cup extra-virgin olive oil

2 tablespoons balsamic vinegar

1 tablespoon red wine vinegar

2 garlic cloves, minced

$\frac{1}{4}$ cup capers, drained

3 salt-packed anchovies, rinsed and finely chopped

2 teaspoons Dijon mustard

2 roasted red bell peppers, cut into small dice

$\frac{1}{4}$ cup pitted, chopped olives

$\frac{1}{4}$ cup coarsely chopped flat-leaf parsley

Jean's Potato Salad

Serves 16, leftovers keep well for a week

This is hands-down the best potato salad you'll ever eat. I got the recipe from Jean Lynn more than a decade ago when she and her husband, Hugh, were still living in Raleigh. Hugh was my golfing buddy, and many Saturday nights we all gathered at his house to throw something on the grill. Quite a few times this potato salad was on the menu. I love it, make it often, and take it to lots of potlucks. Do not try to substitute mayonnaise for Miracle Whip—it does not work.

5 pounds russet potatoes, peeled and cut into large chunks

Water

1 tablespoon kosher salt

5 large eggs, hard-boiled, peeled, and cut into chunks

2 cups chopped sweet onions

1 24-ounce jar whole sweet gherkins, drained and chopped (I use a food processor), juice reserved

2 cups Miracle Whip

$\frac{1}{2}$ cup granulated sugar

1 tablespoon distilled white vinegar

$\frac{1}{2}$ teaspoon yellow mustard

1 Place the potatoes in a large Dutch oven or soup pot and cover with water by 1 inch. Add the salt. Bring to a slow boil over low heat and cook uncovered until the potatoes are soft when pierced with a fork, about 20 minutes. Drain the potatoes, return them to the pot, and mash them coarsely. Stir in the eggs, onions, and gherkins.

2 In a large bowl, whisk the Miracle Whip, sugar, vinegar, and mustard. You're looking for a sweet/tart taste, so adjust as necessary with sugar and vinegar. Add the potatoes to the dressing and stir to combine. Serve warm or cold.

ROOTIN' AROUND

Turnips, Onions, Carrots, & Their Cousins

Root vegetables make up a strong segment of southern foodways. While for most of the last century we treated turnips, onions, carrots, and such relatively simply, inventive chefs and food writers have more recently taken these humble roots and turned them into some amazing mouthfuls. I've discovered a much broader playing field of root vegetables than I ever thought existed and continue to play with these items to come up with recipes that fascinate, surprise, and just plain taste good.

We are now privileged to have more root-vegetable bounty. Baby turnips, with their unique, sweet bitterness, are available to everyone. Europeans have long recognized the value of leeks, and we need to make them more involved in our cooking.

When I first printed a recipe for a sunchoke, I received amazingly positive responses. Jerusalem artichokes, as many of us know them, have a crunchy starchiness that blends with many foods. If white potatoes are medically unsound for you, sunchokes might be a godsend.

I have yet to meet a beet I didn't like. The flavors of the classic reds, the beautiful goldens, and the heirloom stripes fascinate me. I grew up in a home where pickled beets were a regular tabletop item, but my first bowl of borscht, at the Russian Tea Room in Manhattan, showed me a beet was much more than a pickle. Ben Barker's pairing of roasted beets and goat cheese intrigued me even more. Don't tell me you hate beets until you've tried some of these recipes.

Think about the simple onion. We cook with it every day, chopping it, dicing it, and using it to season our other vegetables and meats. But by itself, an onion can be a monumental side dish, stuffed with cheese or fried into beautiful, lacy onion rings.

Like most children, I didn't care how much carrots were supposed to help my eyesight: I didn't particularly like them. When Mama served mixed peas and carrots, I struggled to get them down. That all changed with my first taste of copper pennies. From that moment on, I realized that carrots didn't have to be some bland, mushy thing. I'm sure we had rutabaga growing up, and I probably didn't like it either, but with maple syrup and chives, I could eat it every night. I now wonder at these vegetables that hide in the dirt.

Frisée Salad with Roasted Shallot and Bacon Vinaigrette

Serves 6

If you like poached eggs, you'll like this salad. It's a takeoff on a more involved French bistro salad.

½ pound thick-cut bacon strips

1 shallot, finely chopped

¼ cup bacon fat

3 sprigs thyme

2 tablespoons Dijon mustard

6 tablespoons red wine vinegar

¼ cup extra-virgin olive oil

4¼ cups water, divided

Kosher salt and freshly ground black pepper

½ cup distilled white vinegar

6 large eggs, preferably farm raised

3 heads frisée

1½ cups croutons

1 Cook the bacon in a large sauté pan over medium heat until the meat is crisp and the fat is rendered. Remove the bacon with a slotted spoon and drain on paper towels. Crumble and reserve. Reserve the fat for the vinaigrette.

2 In a bowl, combine the shallots, bacon fat, thyme, mustard, and red wine vinegar. Using an emulsion blender or a regular blender, purée until smooth. While the blender is still running, slowly add the oil and ¼ cup of the water. Season with salt and pepper. The dressing can be covered and chilled for up to 4 days.

3 Bring the remaining water to a slow simmer in a 3-quart saucepan and add the white vinegar. Break each egg and carefully drop it into the water. (I find a teacup helps.) Poach for 5–6 minutes. The yolks should still be runny, but the whites should be fully cooked. Remove the eggs from the water and set aside.

4 Divide the frisée equally among 6 salad plates. Sprinkle the greens with the bacon and croutons and drizzle with the vinaigrette. Top each salad with a poached egg and serve.

Vidalia Onions with Blue Cheese

Thank goodness for the soil in Vidalia, Georgia. Good gracious, it can grow beautiful sweet onions. When Vidalias are in season, I can't seem to use them enough. This hearty dish amplifies the sweetness of the onions as they mingle with the blue cheese. I love to serve these with a perfectly grilled porterhouse steak.

Serves 4

1 Preheat your oven to 425 degrees.

2 Arrange the onion slices in a 9 × 13-inch baking dish. Combine the blue cheese, butter, Worcestershire, dill, and several grindings of pepper in a bowl. Spread this mixture over the onions.

3 Bake for 20 minutes. The onions can be prepared up to this point several hours in advance. Switch your oven to broil and cook the onions until the top is brown and bubbly, usually no more than 5 minutes. Serve immediately.

2 large Vidalia onions, sliced

¾ cup crumbled blue cheese

2 tablespoons unsalted butter, softened

2 teaspoons thick-style Worcestershire sauce

½ teaspoon dried dill

Freshly ground black pepper

Baby Roasted Turnips That You'll Really Like

Serves 4

Turnips are one of those vegetables that people either love or hate. I fall into the first category, but I'm particularly fond of baby turnips, which are less bitter than mature turnips. Serve these to your family but don't tell them what it is, and there won't be any leftovers.

15–20 baby turnips, greens removed and peeled

1 tablespoon unsalted butter

3 sprigs thyme

1 sprig rosemary

2 garlic cloves, sliced in half

¼ cup water

Kosher salt and freshly ground black pepper

Extra-virgin olive oil

1 Preheat your oven to 325 degrees.

2 Place a 12 × 12-inch piece of aluminum foil on your counter. Put the turnips, butter, thyme, rosemary, and garlic in the middle of the foil. Pull up the sides, pour in the water, and then close the packet. Place on a baking sheet.

3 Bake for 30 minutes. Remove from the oven and let rest for 5 minutes.

4 Unwrap the packet, being careful to avoid the hot steam, and spoon the turnips into a serving bowl. Discard the herbs and the garlic. Give the turnips a generous sprinkling of salt and a few grindings of pepper. Drizzle with olive oil and toss. Serve immediately.

Mashed Turnips and Sweet Potatoes

This interesting combination balances the flavors of the sweet potatoes and the turnips. I enjoy serving these mashers in early fall with a pork roast and collards.

Serves 4

1 Place the turnips and sweet potatoes in a 3–4 quart saucepan and cover with water. Bring to a boil over medium-high heat, reduce heat, and simmer for 20–30 minutes or until vegetables are easily pierced with a knife.

2 Drain the vegetables and return them to the pan. Place back on the heat and shake for 1 minute. Remove from heat.

3 If you want a nice smooth purée, run the turnips and potatoes through a ricer or a food mill. Otherwise, mash the vegetables with a hand masher. Stir in the butter and then the milk and bacon fat. Mash and stir until the vegetables reach the desired texture. Add a generous pinch of salt and several grindings of pepper. Give the mixture a few dashes of hot sauce and stir to combine. Serve hot.

2 large turnips, peeled and cut into 1-inch cubes

2 large sweet potatoes, peeled and cut into 1-inch cubes

Water

6 tablespoons unsalted butter

½ cup milk or half-and-half

1 teaspoon bacon fat (optional but really good)

Kosher salt and freshly ground black pepper

Texas Pete or Tabasco sauce

"Confit" of Turnips and Leeks

Serves 4–6

This dish is heavenly. The bitterness of the turnips and the sweetness of the leeks combine forces to give you an awesome taste experience. I don't care if you think you hate turnips—you won't after you try this dish.

8 tablespoons butter

4 medium turnips, diced

2 large leeks, white and
   light green parts only,
   trimmed and thinly sliced

3 garlic cloves, minced

1 bay leaf

¾ cup homemade or low-
   sodium chicken broth

¼ cup dry white wine

½ cup heavy cream

4 sprigs thyme, leaves
   stripped and minced

Kosher salt and freshly
   ground black pepper

A few lemon wedges

1 Melt the butter in a large pan such as a Dutch oven over low heat. Add the turnips, leeks, garlic, bay leaf, broth, and wine. Cover and cook for 10–15 minutes or until the turnips are tender.

2 Add the cream and cook, uncovered, until thickened. Stir in the thyme and continue cooking for about 1 minute. Remove the bay leaf and discard. Season with salt, pepper, and lemon juice as necessary. Serve immediately.

Leeks Vinaigrette

Serves 6

I first had this dish at Patis, a French bistro in Manhattan's meatpacking district, and found it so interesting that I did a little research. Leeks vinaigrette can be used as a first course, salad, or side dish. If you're not familiar with leeks, this is a great place to get introduced.

1 Place the leeks in a 3-quart saucepan and cover with water. Add 2 pinches of salt and bring to a boil over medium-high heat. Reduce heat, cover, and simmer for 10 minutes until the leeks are tender but still retain their shape.

2 Whisk together the mustard and vinegar in a medium bowl. Slowly whisk in the olive oil. Season with salt and pepper.

3 Remove the leeks from the water and cut off the strings. Place the leek halves around a platter. Rewhisk the vinaigrette and pour over the top. Sprinkle on the eggs and top with the parsley. Serve immediately.

3 leeks, white and light green parts only, sliced in half and then tied back together with kitchen twine

Water

Kosher salt

1 teaspoon Dijon mustard

2 tablespoons white wine vinegar

½ cup extra-virgin olive oil

Freshly ground black pepper

3 hard-boiled eggs, yolks and whites separated, chopped

¼ cup chopped flat-leaf parsley

Apple-and-Leek Smashed Potatoes

Serves 6–8

I developed this recipe as part of a St. Patrick's Day meal. I wanted a new flavor on the plate, something different from boiled or regular mashed potatoes. The result surprised even me. With sweetness from the leeks and the apples and sharpness from the grainy mustard, this is a wonderful side dish for days other than St. Patrick's.

4 cups water

3½ pounds russet potatoes, peeled and cut into cubes

12 tablespoons unsalted butter, divided

3 leeks, cut in half, white part only, thinly sliced

2 Granny Smith apples, peeled and cut into small dice

2 cups heavy cream

3 tablespoons coarse-grained Dijon mustard

Kosher salt and freshly ground black pepper

1 Bring the water to a boil in a 3-quart saucepan over medium-high heat. Add the potatoes and cook until easily pierced with a knife, about 20 minutes. Drain the potatoes, return to the pan, and cover.

2 Melt 2 tablespoons of the butter in a sauté pan over medium heat. Cook the leeks and the apples until they take on a little color, 7–10 minutes.

3 With a potato masher, coarsely smash the potatoes. Stir in the leeks and apples. Stir in the remainder of the butter, the cream, and then the mustard. You want this dish to be lumpy, not perfectly puréed. Add salt and pepper to taste. Serve immediately or at room temperature.

Grilled Fennel

This may be one of my favorite grilled vegetables. Grilling brings out the sweetness of the fennel against its natural anise flavor. Serve this with pork chops, fish, and especially lamb.

Serves 4

1 Toss the fennel in a large bowl with the olive oil. Sprinkle a good pinch of salt and several grindings of pepper over the fennel and toss again.

2 Preheat your grill to medium high.

3 Place the wedges on the grill and cook for about 6 minutes, then turn and cook for another 6 minutes. When the core is easily pierced with a knife, they're done. Serve immediately.

2 large fennel bulbs, fronds removed, cut into eight wedges each with core intact on each wedge

2 tablespoons olive oil

Kosher salt and freshly ground black pepper

Lemon-Braised Fennel

Serves 4

Fennel is one of those misunderstood vegetables. Too many people only know fennel in its raw state, where its licorice flavor is very pronounced. Once you cook fennel, though, you get a delicate, earthy flavor with just a hint of licorice. Fennel is wonderful alongside most any fish but especially whitefish such as flounder, bass, and grouper or shellfish.

2 medium fennel bulbs, fronds removed and cut into 6 wedges each

6 cups water

3 tablespoons extra-virgin olive oil

2 teaspoons ground fennel

Generous pinch of kosher salt

½ lemon

1 Place all the ingredients except the lemon in a 3-quart saucepan. Bring to a boil over high heat, reduce heat, and simmer for about 20 minutes or until a knife easily pierces the fennel.

2 Remove the fennel, leaving the liquid. Bring the liquid to a boil and reduce by half, about 5 minutes. Squeeze the lemon juice into the broth and pour over the fennel. Serve immediately, making certain that everyone gets some of the lemony broth.

Fennel Hash

Serves 4

When I'm grilling salmon, I alternate between this hash and my sweet potato hash. Both are natural side dishes for salmon, but I tend to use this one more frequently during the summer.

1 pound Yukon Gold potatoes, peeled and cut into small cubes

Water

Kosher salt

2 tablespoons canola oil

4 tablespoons unsalted butter, divided

1 fennel bulb, top removed, cored, and diced

1 cup diced onions

1 tablespoon dry vermouth (like Pernod)

2 garlic cloves, minced

1 tablespoon chopped tarragon

1 Place the potatoes in a 3-quart saucepan and cover with cold water. Add 2 or 3 pinches of salt. Bring to a boil over medium heat and then parboil for about 5 minutes. The potatoes should retain their shape. Drain.

2 Heat the oil and 2 tablespoons of the butter in a large sauté pan over medium-high heat. When the butter foams, add the fennel and onions. Cook, stirring, until the vegetables are soft and begin to take on a little color, 8–10 minutes. Add the vermouth and cook for another 2 minutes. Add the garlic, potatoes, and remaining butter. Increase heat to high and cook, occasionally stirring gently, until the vegetables are soft and caramelized, 7–8 minutes. Sprinkle with the tarragon and remove from heat. Serve immediately or at room temperature.

Grilled Barbecue Sunchokes

This dish goes great with just about any grilled food. While you've probably figured out by now that I'm an outdoor grill fanatic, using a grill pan is a necessary evil here, since sunchokes are hard to put on a skewer without cracking them. These chokes are so good that you won't miss cooking them outside.

Serves 4

1 In a medium bowl, toss together the sunchokes and olive oil. Sprinkle the barbecue spice over the chokes and toss to coat.

2 Place a large grill pan over medium heat. Spray with vegetable cooking spray. Add as many of the sunchokes as will fit comfortably in the pan. (You may need to cook them in batches.) Cook the chokes, turning occasionally, until all sides get a bit of caramelization, 20–25 minutes. The tip of a knife should slide in easily. Brush with the barbecue sauce and cook for another 3–4 minutes, allowing the sauce to form a glaze. Serve immediately or at room temperature.

1 pound sunchokes, cut into 1-inch slices

2 tablespoons olive oil

½ cup of your favorite barbecue spice

Vegetable cooking spray

½ cup slightly sweet barbecue sauce (try East Tennessee–Style Barbecue Sauce, page 306)

Pan-Roasted Sunchokes

Sunchokes, also known as Jerusalem artichokes, should be in the center of the plate and not just pickled, which is the traditional southern way with this vegetable. Sunchokes have a pleasant potato-like texture and earthy flavor. Sunchokes also make a good stand-in for potatoes if you're trying to control your blood sugar. With a sunchoke, eating healthy never tasted so good.

Serves 4

1 Place a large skillet over medium heat. When the pan is warm, add the oil. When the oil shimmers, add the sunchokes and cook until well caramelized and fork-tender, 15–20 minutes. They should look like skillet potatoes.

2 Reduce heat to low. Add the butter, garlic, and herbs. Toss to coat the sunchokes and cook for 3 minutes.

3 Remove from heat. Sprinkle on a little lemon juice, salt, and pepper. Serve hot or at room temperature.

¼ cup canola oil

1 pound sunchokes, cut into chunks

1 tablespoon unsalted butter

2 garlic cloves, minced

2 sprigs rosemary, leaves stripped and minced

3 sprigs thyme, leaves stripped and minced

1 sprig oregano, leaves stripped and minced

Fresh lemon juice

Kosher salt and freshly ground black pepper

Oven-Roasted Sunchokes with Warm Bacon Vinaigrette

Serves 4–6

What can I say—put bacon on anything, and it's great. I love serving these sunchokes alongside a marinated and grilled London broil. The two dishes have a boldness and complement each other. There also have been times when I've eaten a whole batch of this for supper.

1 pound sunchokes, cut
    into chunks

1 tablespoon olive oil

1 tablespoon plus ¼ cup
    bacon fat

3 sprigs oregano

2 sprigs rosemary

5 sprigs thyme

Kosher salt and freshly
    ground black pepper

1 shallot, cut into ¼-inch
    slices

2 garlic cloves, finely chopped

1 teaspoon grainy mustard

2 tablespoons apple cider
    vinegar

½ cup extra-virgin olive oil

Kosher salt and freshly
    ground black pepper

3 strips thick-cut bacon,
    cooked and crumbled

1 Preheat your oven to 375 degrees.

2 Toss the sunchokes with the olive oil and 1 tablespoon of the bacon fat. Spread on a baking sheet and sprinkle with the oregano, rosemary, and thyme. Add a generous pinch of salt and a few grindings of pepper. Roast for 30–35 minutes, stirring every 10 minutes.

3 Melt ¼ cup of the bacon fat in a sauté pan over medium-low heat. Add the shallots and cook for about 1 minute. Throw in the garlic and cook until fragrant. Stir in the mustard and vinegar. Slowly stir in the olive oil. Season with salt and pepper. Stir in the bacon.

4 Pick the herbs out of the roasted chokes and discard. Pour the hot dressing over the chokes and toss to coat. Serve immediately.

Baked Onions

Serves 4–6

Dad was one of the original folks hired by Herman Lay when he started his potato chip company. Dad worked there until his death thirty-seven years later, and the company grew and prospered. Not surprisingly, we always had snack foods around the house, especially potato chips. I can't tell you the number of potato chip sandwiches I've had. Mom was always trying to come up with something to do with the chips. She tried something similar to this, and I've sort of refined it. This soup-based casserole is exceptional with a Sunday roast or as part of a spread with barbecue and other grilled items.

1 Preheat your oven to 350 degrees.

2 Spray a 9 × 13-inch casserole dish with vegetable spray.

3 Layer the onions, potato chips, and cheese in the casserole dish. Repeat. In a 4-cup measuring cup, combine the soup and milk and pour the mixture evenly over the casserole. Bake for 1 hour or until firm. Serve hot or at room temperature.

Vegetable cooking spray

4 cups thinly sliced onions

1 8½-ounce bag kettle-cooked potato chips, crushed

2 cups shredded Colby Jack cheese

1 10½-ounce can cream of mushroom soup

½ cup milk

"Tobacco" Onions

Serves 4–6

I love fried onions, but they've got to be doggoned good fried onions. These delicately breaded onion slices fry up quickly and are extremely crisp. The name comes from the slightly aged tobacco color that the onion rings take on. My first experience with this type of onion rings was at the storied Tobacco Company in Richmond, Virginia. More than just a side dish, these onions are great on sandwiches, atop salads, and as a topping for your green bean casserole.

2 large sweet onions, thinly sliced and rings separated

2 cups all-purpose flour

1 teaspoon kosher salt

1 tablespoon freshly ground black pepper

1 teaspoon onion powder

1 teaspoon garlic powder

1 teaspoon smoked paprika

1 tablespoon dried thyme

Canola oil for frying

1 Place the onions in a large mixing bowl. In another bowl, combine all the remaining ingredients except the oil. Sprinkle some of the mixture over the onions. Toss, add a little more of the flour mixture, and toss again. Add the rest of the flour mixture and toss once more. (This will help the flour coat the onions better.) Let the onions sit for at least 5 minutes.

2 Fill a 3- or 4-quart saucepan about half full with oil and heat to 350 degrees over medium heat. Place a wire rack on top of a baking sheet. Fry the onions in batches for 5–6 minutes or until crispy. Remove from the oil and place on the wire rack to drain. Continue until all the onions are fried. Serve immediately.

Southern-Fried Onion Rings

Serves 4–6

This recipe for traditional onion rings takes a southern twist with the inclusion of cornmeal. I find this recipe works better with a water-ground fine or extrafine cornmeal. That way, you get the flavor of the corn without an overly thick coating on the onion rings.

1 cup buttermilk

1 cup water

Hot pepper sauce

2 large sweet onions, cut into ½-inch rings and separated

2 cups all-purpose flour

2 cups cornmeal

Canola oil for frying

1 Pour the buttermilk, the water, and 3 dashes of hot sauce into a large mixing bowl. Add the onions and toss to coat. Set aside at room temperature for at least 1 hour; 2 is better.

2 In another bowl, combine the flour and cornmeal.

3 Fill a 3- to 4-quart saucepan half full with oil and bring to 350 degrees over medium heat.

4 Drain the onions but reserve the buttermilk mixture. Dip a handful of onions quickly into the buttermilk mixture and toss them in the flour mixture. Fry for about 6 minutes or until the coating is golden brown. Place a wire rack over a baking sheet. Remove the onions from the oil and drain them on the wire rack. Serve immediately.

Scuppernong-Glazed Carrots

Scuppernong is a native grape of North Carolina. At one time, every farmhouse had a scuppernong grape arbor. They were a great place to play during the hot summer because of the shade, so this recipe has a little bit of nostalgia for me.

Serves 6–8

1 Melt the butter in a large sauté pan over medium heat. When the butter stops foaming, add the carrots. Toss to coat and cook for 8–10 minutes until they are slightly tender. Pour in the grape juice and cook for another 4–5 minutes, stirring to let the juice glaze the carrots. Remove from heat. Add the thyme and vanilla. Stir in 1–2 dashes of vinegar and season with a generous pinch of salt and several grindings of pepper. Serve hot or at room temperature.

3 tablespoons unsalted butter

1 pound carrots, peeled and cut on the bias

1 cup scuppernong grape juice

1 tablespoon thyme leaves

2 drops vanilla extract

Apple cider vinegar

Kosher salt and freshly ground black pepper

Old-Fashioned Glazed Carrots

Serves 6

Mama first got me to eat carrots using this recipe. While it's a throwback to the sixties, it's still viable today, especially with barbecue or anything grilled. Laugh if you want to, but you'll be glad to reconnect with this recipe.

2 pounds carrots, peeled
    and cut into ¼-inch
    rounds

Water

1 10¾-ounce can condensed
    tomato soup

1 cup granulated sugar

¾ cup red wine vinegar

½ cup canola oil

1 teaspoon kosher salt

1 teaspoon prepared yellow
    mustard

1 teaspoon Worcestershire
    sauce

Several grindings of black
    pepper

3 cups chopped onions

1 Place the carrots in a large saucepan and cover with water. Bring to a boil over medium-high heat, reduce heat, and simmer for 10–15 minutes. The carrots should be soft but not mushy. Drain.

2 Combine the remaining ingredients in a large bowl. Pour the carrots into the soup mixture and toss to combine and coat. Cover and refrigerate for 48 hours before serving either chilled or at room temperature.

Carrots and Grapes

The textures and tastes of this recipe are marvelous. The crisp-tender carrots combine superbly with the yielding grapes. This recipe goes great with any kind of seafood except oysters, clams, and mussels; when I sauté shrimp, this dish always seems to be on the side.

Serves 4

1 Fill a 3-quart saucepan half full with water and bring to a boil over medium heat. Add the carrots, reduce heat, and simmer vigorously for about 8 minutes. The carrots should still be crisp-tender. Drain and rinse with cold water.

2 In a large sauté pan, melt the butter over medium heat. Stir in the brown sugar and vermouth. Add the cornstarch and 3 tablespoons of water. Cook, stirring constantly, until thickened. You may have to add some more water to maintain the desired consistency. Stir in the carrots and cook until heated through and nicely glazed. Stir in the grapes and remove from heat. Serve immediately or at room temperature.

Water

8 medium carrots, peeled and cut on the bias

2 tablespoons unsalted butter

2 tablespoons light brown sugar

3 tablespoons vermouth or other dry white wine

2 teaspoons cornstarch

3 tablespoons water

¾ cup green grape halves

¾ cup red grape halves

Grilled Beets and Onions

Serves 8

Winnie Bolton of Raleigh, North Carolina, shared this recipe that she served at an arts council fund-raiser dinner. I had never thought about grilling beets until then, but it gives the root vegetable another dimension. Try these with catfish or steamed oysters or a nice grilled chicken.

8 large beets, peeled and cut into ¼-inch rounds

4 large onions, cut into ¼-inch rounds

Kosher salt and freshly ground black pepper

Extra-virgin olive oil for drizzling

1–2 tablespoons balsamic vinegar

1 Place the beet and onion slices on a baking sheet in one layer. Generously sprinkle the slices with salt and pepper on both sides. Drizzle with the olive oil.

2 Place the beets and onions on the grill in a single layer over medium heat. Cook, turning several times, until the onions are soft and the beets are tender when pierced with a knife, about 15 minutes total. You may need to lower the temperature to avoid burning the vegetables.

3 Remove the onions and beets from the grill. Drizzle with some more olive oil and splash with the vinegar. Toss to coat and serve hot or at room temperature.

Jicama Ginger Slaw

Jicama is often called a Mexican potato. It's low in sugars, making it a good choice for people who are watching such things. Jicama likes to play with other flavors and absorbs them well. This is another good side dish with seafood, chicken, or Asian-style grilled ribs.

Serves 6

1 Toss the vegetables and the ginger in a large bowl to combine. In a separate bowl, whisk together the vinegar, sugar, and lemon zest.

2 Pour the vinegar mixture over the vegetables and toss to combine. Season with a generous pinch of salt and a few grindings of pepper. Cover and refrigerate for 2 hours, tossing occasionally. When ready to serve, drain the vegetables and place in a bowl. Serve cold or at room temperature.

2 cups jicama, peeled and cut into matchstick-sized strips

2 cups carrots, peeled and cut into matchstick-size strips

2 cups red bell peppers, cut into matchstick-size strips

1 quarter-size piece of ginger, peeled and cut into matchstick-size strips

½ cup rice vinegar

1 tablespoon granulated sugar

Grated zest of ½ lemon

Kosher salt and freshly ground black pepper

Lovely Roasted Beets

Serves 4

There are lots of ways to roast beets, but this is my favorite. I enjoy roasting a combination of red, golden, and other beets, but I always roast the red beets separately to maintain the color of the other varieties. Of course, just one type is always welcome. You can use this method to roast beets for pickled beets. When handling beets, especially red ones, it's a good idea to slide on a pair of inexpensive plastic painters' gloves—unless you particularly like having red fingertips.

8 medium beets, peeled with 1 inch of the stem remaining and cut into quarters

¼ cup chopped shallots

2 sprigs rosemary

2 sprigs thyme

1 tablespoon plus 1 teaspoon olive oil

1 Preheat your oven to 400 degrees.

2 Combine all the ingredients in a large bowl and toss several times to combine and coat.

3 Pull off a 17 × 24-inch piece of foil. Pour the ingredients into the middle of the foil and pull up the sides to make a pouch. Roast in the oven for 50–60 minutes or until the beets are easily pierced with a knife. Remove from the oven and let the beets steam inside the pouch for another 10 minutes. Transfer the beets to a serving dish or platter. Discard the herbs and pour the liquid and shallots over the beets. Serve hot or at room temperature.

Tarragon Pickled Beets

I think tarragon is an underused herb in this country. Its licorice her-baciousness adds interest to many foods, and it can be the mystery ingredient in lots of dishes. So why is this recipe not in the pickle chapter? Because I like to heat these up in a microwave when I serve them. The warmth tends to bring out the sweetness and the acidity in a very pleasant way.

Makes about 2 pints

1 Layer the beets and onions in 2 pint jars. Pack down tightly.

2 Bring the remaining ingredients to a boil in a small pot over high heat, stirring to dissolve the salt and sugar. Pour the mixture into a 2-cup measuring cup. Slowly pour the mixture down the inside of each jar. The liquid should come right to the top. Place lids on the jars and tighten. Refrigerate for at least 4 days before using, 7 or 8 days is better.

3 To warm the pickles, place them in a microwave-proof bowl. Drizzle with some of the liquid and microwave on high for 1 minute. Stir and heat for another minute if necessary, but don't make them scalding. Serve warm, at room temperature, or straight from the refrigerator. And yes, you eat the onions, too.

6 roasted beets, peeled and cut into ¼ inch rounds

2 cups red onions, sliced thinly into half moons

1 cup tarragon vinegar

1 tablespoon roughly chopped tarragon

1 teaspoon kosher salt

½ cup granulated sugar

1 cup water

Roasted Beets with Goat Cheese and Tarragon Vinaigrette

From the humble beet comes a classic salad. When you combine beets with the earthy tang of goat cheese, some pecans, and tarragon, you create flavors fit for company, but this salad is also simple enough for every day.

Serves 4–6

1 Preheat your oven to 375 degrees.

2 Place the beets in the middle of a sheet of aluminum foil. Pull the edges of the foil up and add the garlic and water. Seal the packet and roast for about 1 hour or until the beets are tender when pierced with a knife.

3 Mix the tarragon, lemon juice, and vinegar in a medium bowl. Slowly whisk in the olive oil to create an emulsion. Season with salt and pepper.

4 Open the foil and allow the beets to cool slightly. Use your fingers to pull off the skin. (A pair of disposable gloves is a nice accessory here.) Cut the beets however you would like—cubed, sliced, or (my preference) in a julienne about the thickness of a french fry. Add the beets to the vinaigrette and toss. Divide the salad greens among the plates and top with the beets. Add the goat cheese and pecans and another tablespoon of the vinaigrette to each plate. Serve slightly warm or cool.

1 pound golden or assorted medium-size beets, tops trimmed

3 garlic cloves

2 tablespoons water

¼ cup minced tarragon

2 tablespoons fresh lemon juice

¼ cup champagne vinegar

1 cup fruity extra-virgin olive oil

Kosher salt and freshly ground black pepper

2 bunches local salad greens (whatever is freshest at the market)

8 ounces crumbled goat cheese

½ cup chopped and toasted pecans

Saucy Beets with Sour Cream

Serves 4

This recipe came from Boris, the Russian doorman at my apartment in Manhattan. When he found out that I was a foodie, he brought me all manner of Russian specialties. He loved his beets, and I think you will be surprised to see how close this recipe is to southern beet recipes. After all, he was from Georgia—you know, the other one.

3 cups cubed cooked beets

½ cup granulated sugar

1 tablespoon all-purpose flour

¼ teaspoon kosher salt

½ cup red wine vinegar

2 tablespoons unsalted butter

½ cup sour cream

Caraway seeds for garnish (optional)

1 Place the beets in a large mixing bowl.

2 Place the sugar, flour, and salt in a small saucepan. Add the vinegar and whisk. Bring to a boil over medium heat, whisking constantly, and cook for 5 minutes. Remove from heat and whisk in the butter. Pour this mixture over the beets, toss, and then transfer everything to a serving dish. Top the beets with the sour cream and sprinkle with caraway seeds. Serve immediately.

Maple-Glazed Rutabagas

Bitter and sweet. Earthy and bright. That's the best way to describe these glazed rutabagas. This is one of the first recipes I learned during my culinary training, but I make it a lot more now that I can buy peeled and chunked rutabagas. This fall recipe can blend with most any protein or any sauce. If you have any leftovers, reheat them with a little cream and purée them.

Serves 4–6

1 Place a large sauté pan over medium heat. Add the rutabaga and enough water to come about ¼ inch up the side of the pan. Cover, reduce heat to medium low, and cook until just tender, 8–10 minutes. Remove the cover, and if any water remains in the pan, continue cooking until the water has evaporated. Add the butter and toss the rutabagas until the butter melts and they get a little color, 2–3 minutes. Pour on the maple syrup, tossing to coat, and remove from heat. Add a generous pinch of salt and several grindings of pepper and sprinkle with the chives. Serve immediately or at room temperature.

2 large rutabagas, peeled and cut into 1-inch dice

Water

2 tablespoons unsalted butter

4 tablespoons Grade B maple syrup

Kosher salt and freshly ground black pepper

¼ cup roughly chopped chives

ALL PRAISE TO THE BITTER GREENS

Collards, Kale, Turnips, & Cabbage

The soul of southern cooking is its worship of bitter greens. Collards, mustard, kale, and most other greens are descendants of wild cabbage, and they are among the oldest cultivated vegetables in the world. The Bible talks about the growing season for mustard greens. Europeans were farming collards in the first century. Since the days of plantations, the Civil War, and Reconstruction, bitter greens have been a stalwart of southern fare. They are both part of our everyday life and a holiday standard. Would you dare tempt fate by not having slow-braised greens, black-eyed peas, and hog jowls for luck and wealth on New Year's Day? I doubt it.

We've let a few other bitter greens and their relatives sneak into our lifestyle. Spinach, which originated in Southeast Asia before traveling to the Mediterranean, especially Spain, used to be considered highfalutin in the southern diet, but it's my green of choice when I need something quick and delicious to go with that piece of grouper just caught off the coast or with grilled chicken. Spinach needs little more than olive oil and garlic to heighten its goodness.

Most greens are interchangeable. Collards and kale need a little more cooking time than the others, and I'm really picky about varieties of collards. For years, my mother would drive from Greensboro to a collard patch just inside Johnston County, near the split between the Highway 70 bypass and the business route near Smithfield. After much trial and error, she had anointed this collard patch as superior to all others. She would fill up her trunk, take the collards back to Greensboro, and clean, cook, and freeze them. I know of no one who has tasted my mother's collards who has not thought that they were sublime. As my culinary explorations reached new borders, I became a student of old recipes and decided that I should be able to cook collards as well as my mother does. Her recipe sounded simple enough: Make a pot likker with a ham hock, chop your collards, throw them into the pot likker, and slowly simmer them for a couple of hours. I tried and tried, but I never got close to the flavor of my mother's collards. Then I found out that she had left out one of her secrets. She drains the pot likker from the collards and lets it cool until a thin white crust forms on the top; then she scrapes the crust off and stirs it back into the collards. "Mama, that's the fat that's rising to the top," I explained. She responded, "No, son, that's the flavor." I came home, bought a mess of "frostbitten" collards, and proceeded to put the fat back into them, thinking that now I had everything figured out. Nope—they were better but still not as good as my mother's. She

apparently wasn't going to tell me the real secret. Then one day, while I was shopping at the Carrboro Farmers' Market and admiring some of the fall crops from Stanley Hughes's stand, I noticed this green thing that sort of looked like it had a type of cabbage in the middle of it, but it wasn't as tight as a head of cabbage typically is. When I asked what it was, Mr. Hughes said, "Those are cabbage collards." The lightbulb went on in my head. She was using a specific type of collards. I bought some collards from Mr. Hughes and prepared them with all my mother's tricks. When my mother declared my collards pretty close to hers—while shoveling them into her mouth just as fast as she could eat—I figured I had finally come into her league as a collard cooker.

Mama's Collards, with One of My Twists

Serves 8–10

Mama drove me crazy as I tried to find out every trick she had for making her collards. I'll be more kind and not torture you for 20 years the way Mama did me. This recipe was featured on the Live Well Network's *My Family Recipe Rocks*. The fame for these greens is well deserved.

4 strips thick-cut bacon, chopped

1 large onion, chopped

1 quart water, vegetable broth, or low-sodium chicken broth

4 garlic cloves, peeled

1 teaspoon crushed red pepper

2 tablespoons cider vinegar

1 large meaty smoked ham hock, or if you must, a smoked turkey part

2 bunches cabbage collards (about 5 pounds), cleaned in several rinses of water, stems removed, and roughly chopped

Kosher salt and freshly ground black pepper

Vinegar and hot sauce for serving

1 Place a stockpot over low heat. Add the bacon and slowly cook to render the fat. When the bacon is crisp, remove and reserve.

2 Cook the onion in the bacon drippings until "lazy" and slightly colored, about 5 minutes. Pour in the liquid and add the remaining ingredients except the collards. Increase your heat and bring to a boil. Reduce to a simmer and continue cooking for 20 minutes. This is the "pot likker."

3 Add the collards, a handful at a time, stirring each addition until wilted. Believe it or not, they will all go in the pot. Cook over low heat for 2 hours or until tender.

4 Remove the hock and let cool. Drain the collards, reserving the liquid. Place the liquid in the refrigerator for a quick cool down.

5 Chop the collards if desired. Taste for salt and pepper. Break apart the hock, separating the fat and meat, finely dice the meat, and stir into the collards. Remove the "pot likker" from the refrigerator, skim the white stuff off the top, and stir it into the collards. Reserve the liquid for dipping cornbread.

6 Transfer the collards to a bowl and top with the crumbled bacon. Serve with vinegar and hot sauce for the table. Freeze any leftovers.

Southern Greens with Hot Bacon Vinaigrette

Serves 4–6

A hot bacon vinaigrette is expected with a spinach salad, but I like to use it as a way of seasoning most any quick-cooking green. Though spinach is a good start, it can be mixed with finely chopped kale or mustard greens to create a nice variety of flavors and textures, and they all hold up to the soul-soothing hot bacon dressing. Heck, you can even do this with green beans if you want.

8 slices hickory-smoked bacon

¼ cup roughly chopped shallots

2 garlic cloves, chopped

¼ cup vinegar (apple cider, red wine, or sherry vinegar works well)

½ teaspoon freshly ground black pepper

1 pound stemmed greens, roughly chopped

½ cup toasted pecan halves

Kosher salt

1 In a large sauté pan, slowly cook the bacon until crisp. Remove the bacon from the pan, leaving the fat, and drain on paper towels. Add the shallots and sauté until soft and translucent, 2–3 minutes. Throw in the garlic and cook until fragrant.

2 Immediately add the vinegar and pepper. Using tongs, stir in the greens and continue to stir and coat with the vinaigrette until they're slightly wilted. Depending on the greens you use, this could be as short as 4 minutes (spinach leaves alone) or as long as 10 minutes (collard greens). When the greens are wilted, remove from heat and transfer to a serving bowl. Pour any remaining vinaigrette from the pan over the greens. Crumble the bacon and sprinkle it and the pecan halves over the greens. Season with salt. Serve immediately.

Beer-Braised Collard Greens

Collard greens' affinity for beer is amazing. Something from the hoppiness of beer seems to deepen and sweeten the flavor of collards and to tenderize them in some weird way. This is a really good method to use on "pre-frostbitten" collards, which generally seem to need a little flavor boost. If you have a vegetarian in your family, leave out the meat, up the amount of onions, and you'll get a smokiness that's very appealing and satisfying.

Serves 6–8

1 Cook the bacon slowly in a 5-quart Dutch oven over medium-low heat. Remove the bacon from the pan, leaving the fat, and drain on paper towels. Add the onions and cook for 3–4 minutes or until translucent and soft. Add the chicken wing, cayenne pepper, and chicken broth. Bring to a rolling boil, reduce heat, and simmer for about 30 minutes.

2 Stir in the collards until they've all wilted into the pot likker. Slowly add the beer and stir gently to combine. Cook uncovered for 1–1½ hours or until the collards are tender. Remove the chicken wing. Pull off any meat, chop it finely, and stir it back into the collards. Crumble and stir in the bacon. Serve immediately.

3 slices thick-cut hickory-smoked bacon

2 large onions, chopped

1 smoked chicken wing

½ teaspoon cayenne pepper

4 cups homemade or low-sodium chicken broth

1 pound collard greens, stemmed and torn

12-ounces beer (not "lite"; for a bolder experience, use a dark beer)

Creamed Turnip Greens

Serves 4

Frank Stitt, chef-owner of Highlands Bar and Grill in Birmingham, Alabama, put this thought in my head. These turnip greens are a southern spin on a steakhouse favorite, and they are superb with grilled steak, lamb chops, or highly seasoned pork. You can cut the calories by using 2 percent milk and reduced-fat cream cheese without losing too much lusciousness.

1 tablespoon unsalted butter

1 cup finely chopped onions

2 garlic cloves, finely chopped

1 pound turnip greens, stemmed and roughly chopped

½ cup homemade or low-sodium chicken broth

½ teaspoon crushed red pepper flakes

2 tablespoons all-purpose flour

1 cup milk

5 ounces cream cheese, cut into small pieces

Kosher salt

1 Melt the butter in a large skillet over medium-high heat. When the butter quits foaming, add the onions and garlic and sauté for about 3 minutes. Toss in the turnip greens, chicken broth, and pepper flakes. Use tongs to toss the greens around until everything fits in the pan. Cook for 4–5 minutes or until most of the liquid has evaporated.

2 Sprinkle the turnip green mixture with flour and sauté for 2 minutes. Gradually stir in the milk and cook, stirring occasionally, for another 3 minutes. Add the cream cheese and gently stir until melted. Season with salt. Serve immediately.

Southern Greens and Beans

Cold-weather greens and dried beans have kept many a rural family alive during the southern winter. This recipe is an homage to the struggles of those country folks. You can use dried October beans that have been soaked overnight and drained, but freshly shelled October beans, which you can usually find in the late fall, will add a smoothness to this recipe that you won't get with dried beans. The key to success here is to finely shred the collard leaves much like you would cabbage to make slaw. That way, they will become tender more quickly. I find this recipe marvelous and unexpected next to a piece of grilled striped bass or pan-seared scallops.

Serves 6–8

1 Bring the greens, beans, garlic, and broth to a boil in a large pot or Dutch oven over medium heat. Reduce heat and simmer for about an hour, checking the beans for doneness. They need to retain their shape and be tender yet a bit firm. Season with salt. Remove from heat and stir in 1 tablespoon each of the vinegar and sugar. Taste and add more vinegar and sugar as necessary. Serve immediately.

4 cups stemmed and finely shredded collards or other bitter greens or a mix of greens

2 cups fresh October beans

5 garlic cloves, roughly chopped

4 cups homemade or low-sodium chicken broth

Kosher salt

1–2 tablespoons balsamic vinegar

1–2 tablespoons granulated sugar

Turnip, Collard, and Leek Gratin with Blue Cheese Topping

This recipe was a total accident. I was goofing around trying to figure out how to use some leftover greens. This was the result. I now cook greens just to make this gratin. This is an elegant presentation of good old country food.

Serves 4–6

1 Preheat your oven to 400 degrees.

2 Melt 3 tablespoons of the butter in a large sauté pan over medium heat. Stir in the coarse-grained mustard and then the bread crumbs. Sauté until the bread crumbs are golden, about 5 minutes. Remove from the pan, let cool for a minute, and then stir in the cheese.

3 Melt the remaining 2 tablespoons of the butter in the same pan over medium-high heat. Add the leeks and sauté for 4–5 minutes until they take on a little bit of color. Reduce heat to medium low and pour in the half-and-half, hot mustard, and mixed greens. Toss to combine and cook until thickened, about 2 minutes. Transfer to a 2½-quart or 7 × 11-inch baking dish. Top with the bread crumbs and bake for about 10 minutes or until bubbly. Let cool for 10 minutes before serving.

5 tablespoons unsalted butter, divided

2 tablespoons coarse-grained mustard

2½ cups bread crumbs (leftover French bread works nicely)

1 cup crumbled blue cheese (any variety works, including goat blue cheese)

3 cups leeks, thinly sliced crosswise

¾ cup half-and-half

1½ tablespoons hot English-style mustard or Dijon mustard with horseradish

4 cups chopped cooked greens (a mixture is excellent)

Turnips, Turnip Greens, and Gnocchi

Serves 4

I've had to teach myself to eat greens other than collards. Growing up I hated all these bitter greens and fussed when I was forced to eat them. Then when I was about twenty my taste buds changed and I couldn't get enough, first, of collards, then, of mustard and turnip greens. This playful way to eat bitter greens works as a side dish or as a vegetarian entrée.

Vegetable cooking spray

1 tablespoon unsalted butter

$\frac{1}{2}$ cup chopped onions

1 tablespoon all-purpose flour

1$\frac{1}{4}$ cups milk

1 16-ounce package shelf-stable gnocchi (in your pasta section)

1 cup shredded Gruyère cheese

$\frac{1}{2}$ cup shredded mozzarella cheese

Fresh nutmeg

2 cups cooked, chopped turnip greens

1 Preheat your oven to 350 degrees. Spray a 1$\frac{1}{2}$-quart casserole with vegetable spray.

2 In a 3-quart saucepan, melt the butter over medium heat. Add the onions and cook until tender, about 3 minutes. Stir in the flour and cook, stirring, for about another minute. Gradually whisk in the milk. Add the gnocchi and bring to a boil. Remove from heat and stir in the cheeses and a few grindings of nutmeg.

3 Spoon about half of the gnocchi mixture into the casserole. Top with turnip greens and finish with the remaining gnocchi.

4 Bake uncovered for 25–30 minutes or until bubbly and slightly browned and the gnocchi are tender. Serve hot.

Oven-Roasted Broccoli with Black Truffle Oil

In an effort to extend her culinary awareness, my mother would occasionally try to cook broccoli. Being a good rural cook and a child of the Depression, she cooked her broccoli like she did everything else—to death. Ugh! After I left home and realized that broccoli was much better when it was still a little crunchy or generally cooked less, I became a fan of the vegetable. Roasting brings out a natural sweetness, and when company is coming, I drizzle on a little truffle oil to gild the lily.

Serves 4

1 Preheat your oven to 375 degrees.

2 In a large mixing bowl, toss the florets, a generous pinch of pepper flakes, and a little salt and black pepper with the olive oil, making sure to coat the broccoli completely. Add additional oil if necessary.

3 Spread the broccoli in a single layer on a rimmed baking sheet. Bake for 15–18 minutes until just tender. It should look roasted. Transfer to a platter. Drizzle the broccoli with the truffle oil and serve immediately.

2 bunches broccoli, cut into florets

Crushed red pepper flakes

Kosher salt and freshly ground black pepper

4 tablespoons (or more) olive oil

2 tablespoons black truffle oil

Sweet and Crunchy Broccoli Salad

Serves 6

In my part of the world, broccoli salad recipes are highly guarded family secrets. Enough of that. Here's a recipe that I think will rival any you've ever had. Not only does it make a good side dish for grilled meats, but it can be a full meal as well. Take some on your next picnic.

1 cup good-quality
  mayonnaise

¼ cup white wine vinegar

¼ cup granulated sugar

1 bunch broccoli, cut into
  bite-size florets

½ cup chopped red onions

2 green onions, roughly
  chopped

½ cup golden raisins

½ cup peanuts

8 slices bacon, cooked until
  crisp, then crumbled

1 In a medium bowl, combine the mayonnaise, vinegar, and sugar. Cover with plastic wrap and refrigerate for several hours (overnight is better).

2 Combine the remaining ingredients in a large bowl. Pour the dressing over the salad and mix until combined and nicely coated. Serve immediately or refrigerate in an airtight container until ready to serve. This keeps a couple of days refrigerated.

Spinach Paneer

Indian and other subcontinent peoples have congregated in our larger southern cities, especially those blessed with colleges or universities, and their foodways have begun to assimilate into southern culture. This is one of my favorite Indian dishes, and I don't hesitate to serve it alongside grilled chicken or a standing rib roast. The flavors are subtle, and with the addition of the cheese, you almost wind up with a spiced creamed spinach.

Serves 4–6

1 Combine the garlic, ginger, tomato sauce, water, coriander, cumin, and garam masala in a 3-quart saucepan and bring to a boil over medium-high heat. Reduce heat to low and simmer for about 5 minutes. Stir in the spinach until it completely wilts. Add the cheese and cook for another 2–3 minutes. Stir in the whipping cream. Season with salt and pepper. Remove from heat. Place in a serving dish and squeeze the lime wedges over the spinach. Serve immediately.

3 garlic cloves, minced

1 tablespoon ginger, peeled and minced

½ cup tomato sauce

4 tablespoons water

2 teaspoons ground coriander

½ teaspoon ground cumin

½ teaspoon garam masala

1 pound fresh spinach, stemmed

1 cup paneer cheese, cut into ½-inch cubes (available at Indian and most Asian markets)

¼ cup whipping cream

Kosher salt and freshly ground black pepper

2 lime wedges

Golden Raisin Cabbage

Serves 4–6

I love quail, and I've always wanted a really great side to go with it. My son-in-law and I were working on a quail-based dinner for *Edible Piedmont* magazine when we came up with this idea. It's got everything—sweet, sour, bitter, and of course some pork thrown in for good measure. It's a very soulful recipe that works wonderfully with quail and duck.

2 tablespoons bacon fat

3 garlic cloves, minced

1 head green cabbage
    (about 1½–2 pounds),
    cored and shredded

6 cups homemade or low-
    sodium chicken broth

1 cup golden raisins

2 tablespoons sherry vinegar

½ teaspoon ground cumin

½ teaspoon curry powder

Kosher salt and freshly
    ground black pepper

A few lemon wedges

1 Heat the bacon fat in a 3- or 4-quart saucepan over medium heat. Add the garlic and cabbage and cook for 6–7 minutes. Pour in the broth and raisins and continue cooking until the cabbage is very tender, 45 minutes to 1 hour. During the last 15 minutes of cooking, add the vinegar, cumin, and curry powder. Cook until most of the liquid in the pan is gone, then add a generous pinch of salt and a few grindings of pepper and season with lemon juice. Serve immediately or at room temperature.

Quick-Braised Red Cabbage

Red cabbage, especially when braised, takes on some Bavarian influences. This recipe is perfect for a weeknight since it has very few ingredients and comes together extremely quickly. If you like red cabbage, this one's a winner. Serve with pork chops or European-style sausages.

Serve 4–6

1 Heat the oil in a large sauté pan over medium heat. When the oil begins to shimmer, add the cabbage, the caraway seeds, the paprika, a generous pinch of salt, and several grindings of pepper. Toss the cabbage to coat. Reduce heat to medium low and cook for about 8 minutes, stirring often. Then add ¼ cup apple cider and cook for an additional 2 minutes. Stir together the remaining apple cider and ¼ cup mustard. Pour this mixture into the cabbage and cook for another 2–3 minutes, stirring occasionally. Remove from heat and add the vinegar. Taste and add more mustard if necessary. (I usually do.) Serve immediately or at room temperature.

2 tablespoons olive oil (not extra-virgin)

1 head red cabbage (about 1½ pounds), cored and coarsely shredded

1 tablespoon caraway seeds

1 teaspoon sweet paprika

Kosher salt and freshly ground black pepper

1¼ cups apple cider or apple juice, divided

¼ cup plus 1 tablespoon grainy Dijon mustard, divided

1 tablespoon red wine vinegar

Beer-Braised Cabbage

Serves 8

I know this sounds a little funny, but it certainly tastes good. Just think of it as a tip to the Irish and serve it with pot roast, corned beef, or brisket.

6 slices bacon, chopped

2 cups thinly sliced onions

Freshly ground black pepper

$\frac{1}{4}$ cup coarse-ground mustard

$1\frac{1}{2}$ pounds white cabbage, thinly shredded

1 tablespoon chopped garlic

12-ounces beer, preferably dark

$\frac{1}{4}$ cup heavy cream

1 Cook the bacon in a large sauté pan over medium heat until crisp, about 8 minutes. Remove the bacon from the pan, leaving the fat, and drain on paper towels. Add the onions to the pan and season with several grindings of pepper. Cook until soft, about 5 minutes. Stir in the mustard and the cabbage and cook for an additional 3 minutes. Add the garlic and the beer, cover the pan, and cook for about 30 minutes, stirring occasionally. Mix in the cream and continue cooking, covered, for an additional 10 minutes. Garnish with the bacon and serve warm or at room temperature.

Appalachian Cabbage Pudding

Food writer Jim Villas and East Tennessee food radio personality Fred Sauceman introduced me to this wonderful cabbage dish. It's become one of my holiday favorites.

Serves 4–6

1 Preheat your oven to 350 degrees.

2 Bring the water, bacon, and pepper flakes to a boil in a large pot over high heat, then add the cabbage. Continue to boil for 15 minutes. Drain the cabbage, run under cold water, then drain again. Reserve the bacon.

3 Roughly chop the cabbage and squeeze it to remove the excess water. Place in a large bowl.

4 Whisk together the milk, eggs, salt, mustard, and pepper. Pour this mixture over the cabbage. Cut the reserved bacon into small chunks. Combine the bacon in a small bowl with the bread cubes and thyme. Toss to blend.

5 Butter a 1½-quart casserole dish with 3 tablespoons of the melted butter. Sprinkle the bread crumbs evenly over the bottom and sides of the dish. Pour the cabbage into the dish and top with the bread cube mixture. Drizzle with the remaining melted butter and bake until the custard is set, 50–60 minutes. Serve hot.

2½ quarts water

2 × 2-inch piece of slab bacon

1 teaspoon crushed red pepper flakes

1 medium head of cabbage (about 2 pounds), trimmed, cored, and quartered

2 cups whole milk

3 large eggs

1 teaspoon kosher salt

½ teaspoon dry mustard

Freshly ground black pepper

1 cup small bread cubes

½ teaspoon dried thyme

5 tablespoons unsalted butter, melted, divided

¼ cup fine bread crumbs

Fred's Favorite Brussels Sprouts

Serves 4–6

If you had asked me a few years ago what my favorite brussels sprouts recipe would be, I would have laughed and told you there was no such thing as a good brussels sprouts recipe. This one changed my mind, and all credit goes to Kyle Wilkerson. Now I can't wait for brussels sprouts to come into season, and I eat this dish nearly once a week through the late fall and winter.

Water

1 pound brussels sprouts, trimmed

4 slices heavily smoked bacon, like Allan Benton's from Tennessee, diced

2 tablespoons olive oil

3 garlic cloves, minced

Kosher salt and freshly ground black pepper

A few lemon wedges

1 Fill a 3-quart saucepan about half full of water. Bring to a boil over high heat, add the brussels sprouts, and cook for 4–5 minutes. Drain the brussels sprouts and run them under cold water for a couple of minutes, then allow them to dry on paper towels.

2 Place the bacon in a cold sauté pan and cook over medium-low heat until crisp. Remove the bacon from the pan, leaving the fat, and drain on paper towels. Add the olive oil to the pan and increase heat to medium high. When the fats begin to shimmer, throw in the sprouts and garlic and cook until they begin to caramelize, about 15 minutes. Be sure to shake the pan occasionally so that all sides of the sprouts are browned. When the sprouts are tender, add the bacon. Season with a generous pinch of salt and pepper. Remove from heat and season with lemon juice. Serve hot.

Spinach and Noodles

Sometimes convenience is a good thing. I always keep a package of spinach soufflé in my freezer in case unexpected company drops by. Although this recipe is a little bit of a cheat, no one will ever know it by the taste. Just tell them it took hours to do.

Serves 4–6

1 Preheat your oven to 350 degrees.

2 Butter an 8 × 8-inch or 2-quart baking dish.

3 Place the soufflé in a large bowl and mix in the cooked noodles. Fold in the sour cream, the pesto, and several grindings of nutmeg. Spoon the mixture into the baking dish and sprinkle cheese evenly on top. Bake for 45 minutes or until firm. Let stand for 10 minutes before serving.

1 tablespoon unsalted butter

1 12-ounce package frozen spinach soufflé, thawed

8 ounces wide egg noodles, cooked according to package directions and drained

1 cup sour cream

3 tablespoons pesto sauce

Fresh nutmeg

1 cup shredded Italian-blend cheese

Creamed Spinach and Pearl Onions

Serves 6–8

Creamed spinach was not in my repertoire until I started working in Manhattan and discovered how inviting the dish could be. Put it underneath a steak or pork chop, and you have a tasty duo. While some may consider this a northern dish, I think it's eloquently southern.

Water

20 ounces pearl onions, loose ends chopped off

5 tablespoons unsalted butter

2 tablespoons all-purpose soft wheat flour

1¼ cups milk

Fresh nutmeg

Kosher salt

2 tablespoons olive oil (bacon fat works well, too)

3 garlic cloves, finely chopped

1 pound spinach, stemmed and roughly chopped

Freshly ground black pepper

A few lemon wedges

1 Fill a 3-quart saucepan half full of water and bring to a boil over high heat. Add the onions and cook for 3–5 minutes. Drain and run under cold water until the onions are cool enough to handle. Peel and set aside.

2 Melt the butter in a 2-quart saucepan over medium heat. Whisk in the flour and cook for about 2 minutes. Slowly add the milk, whisking, until a thick white sauce has developed. Add a grinding or two of nutmeg and a little salt. Reduce heat to low.

3 Heat the olive oil in a large sauté pan over medium heat. When the oil begins to shimmer, add the garlic. Cook for about a minute, throw in the onions, and cook for another 2–3 minutes. Add the spinach and mix with tongs until it wilts, usually 5–7 minutes. Stir in the white sauce and cook a few minutes longer. Season with salt, pepper, and lemon juice. Serve immediately.

Umbrian Spinach

Serves 6–8

When a bunch of foodies rent a farmhouse in Umbria, guess what they do. Yep—they cook. I've been fortunate enough to make that trip three times. To me, cooking in the Italian countryside is like being a kid in a candy store. This recipe came from those hills, and because it is quick and a tad unusual, I use it all the time. I've put in capers instead of black olives and substituted sun-dried tomatoes for the raisins. It's very versatile.

4 large bunches spinach, trimmed and left wet

2 tablespoons olive oil

4 large garlic cloves, roughly chopped

⅓ cup pitted Italian olives, quartered

⅓ cup golden raisins

¼ cup toasted pine nuts

1½ tablespoons balsamic vinegar

Kosher salt and freshly ground black pepper

1 Heat ⅓ of the spinach in a large sauté pan over high heat. Using tongs, stir the spinach until it wilts, about 3 minutes. Place the spinach on paper towels. Repeat with the remaining spinach.

2 Heat the olive oil in the pan. When it begins to shimmer, add the garlic, olives, and raisins. Reduce heat to medium and cook for 3–4 minutes, but do not allow the garlic to brown. Add the spinach and pine nuts and heat for about 2 minutes. Remove from heat, stir in the vinegar, and season with salt and several grindings of pepper. Toss to mix, and serve immediately.

Brazilian-Style Collards

On Manhattan's Ninth Avenue, the street with every ethnic cuisine, there's a small little place called Rice and Beans. The 16-seat café serves primarily Brazilian-influenced food, and I particularly love their collards. After a little finagling, I got the gist of the recipe. This style of cooking collards works better with dark-leafed collard greens than with sweeter cabbage collards.

Serves 4–6

1 Cook the bacon in a large pot such as a Dutch oven over medium-low heat until the bacon is crispy, 5–8 minutes. Remove the bacon from the pan, leaving the fat, drain on paper towels, and crumble.

2 Add the oil olive to the pot and increase heat to medium. Throw in the garlic and sauté for about 1 minute. Sprinkle in the pepper flakes and add the collards, tossing with tongs until the greens are coated with the oil and wilted. Cook until crisp-tender, about 10 minutes. If the collards start to stick to the pan, add a little water. Stir in the cooked bacon. Remove from heat and season with salt, pepper, and lemon juice. Serve immediately with rice and beans.

2 strips thick-cut smoked bacon

3 tablespoons olive oil, preferably Spanish

10 garlic cloves, smashed and finely chopped

¼ teaspoon crushed red pepper flakes

1 bunch collards, stemmed and cut into thin slices or a chiffonade (about 8 cups)

Kosher salt and freshly ground black pepper

A few lemon wedges

Smoked Hog Jowl and Black Kale

Serves 4

This recipe includes two ingredients that may not be familiar to you—black kale and guanciale, which is bacon made from the hog's jowl. This meat takes smoke a little differently than other parts of the pig, which makes it delightful to cook with. If you've never had black kale, you'll find it is less bitter than regular kale and much more versatile as a side dish.

4 thick slices guanciale, cut into small dice

5 garlic cloves, cut in half

2 shallots, sliced

½ cup white wine

1 bunch black kale, stemmed and coarsely chopped

1 cup homemade or low-sodium chicken broth

5 sprigs oregano, tied

Kosher salt and freshly ground black pepper

Balsamic vinegar

1 Cook the guanciale in a large sauté pan or Dutch oven over medium heat until crisp. Remove the guanciale from the pan, leaving the fat, and drain on paper towels.

2 Add the garlic and shallots to the pan and cook until both are soft, about 5 minutes. Add the wine and reduce by half. Throw in the kale and the broth and reduce heat to low. Add the oregano, cover, and cook for 30 minutes or until the kale is tender. Remove the oregano and season with salt, pepper, and vinegar. Serve immediately.

Benne Seed Collards with Hot Chili Vinegar

In my ongoing quest to find different ways to cook collards and other bitter greens, this recipe has become a favorite, not only of mine but also of many people who have sat at my table. I have added a little low-country flavor and some Asian heat.

Serves 6–8

1 Bring a large pot of water to a boil over high heat. Add the collards a few at a time until they wilt into the water. Reduce heat to medium and cook for 6–8 minutes. Drain the greens, run cold water over them, and let them set for 4–5 minutes. Squeeze out as much water as you can.

2 Heat the oil in a Dutch oven or other large pot over medium heat. When the oil begins to shimmer, add the onions and cook until they begin to take on color, 5–8 minutes. Add the garlic and cook for another 1–2 minutes. Add the collards, being careful in case they have any water residue that might cause the oil to spit. Cook for about 5 minutes. Add the chicken broth and the benne seeds and cook for another 5 minutes, stirring constantly.

3 Remove from heat and add the vinegar as well as salt and pepper to taste. Strain into a serving bowl and serve immediately with a little more chili vinegar at the table.

Water

1–2 bunches collards, stemmed and cut into a chiffonade

¼ cup canola oil

1 cup chopped onions

4 garlic cloves, thinly sliced

1 cup homemade or low-sodium chicken broth

⅓ cup toasted benne seeds (sesame seeds)

6 tablespoons Asian chili vinegar

Kosher salt and freshly ground black pepper

As Close As I Can Get to Calhoun's Spinach Maria

Serves 12, leftovers freeze well

Calhoun's restaurant sits on the river in Knoxville, snuggled up to the University of Tennessee's campus. All the food is good, but the Spinach Maria has been one of Calhoun's signature dishes for a long time. It's sort of mandated that at least one person at your table order this as a side dish. Replicating the recipe requires using Velveeta cheese, so don't give me any flack about it. It really does make a difference in this rich and satisfying dish.

5 10-ounce packages frozen chopped spinach

1½ cups whole milk

1 teaspoon dry mustard (I like Colman's)

2 teaspoons minced garlic

1 teaspoon crushed red pepper flakes

6 tablespoons unsalted butter, divided

1 cup finely chopped sweet onions

6 tablespoons all-purpose flour

8 ounces Velveeta cheese, cut into small cubes

8 ounces sharp cheddar cheese, cut into small cubes

4 ounces Monterey Jack cheese, cut into small cubes

2 cups shredded Monterey Jack cheese

1 Thaw the spinach in the refrigerator for 24 hours. Place the spinach in a colander lined with several layers of paper towels. Ball up the paper towels and squeeze as much excess water out of the spinach as possible. Spread the spinach on a baking sheet to dry further.

2 Add the milk, mustard, garlic, and pepper flakes to a 5-quart Dutch oven and bring to a hard simmer (not a boil) over medium heat. Reduce heat and let the milk continue to simmer.

3 Melt 1 tablespoon of the butter in another pan over medium heat. Add the onions and cook until translucent, 5–8 minutes. Pour the onions and butter into the Dutch oven. Using the same pan as for the onions, melt the remainder of the butter and whisk in the flour until completely blended. Cook over low heat for 3–4 minutes. Briskly whisk the flour mixture into the milk and onions and cook until the sauce thickens, about 5 minutes.

4 Using a wooden spoon, stir in all the cubed cheese. Continue to stir until the cheese is completely melted and blended into the sauce. Be careful—you don't want the sauce to burn while the cheese is melting. Remove from heat and allow to cool for 15 minutes.

5 Preheat your oven to 350 degrees.

6 Add the drained spinach to the cheese sauce and stir until completely blended. Spoon into an 11 × 9 × 2-inch casserole or baking dish. Spread the shredded cheese evenly over the top. Bake for 12–15 minutes or until bubbly. Serve immediately.

Baked Belgian Endive

Belgian endive is something I got more acquainted with while working in New York City. I like its bitterness when it's raw. The leaves are marvelous little spoons for a tidbit of something good. When I had baked endive at a dinner party, I found it still tart but sweeter, sort of a high-class turnip green. Since I have to southernize everything, a little pork goes into this dish, too.

Serves 4–6

1. Preheat your oven to 375 degrees.
2. Heat the olive oil and butter in a large sauté pan over medium heat. Place the endive in a single layer, cut side down. Add a generous pinch of salt and several grindings of pepper. You will more than likely have to cook the endive in batches. Cook the endive for about 5 minutes or until it's lightly browned. Flip and cook for about 3 minutes longer.
3. Spray a 9 × 13-inch baking dish with vegetable spray and place the endive in the dish. Put the chicken broth and the bacon into the same sauté pan and bring to a boil for 1 minute. Pour the broth over the endive and top with the roasted peppers and parsley. Cover with foil and bake for 30 minutes. Uncover and cook for an additional 10 minutes until the casserole is slightly browned and bubbly. Serve immediately or at room temperature.

1 tablespoon olive oil

2 tablespoons unsalted butter

1½ pounds Belgian endive, sliced in half lengthwise

Kosher salt and freshly ground black pepper

Vegetable cooking spray

¾ cup (or more) homemade or low-sodium chicken broth

3 tablespoons crumbled cooked bacon (about 2 slices)

2 tablespoons diced roasted red bell peppers (ones from the jar work fine)

3 tablespoons chopped flat-leaf parsley

Fried Cauliflower with Asiago Cheese

Serves 4

During my three trips to Italy, I ran across fried cauliflower at almost every restaurant. Now, cauliflower was another one of those vegetables that I didn't want to see on my plate when I was growing up. Later, when my daughter was young, we would pour Velveeta all over cauliflower in an effort to get her to like it. Since then, we've both expanded our horizons, and I use cauliflower in many different ways. But if you want to see us pig out, then watch us eat this adult version of cauliflower and cheese.

Canola oil for frying

2 heads cauliflower, cut into medium-size florets and completely dry

2 cups finely grated Asiago cheese

½ teaspoon dried oregano

Kosher salt

1 Fill a 3-quart saucepan about 3 inches deep with oil and heat to 375 degrees over medium heat. Add handfuls of cauliflower to the oil and fry 5–7 minutes or until golden. Remove the cauliflower from the oil with a slotted spoon or spider and drain on paper towels. Sprinkle each batch with some cheese. When all the cauliflower is cooked, sprinkle with the oregano and add salt to taste. Serve immediately.

Broccoli Rabe and Potato Bake

Serves 4–6

I discovered broccoli rabe during my first excursion to the Culinary Institute of America. Ten years ago, broccoli rabe was extremely hard to find in the South, but now most major supermarkets and definitely Whole Foods and other such places carry it. Be sure you're buying broccoli rabe, not some other mutation of broccoli. Broccoli rabe is bitter, earthy, strong, and delicious. I use it quite a bit to make pasta sauces with some of our good local Italian sausage, but I also think it's great just steamed and drizzled with a little olive oil and balsamic vinegar. This broccoli rabe–potato combination is truly amazing, good not only the first time but also reheated and even served right from the refrigerator.

4 tablespoons olive oil

4 garlic cloves, smashed

1½ pounds Yukon Gold potatoes, sliced into ¼-inch half moons

Kosher salt

1 bunch broccoli rabe, stems peeled

1½–2 cups water

¼ cup chopped toasted pecans

Hot pepper sauce

1 Heat the olive oil in a large sauté pan over medium heat. When the oil begins to shimmer, throw in the garlic and cook for about 2 minutes or until it turns brown. Use a slotted spoon to remove the garlic and then add the potatoes. Toss to coat with the oil and cook for 6–7 minutes, without stirring, until the potatoes begin to brown. Season with salt. Add the broccoli rabe in a single layer over the potatoes. Pour in the water and cover.

2 Preheat your broiler.

3 After the broccoli has steamed for 2–3 minutes, remove the cover and place the pan under the broiler. Broil until the broccoli rabe begins to turn brown and the leaves char, usually 10–12 minutes. Remove from the broiler. Sprinkle on the pecans and toss the vegetables to mix. Place the pan back under the broiler for another 4–5 minutes. Don't let the pecans burn, but don't be afraid to get a little char on the vegetables. Remove the pan from the oven and add 3–4 dashes of hot sauce. Toss to combine. Serve immediately.

DRIED & DELICIOUS

A Tribute to Dried Beans, the Savior during Hard Times & Good

One of my favorite meals growing up was when Mama would stew some dried white beans. I think what I really liked was that we got to stir ketchup in with our white beans. All I really knew about our white bean supper was that the beans were creamy and the ketchup added a little kick. I didn't know at the time that Mom and Dad were saving every nickel they possibly could for a down payment on their first house. I can remember both of my parents talking about the Great Depression. Both were younger than twelve during that time, but I know that the hardships of that decade had a major impact on my folks. Pinto beans, white beans, and what they could raise in the garden were their staples. Meat was scarce, and fish, other than local lake fish such as brim or perch, were nonexistent. People were sustained by dried beans, along with things like hog jowl and potatoes. In other parts of the South—the mountains of East Tennessee and the northern regions of Alabama—a bowl of pinto beans cooked in a little pork fat with a cast-iron skillet of cornbread was often served three times a day. Tough times made that generation tough. Tom Brokaw has called these people the "Greatest Generation," and we should be thankful for what they sacrificed and what they learned and passed on to us.

Mom still loves a pot of stewed beans, as do Keith Parrish in Cullman, Alabama, and Belinda Ellis and Fred Sauceman in East Tennessee. Down in Louisiana, red beans and rice are still a Monday must-have. I'm a huge fan of dried beans, and since I've learned the ease with which they can be cooked in a slow-cooker, I have them quite frequently. I love them in all manner of ways. White beans or great northerns now get gussied up with Italian touches. Pintos might have a little tasso ham as opposed to a ham hock. Be sure to try the Lentil "Risotto" (page 210) for an appealing and delicious twist on a classic. I learned to use dried butterbeans in baked beans from my food-styling mentor, Delores Custer, who ate them a lot while growing up in Oregon. Another recipe not to be missed is Not Quite the Bean Barn's Pinto Beans (page 199). The Bean Barn in Greenville, Tennessee, is worth a side trip if you ever find yourself on I-81 between Johnston City and Morristown. Get the beans mixed with their beef stew. It's good!

Dried beans today are just as hearty, filling, and nutritious as they were eighty-plus years ago. They are still a great way to save money, but they are an even better way to add enormous flavor and fiber to your plate. No longer are they poor man's food—they're just darned good eating.

The Original Hoppin' John

Serves 6–8

Most of us prepare our hoppin' John for New Year's Day using black-eyed peas, and I'm including a wonderful recipe for Good Luck Black-Eyes (page 209). You cook the peas, you cook the rice, and you toss them together. It's better than good. But what if there was a predecessor to the black-eyed pea and hoppin' John? Would you try it? Well, there is. It's called a cowpea. Honestly, cowpeas cooked by themselves taste like dirt, and that's probably why they were slaves' food. Cooking them with rice in this concoction brings a different balance to the table. When I prepare this dish, it's easy to rethink the history of the South, and I like eating this dish to celebrate our heritage.

9 slices smoky old-style bacon, like Allan Benton's, divided

1 cup chopped onions

1¼ cups dried cowpeas, soaked in water overnight and drained

1 tablespoon garlic powder

1 tablespoon hot pepper sauce

12 cups homemade or low-sodium chicken broth, divided

1 cup thinly sliced sweet onions

2 cups long-grain rice, like Carolina Gold

1 Cook 6 slices of the bacon in a skillet over medium-low heat until crisp. Remove the bacon from the pan, leaving the fat, and drain on paper towels. Crumble the bacon and set aside. Cook the chopped onions in the bacon fat until translucent, about 5 minutes. Add the peas, garlic powder, hot sauce, and 4 cups of the broth. Bring to a boil, reduce heat, and simmer for 40–45 minutes until the peas are tender but not mushy. Drain and reserve.

2 Cook the remaining bacon in a 3- to 4-quart saucepan over low heat until crispy. Remove the bacon from the pan, leaving the fat, and drain on paper towels. Crumble the bacon. Cook the sliced onions in the bacon fat until they take on some color, 8–10 minutes. Add the remaining broth and the cowpeas and bring to a boil. Add the rice and return to a boil. Cover, reduce heat to low, and cook for 25–30 minutes. Remove from heat and let sit for 10 minutes, covered. Remove the cover and fluff the mixture with a fork. Sprinkle with crumbled bacon and serve hot or at room temperature.

Pableaux's Red Beans and Rice

You want to know Pableaux Johnson, my friend from New Orleans, or at least you want to know someone who knows him. Pableaux is famous for jumping in his car with his pressure cooker, rice steamer, and andouille sausage and embarking on what has become known as the Red Beans and Rice Tour. I've had lots of red beans and rice over the years—some good and some not so good—but I find this one the best. I think it has something to do with the love from the cook that goes into this dish. I know in New Orleans, it's a Monday thing, but I'm not going to relegate this dish to just one day.

Serves 10

1 Heat 1 tablespoon of the olive oil over medium heat in a very large pan, like a Dutch oven. When the oil shimmers, add the sausage and cook until nice and crispy, about 5 minutes. Add a little more oil and the garlic and onions. Cook until the onions, as Pableaux says, "get lazy," or limp and transparent. Throw in the green peppers and celery and sauté for another 5 minutes. Add the beans and cover with water by 1 inch. Simmer until the beans soften, usually 1–2 hours. Pableaux uses a pressure cooker, and if you have one, by all means, go for it. Once the beans have softened, add the bay leaves, all three ground peppers, and the basil, sage, salt, and parsley. Simmer for about 15 minutes. Remove the bay leaves and discard. Remove 1 cup of the beans, mash them with a fork, and return them to the pot. (This will help make your red beans creamy.) Add the green onions and simmer for another 15 minutes. Season with salt and serve immediately over white rice.

4 tablespoons olive oil, divided

1 pound andouille or other smoked sausage, cut into ¼-inch rounds

4 garlic cloves, finely chopped

2 cups diced onions

2 cups diced green bell peppers

3 celery stalks, finely diced

1½ pounds dried red beans, soaked in water overnight and drained

Water

2 bay leaves

1 teaspoon freshly ground black pepper

½ teaspoon freshly ground white pepper

¼ teaspoon cayenne pepper

2 teaspoons dried basil

¾ teaspoon rubbed sage

2 teaspoons kosher salt, plus more

4 tablespoons dried parsley

1 bunch green onions, white and green parts, chopped

White rice

Not Quite the Bean Barn's Pinto Beans and Fred's Favorite Cornbread (page 264)

Not Quite the Bean Barn's Pinto Beans

Appalachian Foodways scholar Fred Sauceman has provided me with guidance about many of the classic foods of the mountain folk. He met me at the Bean Barn in Greenville, Tennessee, for what is undoubtedly the best bowl of pintos I've ever had. You might want to keep in mind that the Bean Barn also mixes their pinto beans with their beef stew as an option. Think about these the next time it's ten degrees outside and you need something warm and filling.

Serves 6–8

1 Cook the bacon over medium heat in a 4-quart or larger saucepan until the bacon is crispy, 5–7 minutes. Throw in the onions and garlic and cook until the onions are translucent, about 5 minutes. Add the beans and chicken broth and nestle the ham hock down in the middle of all of it. Reduce heat to low and simmer, stirring often, until the beans are tender, 1–2 hours depending on the age of the beans. You also can do this in a slow-cooker turned on low for 8–10 hours. Remove the pot from the heat. Use tongs to remove the ham hock. Let it cool slightly and then cut off any lean meat. Finely chop the ham and stir it back into the beans. Serve hot or warm, garnished with onions and parsley. Always serve with cornbread.

3 slices applewood smoked bacon, chopped

1 cup diced onions

1 teaspoon finely minced garlic

1 pound dried pinto beans, soaked in water overnight and drained

4 cups (or more) homemade or low-sodium chicken broth

1 good-sized smoked ham hock

Chopped onions for serving

Chopped parsley for serving

1 batch of cornbread

Barbecued Baked Butterbeans

Serves 8–10

Delores Custer shared this recipe with me when I was her food-styling assistant many years ago in New York City. Delores is an excellent cook and always surprised me with the unique ways she used relatively simple products. I've tinkered with this recipe a bit, and I love the surprised looks I get when people taste it for the first time.

1 pound dried baby lima beans, soaked overnight and drained

Kosher salt

Water

6 strips thick-cut bacon

2 tablespoons unsalted butter

1 cup chopped onions

3 garlic cloves, minced

4 sprigs thyme, leaves stripped and finely chopped

⅔ cup homemade or low-sodium chicken broth

½ cup ketchup

½ cup thick barbecue sauce or Slow-Cooked Memphis-Style Barbecue Sauce (page 307)

¼ cup Worcestershire sauce

2 tablespoons yellow mustard

2 tablespoons molasses

1 tablespoon apple cider vinegar

2 tablespoons light brown sugar

¼ cup brewed coffee

1 Place the butterbeans in a 3-quart saucepan with a pinch of salt and enough water to cover by 1 inch. Bring to a boil over medium heat, reduce heat, and simmer for about 30 minutes or until the beans begin to get tender, though they should still be a little firm. Drain.

2 Cook the bacon in a 12-inch sauté pan over medium heat for 2 minutes on each side. Remove from the pan, leaving the fat.

3 Add the butter to the pan. When the butter foams, throw in the onions, garlic, and thyme. Cook until the onions have become translucent, usually about 5 minutes. Stir in the chicken broth, ketchup, barbecue sauce, Worcestershire sauce, yellow mustard, molasses, vinegar, and brown sugar. Cook until the sugar dissolves and then stir in the brewed coffee and remove from heat.

4 Preheat your oven to 350 degrees.

5 Stir the cooked beans into the sauce. Pour the mixture into a 9 × 13-inch baking dish and top with bacon strips. Bake for about 45 minutes or until the sauce is thickened but still wet. Serve immediately or at room temperature.

Santa Maria–Style Beans

Serves 8–10

During my travels to central California, I've learned to love the style of barbecue made in the Santa Maria Valley. It's not necessarily barbecue as we think of it in the South, but they can grill the tri-tip cut of beef until it's unbelievably moist and flavorful. An absolute must-have with the tri-tip is beans cooked in this style. I sometimes call these cowboy beans, because I always serve them when I smoke a beef brisket. They are also a nice change of pace for cookouts or tailgates.

1 pound dried pinquito or small red beans, soaked overnight and drained

Water

2 strips thick-cut applewood smoked bacon, chopped

½ cup chopped smoked ham

1 garlic clove, finely chopped

¾ cup canned tomato purée

¼ cup prepared chili sauce (I like Bennett's)

1 tablespoon granulated sugar

1 teaspoon dry mustard

1 teaspoon kosher salt

1 Place the beans in a large saucepan or Dutch oven and add enough water to cover by 2 inches. Bring to a boil over high heat, reduce heat, and simmer, covered, until tender, about 2 hours. The exact cooking time will depend on the age of the beans. Older dried beans take longer.

2 Cook the bacon and ham in a medium skillet over medium heat until both are browned, usually 5–7 minutes. Add the garlic and cook for 1 minute. Stir in the tomato purée, chili sauce, sugar, mustard, and salt. Remove from heat.

3 Drain most of the liquid from the beans, reserving 1 cup. Stir that liquid back into the beans along with the sauce. Place back over medium heat and cook until heated through, around 5 minutes. Serve hot or at room temperature.

Pintos and Tasso

If you're a fan of red beans and rice, be sure to try this recipe. The pintos are rich, and the tasso gives the broth a spicy smokiness that you don't get when using andouille. As is the case with all dried bean recipes, seek out the freshest. You're also going to learn my trick for cooking beans—the slow-cooker.

Serves 4–6

1 Place the beans and water in a slow-cooker. Add the salt and stir to dissolve.

2 Melt the bacon fat in a large sauté pan over medium heat. Add the vegetables and the tasso and cook until the vegetables are lightly caramelized, 8–10 minutes. Pour the mixture into the slow-cooker with the beans. Add the mustard, thyme, and Worcestershire sauce. Cover and cook on low for 12 hours. Remove the thyme and season with salt and pepper. Serve hot or at room temperature.

1 pound dried pinto beans

6 cups water

1 teaspoon kosher salt

2 tablespoons bacon fat

1 carrot, peeled and cut into small dice

1 celery stalk, cut into small dice

1 small onion, chopped

2 garlic cloves, minced

1 cup tasso, cut into small dice

1 tablespoon prepared yellow mustard

3 sprigs thyme, tied

2 teaspoons Worcestershire sauce

Kosher salt and freshly ground black pepper

Italian-Style White Beans

Serves 4–6

The flavor of these beans is remarkable with pork, and I pair them often. A simple grilled or pan-seared pork chop leaned up against a pile of these beans will give you monumental eating pleasure.

1 pound dried great northern or cannellini beans

5 cups water

3 sprigs rosemary, tied

2 sage leaves, finely chopped

3 garlic cloves, finely chopped

2 bay leaves

1½ tablespoons coarse-ground mustard

Grated zest of ½ lemon

Kosher salt and freshly ground black pepper

Roasted garlic oil or extra-virgin olive oil (optional)

1 Place the beans, water, rosemary, sage, garlic, bay leaves, and mustard in a slow-cooker. Cover and cook on low for 10–12 hours until the beans are tender but still keep their shape. Remove the rosemary and bay leaves and discard. If you want the beans to be a little stewy, run a potato masher through the pot once or twice. Stir in the lemon zest. Season with salt and pepper and drizzle with garlic oil or olive oil, if desired. Serve hot or at room temperature.

Lima Beans and Ham Hocks

When the book advance has run out and I'm still working on recipes, I turn to this dish for its filling nature and inexpensive cost. But don't let poverty be the only reason you cook this—it's perfect with meat, whitefish, or scallops.

Serves 4–6

1 Combine all the ingredients in a slow-cooker. Cover and cook on low for 10–12 hours. Remove the thyme and bay leaves and discard. Season with salt and pepper. Serve hot or at room temperature.

1 pound dried baby lima beans

1 smoked ham hock

1 onion, cut into eighths

4 sprigs thyme, tied

2 bay leaves

1 teaspoon kosher salt

5 cups water

Kosher salt and freshly ground black pepper

Great Northern Beans with Roasted Tomatoes

Serves 4–6

These beans require two steps: one, cooking the beans themselves; two, roasting tomatoes. You'll be glad you made the effort.

1 pound dried great northern beans

2 chunks country ham

1 tablespoon coarse-ground mustard

6 garlic cloves, finely chopped, divided

4 cups water

12 Roma or plum tomatoes, sliced in half

½ teaspoon dried rosemary

½ teaspoon dried thyme

½ teaspoon dried tarragon

1 small onion, sliced

1 Combine the beans, the ham, the mustard, half of the garlic, and the water in a slow-cooker. Cover and cook on low for 10 hours.

2 Preheat your oven to 250 degrees. Place the tomatoes on a baking sheet, cut side up. Sprinkle the tomatoes with the rosemary, thyme, and tarragon and then with the onion and the remainder of the garlic. Bake for 3 hours or until the tomatoes have slumped and gotten a little soft.

3 Combine the beans and the tomatoes. Serve hot or at room temperature.

Good Old Black Beans

Black beans are good to have around for a number of reasons. You can mash them up and make wonderful bean cakes with them, mix them with rice and serve them with Cuban pork, or use them as a side dish for barbecued chicken. This is my straightforward black bean recipe, so feel free to goose it up.

Serves 4–6

1 Heat the oil in a medium sauté pan over medium-high heat. When the oil begins to shimmer, throw in the onions and cook for 3–4 minutes or until translucent. Add the garlic, chili powder, cumin, paprika, and sugar. Cook for another 3–4 minutes. Pour this mixture into a slow-cooker.

2 Add the black beans, vinegar, and water to the slow-cooker and stir. Cover and cook on low for about 5 hours, checking after 4 hours to see if the beans are tender. Add more liquid if necessary. When the beans are tender but still hold their shape, stir in the chopped cilantro. Adjust seasoning as necessary. Serve hot or at room temperature.

1 tablespoon olive oil

1 small onion, coarsely chopped

3 garlic cloves, minced

1 teaspoon ancho chili powder

1 teaspoon ground cumin

1 teaspoon smoked paprika

1 teaspoon granulated sugar

1 pound dried black beans

¼ cup distilled white vinegar

6 cups water

¾ cup chopped cilantro

Good Luck Black-Eyes

If I didn't eat black-eyed peas on New Year's Day, my mother would have a pure hissy fit. It's been a tradition for as long as I can remember. Hers were a little plainer than this recipe, but I think you'll find the additions welcome.

Serves 4–6

1 Heat the bacon in a large sauté pan over medium heat. Cook until the bacon is crisp, 5–8 minutes. Remove the bacon, leaving the fat, drain on paper towels, and crumble.

2 Add the peppers, fennel, carrots, celery, onions, and garlic to the pan. Sauté until tender, 6–7 minutes. Pour everything from the pan into a slow-cooker. Add the vinegar, herbs, peas, and water. Cook on low 10–12 hours or until the peas are tender but still retain their shape. Remove the thyme and bay leaves and discard. Season with salt and pepper, garnish with the bacon, and serve hot or at room temperature.

3 strips bacon

1 small red bell pepper, cut into small dice

½ fennel head, cut into small dice

4 carrots, peeled and cut into small dice

2 celery stalks, cut into small dice

½ cup diced onions

4 garlic cloves, minced

2 teaspoons red wine vinegar

3 sprigs thyme, tied

2 sage leaves

2 bay leaves

1 pound dried black-eyed peas

6 cups water

Kosher salt and freshly ground black pepper

Lentil "Risotto"

I like lentils, and I don't know why I don't cook them more often. This concoction may perplex you, but only until you taste it. It's a regal dish, unbelievable with lamb chops.

4 tablespoons unsalted butter

1 cup chopped onions

3 garlic cloves, minced

1 pound dried lentils

4 cups homemade or low-sodium chicken broth

2 cups water

½ cup half-and-half

1 cup grated Swiss cheese

2 tablespoons sherry vinegar

1 tablespoon truffle butter

1 Melt the butter in a 3-quart saucepan over medium heat. When the butter stops foaming, throw in the onions and cook until translucent, 3–4 minutes. Add the garlic and cook for an additional 2 minutes. Add the lentils and stir for 5 minutes. Pour in the broth and the water, stirring. Increase temperature to medium high and cook for 30 minutes, stirring as the liquid evaporates. Add the half-and-half and cook, stirring, 5 minutes. Stir in the cheese, vinegar, and truffle butter. Serve immediately.

APPEASING BEANS & PEAS

Shell Beans, Green Beans, May Peas, & *Petits Pois*

"Freddy's coming for a visit. We need to fix some field peas." And with that, my grandmother, Bena Thompson, would head across Stevens Chapel Road in Johnston County to pick peas from her garden. I can still see the sunbonnet she wore when she was working in the field. When she had picked a mess of peas, she would retire to the sanctuary of her kitchen to shell and cook the little brown gems that I only knew as field peas. Those peas were her special gift to me, her second grandson, and I never set foot in her house but what a pot of peas would be cooking. My aunts and cousins carry on this tradition at family reunions, honoring not only me by doing so but also my grandmother. Food has always carried a message of love, and my family has made sure that in this simple way I am a part of them and know I am truly loved. My grandmother didn't live to see how important those field peas became to me, and it took me a while

to realize the impression that her cooking and being in her kitchen would make on me. This chapter holds a special meaning to me for this reason. I've since learned that the peas my grandmother fixed were probably called Dixie Lee. Then upscale chefs introduced me to pink-eyes, lady creamers, and silver crowders. Farmers coached me with six-week peas, white acre peas, and heirloom Emily Lees.

The following pages will take you through my life via my field pea and shell bean adventures. I'll also walk down the garden path of green beans, which I will always consider "snap beans," and explore my more recent affection for May peas and green peas—or, as my mother calls them, English peas. With an ear or two of corn and a garden full of tomatoes, I could live all summer long on the recipes in this chapter. I hope you enjoy them.

Silver Crowder Peas

Serves 4–6

There are many varieties of what people call field peas. The silver crowder is an old-style pea that's making a resurgence with independent farmers. This pea is a good, standard, all-around pea. Don't overcook these peas—they're much better when they have a little bite and a little texture.

2 tablespoons canola oil

½ cup diced green bell peppers

½ cup diced onions

½ cup diced carrots

½ cup diced celery

¼ teaspoon crushed red pepper flakes

3 bay leaves

2 sprigs thyme

2 teaspoons minced garlic

4 cups fresh silver crowder peas

4 cups low-sodium chicken broth or water

1 tablespoon finely chopped flat-leaf parsley

Kosher salt and freshly ground black pepper

1 Heat the oil in a 3-quart saucepan over medium-high heat. When the oil starts to shimmer, add the green peppers, onions, carrots, celery, pepper flakes, bay leaves, and thyme. Cook until the vegetables are tender but haven't taken on any color, about 5 minutes.

2 Add the garlic and cook about 1 minute more until fragrant.

3 Add the crowder peas and chicken broth. Bring to a boil, reduce heat, and simmer for about 25 minutes or until the peas are tender but not mushy. Remove the thyme and bay leaves and discard. Stir in the parsley and season with salt and pepper. Serve immediately or at room temperature.

FIELD PEAS Most southerners use the term "field peas" as a catchall for any fresh, field-grown shell bean that has to be shelled and cooked before it can be eaten. They are totally unlike English or green peas, which can be eaten raw. So for the most part, a field pea is a shell bean, and a shell bean is a field pea—they're just not green peas.

Pea Cakes

When I cook any shell bean, I usually do a double batch, partly because I enjoy these savory little cakes. I serve them with most anything or any topping. Try them with pimento cheese, sausage gravy, or chow-chow relish. Make small ones as a perfect cocktail party nibble.

Makes 8 cakes

1 Purée 1 cup of the beans in a blender or food processor with ⅓ cup of the broth. You can use low-sodium chicken broth if you have lost your cooking liquid.

2 Dump the rest of the beans and the purée into a large bowl and add the cornbread, herbs, Worcestershire sauce, olive oil, and flour. Season with salt and pepper. Stir to combine.

3 Add the egg, working it in with your hands. Adjust the mixture with more broth or cornbread so the cakes hold together.

4 Use a 2-inch biscuit cutter to form the patties.

5 Lightly dust the patties with flour. Heat 2 tablespoons of canola oil in a sauté pan over medium heat. Add a few of the little cakes and lower heat just a smidge. Cook for 3–4 minutes on each side or until a nice golden color has developed. Serve hot or at room temperature.

2 cups cooked shell beans (your choice), cooking broth reserved

1½ cups crumbled day-old cornbread

1 tablespoon chopped chives

1 tablespoon chopped flat-leaf parsley

1 tablespoon Worcestershire sauce

1 tablespoon olive oil

2 tablespoons all-purpose flour, plus some for dusting

Kosher salt and freshly ground black pepper

1 large egg, beaten

Canola oil for pan-frying

Lady Creamer Peas, the Aristocrat

Serves 4–6

For me, lady creamer peas are the stateliest members of the shell bean family. When they cook, they take on a creaminess yet keep their defined shape. Lady creamers are so delicious that very little seasoning is necessary. And while the recipe calls for bacon fat, I often finish these peas with butter.

---

4 cups homemade or low-sodium chicken broth

4 cups shelled lady creamer peas

4 sprigs thyme and 1 sprig rosemary, tied

2 garlic cloves

Kosher salt and freshly ground black pepper

1 teaspoon bacon fat or unsalted butter

1 Bring the chicken broth to a boil in a 3-quart saucepan over medium heat. Pour in the lady creamers and reduce heat to simmer.

2 Add the herb bundle as well as the garlic to the pot and simmer gently for 18–20 minutes or until the peas are tender but not mushy.

3 Remove from heat. Remove the herb bundle and discard. Season with salt and pepper and stir in the bacon fat or butter. Serve immediately or at room temperature.

Spicy Speckled Butterbeans

As far as I'm concerned, there is no such thing as a lima bean, but I do love a butterbean. Speckled butterbeans have an earthiness that I particularly enjoy (along with the mottled colors). They are a perfect candidate for a little extra spice—not heavy-handed, but just a slight bite.

Serves 4–6

1 Heat the chicken broth and ham hock in a 3-quart saucepan over medium heat. Bring to a simmer and cook for 15 minutes. Add the chili and simmer for 5–10 minutes longer. The longer you simmer, the more heat the pot likker will absorb.

2 Pour in the butterbeans and bring the mixture to a boil. Reduce heat and simmer for 16–24 minutes. Start checking for doneness at the 16-minute interval. The peas should be tender but not mushy.

3 Remove from heat and take out the ham hock. Strip any meat from the ham hock and stir it back into the butterbeans. Season with salt as necessary (although both the broth and the ham hock are salty). Serve immediately or at room temperature.

4 cups homemade or low-sodium chicken broth

1 small smoked ham hock

1 green chili, seeded and chopped

3½ cups shelled speckled butterbeans

Kosher salt

STRUTTIN' TOMATOES Struttin' tomatoes are a perfect foil for shell beans and are an excellent choice any other time you want a little sweet/tart flavor mixed in with a vegetable. At my house, we use another name for this—we call it tomato @#$%. A pot of peas doesn't get prepared without this tomato relish. Take one peeled, diced tomato, throw it in a bowl, and add enough white vinegar to cover. Sprinkle in ¼ tablespoon kosher salt, 4 grinds of black pepper, and at least 2 tablespoons granulated sugar. Stir until the sugar has dissolved, cover, and let sit at room temperature for about an hour. Spoon the tomatoes and some of their liquid over the peas. This little mixture does unbelievable things to field peas.

Six-Week Peas

Serves 4–6

With all the fuss over baby vegetables, I guess six-week field peas would be in the "baby" category, though there is nothing baby about their flavor. Six-week peas have a rustic depth that belies their quick maturation. Many folks who claim they don't like field peas go gaga for this recipe.

---

3 cups homemade or low-sodium chicken broth

1 onion, cut into quarters

3½ cups shelled six-week peas

Kosher salt and freshly ground black pepper

1 Bring the broth, onions, and peas to a boil in a 3-quart saucepan over medium heat. Reduce heat to medium low and simmer for 20 minutes. Check for doneness. The peas should be tender but not mushy. Cook up to 10 minutes longer if necessary.

2 Remove from heat. Season with salt and pepper. Serve immediately or at room temperature.

Fred's Favorite Shell Beans—Pink-Eyes

Serves 4–6

Pink-eyes may be the most beautiful of all the field peas, both in their raw state and when they're cooked. Unlike so many of the shell beans, they retain much of their original color, giving them a wonderful plate appearance. And, oh yeah, they're pretty doggoned good, too.

2 slices thick-cut smoked bacon, chopped

½ cup diced onions

3–4 cups shelled pink-eyed beans

3 cups homemade or low-sodium chicken broth

4 sprigs thyme, tied

2 bay leaves

Kosher salt and freshly ground black pepper

1 Spread the chopped bacon evenly across the bottom of a 3-quart saucepan. Place over medium-low heat and cook until crisp, usually 5–10 minutes. Remove the bacon from the pan, leaving the fat, and drain on paper towels.

2 Increase heat to medium and toss in the onions. Cook, stirring occasionally, until translucent, 2–3 minutes. Pour in the pink-eyes and broth. Add the thyme and bay leaves.

3 Bring to a boil over medium-high heat, reduce heat, and simmer for 25 minutes. Taste the peas for doneness. Pink-eyes are often tender yet retain their shape at 25 minutes, but don't be surprised if it takes 35 minutes for them to be completely done.

4 Remove from heat. Remove the thyme and bay leaves and discard. Season with salt and pepper and serve immediately or at room temperature.

NOTE With pink-eyes (or, for that matter, any shell bean), I frequently add several dashes of vinegar before I season with salt and pepper. Acidity is a wonderful seasoning device and usually allows you to cut down on the amount of salt while adding a twang of flavor. Balsamic, sherry, and red wine vinegars are especially useful.

Everybody's Favorite—Dixie Lee Peas

If you plan to have Dixie Lee peas, then get to your farmers' market early, lest you be disappointed. They sell out quick. I don't know what the magic is behind Dixie Lee peas, but folks just seem to love them. I believe there is an inherent sweetness in this shell bean that makes it a palate-pleaser for many folks. I like to emphasize that sweetness by cooking them with sweet onions like Vidalias.

Serves 4–6

1 Bring the broth, ham hock, thyme, onions, and bay leaves to a boil in a 3-quart saucepan over medium heat. Reduce heat to medium low and simmer for 10–15 minutes.

2 Stir in the peas. Return the pot to a boil, then reduce heat to medium low and simmer gently for about 25 minutes. Taste for doneness. The peas should be tender but retain their shape. Remove from heat. Remove the thyme and bay leaves and discard. Take out the ham hock, remove the meat, and toss the meat back into the pan. Season with salt and pepper. Serve immediately or at room temperature.

3 cups homemade or low-sodium chicken broth

1 small smoked ham hock or turkey wing

4 sprigs thyme, tied

1 cup finely chopped Vidalia or other sweet onions

2 bay leaves

4 cups shelled Dixie Lee peas

Kosher salt and freshly ground black pepper

Cumin-Scented Crowder Peas

Serves 4–6

You don't always have to think about refried beans or black beans when serving fiesta-style foods. These cumin-scented crowder peas are a perfect stand-in, especially with fish tacos, fajitas, and even barbecued goat.

3 cups homemade or low-sodium chicken broth

½ cup chopped onions

1 poblano chili, roasted, peeled, and sliced

¾ teaspoon ground cumin

⅛ teaspoon smoked paprika

⅛ teaspoon ground coriander

1 garlic clove, smashed

4 sprigs oregano, tied

3½ cups crowder peas

1 tablespoon chopped cilantro

Juice of 1 lime

Kosher salt and freshly ground black pepper

1 Combine all the ingredients except the peas, cilantro, lime juice, and salt and pepper in a 3-quart saucepan and bring to a boil over medium-high heat. Pour in the crowder peas, reduce heat to medium, and cook for about 25 minutes. Taste for doneness. The peas should be tender but still retain their shape.

2 Remove from heat and take out the oregano and discard. Sprinkle with the cilantro and season with lime juice, salt, and pepper. Serve immediately or at room temperature.

NOTE Sometimes it's fun to take a potato masher to these peas to get them a little more like the texture of refried beans.

Luscious Little White Acre Peas

Folks fall over themselves for white acre peas. I can remember my parents thinking they had a special treat when they were able to get some. Nowadays, they're fairly prevalent at farmers' markets, so be sure to enjoy this delicate, small, and oblong little pea. After you've made this basic recipe, try them in White Acre Pea Salad (page 223).

Serves 4–6

1 Bring the broth, ham hock, onions, chili pepper, bay leaf, and vinegar to a boil in a 3-quart saucepan over medium heat. Stir in the peas, reduce heat, and simmer for 20–25 minutes or until the peas are tender but retain their shape. Remove from heat. Remove the bay leaf and discard. Take out the ham hock, remove the meat, and stir the meat back into the peas. Season with salt and pepper. Serve immediately or at room temperature.

3 cups homemade or low-sodium chicken broth

1 small ham hock

¼ cup finely chopped onions

1 small dried hot chili pepper

1 bay leaf

1 tablespoon balsamic vinegar

3½ cups shelled white acre peas

Kosher salt and freshly ground black pepper

White Acre Pea Salad

This is a perfect potluck dish because it blends well with all kinds of other summer veggies and is just what the doctor ordered to go with things like fried chicken, rich pork, or barbecue. Pair this with fried shrimp for an exceptional southern meal.

Serves 6–8

1 Pour the peas into a large mixing bowl. Toss with the chopped tomatoes.

2 In a small bowl, whisk together the mustard, shallots, garlic, and both vinegars. Slowly whisk in the olive oil to form an emulsion. Stir in the chives and parsley. Pour this mixture over the peas and tomatoes. Toss until the peas are well coated with the dressing and everything is nicely combined. Season with salt and pepper. Serve immediately or at room temperature. If you need to refrigerate, let the pea salad sit at room temperature for at least an hour before serving.

NOTE When making this salad, if you can use just-cooked white acre peas that are still warm, the dressing will absorb better, multiplying the flavor.

1 recipe Luscious Little White Acre Peas (page 221), drained

½ cup peeled and chopped heirloom tomatoes or quartered cherry tomatoes

1 teaspoon Dijon mustard

1 tablespoon minced shallots

1 garlic clove, minced

2 tablespoons tarragon vinegar

2 tablespoons raspberry vinegar

½ cup extra-virgin olive oil

1 tablespoon chopped chives

1 tablespoon chopped parsley

Kosher salt and freshly ground black pepper

Heirloom Emily Lee Peas

Serves 1 if that 1 is me but otherwise 4–6

Heirloom varieties are almost clichéd now, but they're important not only for their history but also for their incredibly intense taste. I remember Emily Lees on my grandmother's heavily laden dinner table every time we came to visit. She knew that I loved them and would never let a visit go by without packing me full of Emily Lee peas. I've missed them and am glad to see that many farmers have decided to raise this old-fashioned but yummy shell bean.

4 cups homemade or low-sodium chicken broth

½ cup chopped onions

4 sprigs thyme, tied

3–4 × 1½-inch piece of smoked or double-smoked slab bacon

3½ cups Emily Lee peas

Kosher salt and freshly ground black pepper

1 Bring the broth, onions, thyme, and bacon to a boil in a 3-quart saucepan over medium-high heat. Reduce heat to medium and simmer for 15 minutes.

2 Increase heat to high, return the liquid to a boil, and stir in the peas. Reduce heat to medium and simmer for 30–35 minutes until the peas are tender yet a little firm. Remove from heat. Remove the thyme and discard. Remove the bacon, cut into ¼-inch slices, and stir them back into the pot. Season with salt and pepper. Serve immediately or at room temperature.

NOTE If you're planning to make Emily Lee Pea Risotto (page 225), keep all of the pot likker from these peas.

Emily Lee Pea Risotto

If you've cooked the preceding recipe, you know how delicious Emily Lee peas can be. But I also like to bring these heirloom peas squarely into the moment, and this risotto is one way I advance their cause.

Serves 6–8

1 Melt 2 tablespoons of the butter in a large skillet over medium-high heat. Add the garlic and onions and cook for 6–8 minutes or until the onions are translucent. Pour in the wine and cook until reduced by half.

2 Stir in the rice and cook for 2–3 minutes. Add the pot likker and bring to a low boil. Reduce the liquid, stirring constantly. Add the chicken broth, ½ cup at a time, stirring with each addition, and cook until almost evaporated. Continue until the rice is al dente, 15–20 minutes. Stir in the grated cheese, the peas, and the remainder of the butter. Season with salt, pepper, and lemon juice. Risotto waits for no one—serve it immediately.

3 tablespoons unsalted butter, divided

3 garlic cloves, minced

½ cup finely chopped onions

¼ cup dry white wine

1¾ cups arborio rice

1¾ cups Heirloom Emily Lee Peas pot likker (page 224)

3 cups homemade or low-sodium chicken broth

¼ cup grated Asiago cheese

1 recipe Heirloom Emily Lee Peas (page 224)

1 tablespoon unsalted butter

Kosher salt and freshly ground black pepper

A few lemon wedges

Summer Bean Ragout

Serves 8

Give me a bowl of this ragout with a plate of sliced heirloom tomatoes drizzled with olive oil and basil, and I have the essence of summer on my table. This is a riff on a recipe from John Toler, chef-owner of Bloomsbury Bistro in Raleigh, North Carolina. I make this dish all summer long and am sad when the fresh ingredients leave in the fall.

4 slices pancetta or bacon, finely chopped

2 cups chopped onions

4 cups homemade or low-sodium chicken broth

2 cups assorted fresh summer peas, like purple hulls, Dixie Lees, or butterbeans

1 tablespoon thyme leaves

1/4 teaspoon crushed red pepper flakes

2 cups assorted summer beans, like snap beans, pole beans, or Roma beans, cut into pieces

2 cups peeled, seeded, and diced tomatoes

2 tablespoons chopped flat-leaf parsley

Kosher salt and freshly ground black pepper

1 Cook the pancetta in a 3-quart saucepan over medium heat until crisp, 5–6 minutes. Add the onions and cook until they begin to color, about 8 minutes. Stir the onions often to pick up the brown bits from the bottom of the pot. Pour in the broth and bring to a simmer. Add the summer peas, starting with the larger ones first, and cook for 8–10 minutes. If using Dixie Lees or butterbeans, add them now and continue cooking for another 10 minutes.

2 Stir in the thyme, pepper flakes, and summer beans. Return to a simmer and cook until the beans are tender, about 10 minutes. Stir in the tomatoes and parsley and heat until just warm, about 3 minutes. Season with salt and pepper. Serve hot or warm.

Summer Bean Ragout and True Southern Biscuit (page 242)

October Beans

I first saw October beans at the Union Square farmers' market in Manhattan. These late-harvest beans cause quite a commotion when they hit the market. So not one to be left out, I came up with a recipe for them. Now I'm glad to see that they are available at most farmers' markets and some grocers. October beans are very rustic and yummy. They support any protein that has an Italian flair.

Something smoked, whether it be a turkey wing or some side meat

1 tablespoon olive oil

1 cup chopped onions

1 pound October beans, carefully picked over

3 cups homemade or low-sodium chicken broth, more if necessary

1 sprig rosemary, leaves stripped and roughly chopped

Chopped onions to top the finished beans (optional)

1 Heat the smoked meat and olive oil in a 3-quart saucepan over medium heat. When the oil is hot, add the onions and cook until translucent. Add the October beans and chicken broth. Increase heat to high and bring to a boil. Reduce heat to medium and simmer for 30–35 minutes or until tender.

2 Sprinkle the rosemary over the beans and stir to combine. Transfer to a big bowl, top with chopped onions, if desired, and serve immediately.

Haricots Verts with Balsamic Onions

A decade ago, haricots verts were difficult to find outside of specialty food shops. Now most local supermarkets carry them and they are big sellers at farmers' markets. These tiny little green beans are filled with flavor and are a nice change of pace when you're trying to gussy up a meal.

Serves 4

1 red onion, peeled and sliced

Vegetable cooking spray

2 tablespoons balsamic vinegar

1 pound baby green beans, trimmed

3 cups water

2 tablespoons canola oil

1 tablespoon thyme leaves

Kosher or sea salt

1 Coat the onions with vegetable spray. Preheat your grill to high. Place the onions on the grill (easier to do if you place them on a skewer) and cook until well charred on both sides, usually a total of about 10 minutes. Remove from the grill, separate the rings, and place in a medium bowl. Add the vinegar and toss until coated. Let the onions marinate for at least 30 minutes.

2 Blanch the green beans in the water for 3 minutes. You can do this one day ahead and refrigerate the beans in paper towels.

3 Heat the canola oil in a large sauté pan over medium heat. When the oil begins to shimmer, throw in the green beans and sauté for about 2 minutes. They should be crisp-tender and still bright green. Remove the beans from the sauté pan and toss them with the onions and vinegar. Add the thyme and toss again. Season with salt. Serve immediately.

Green Beans with Brown Butter

Serves 4–6

Regular old green beans take on a European air when served in this manner. I think you'll like the nuttiness that develops as the butter begins to caramelize. Remember, the key word is *brown* butter, not *burnt* butter. If you take it that far, you need to start over.

8 tablespoons unsalted butter, divided

4 shallots, thinly sliced

4 garlic cloves, minced

1 pound green beans, trimmed and blanched for 2 minutes

¼ cup chopped parsley

Kosher salt and freshly ground black pepper

1 tablespoon apple cider vinegar

Hot pepper sauce (optional)

1 Melt 3 tablespoons of the butter in a large sauté pan over medium heat. When the butter foams, throw in the shallots and cook until just softened, 1–2 minutes. Stir in the garlic and cook until you can smell it. Add the green beans, toss with the shallots and butter, and cook until crisp-tender, another couple of minutes. Remove from heat.

2 Melt the remaining butter in another small sauté pan over medium-low heat. Paying close attention, cook the butter until it just begins to turn golden. Remove from heat and pour over the green beans. Then toss the green beans with the parsley. Season with salt and pepper. Pour in the vinegar and toss. Hit the green beans with a dash or two of hot sauce, if desired. Otherwise, serve immediately.

BLANCHING VEGETABLES Sometimes you need to give crispy vegetables like beans, carrots, cauliflower, and potatoes a little bath in some hot water. It sets their color, enhances their flavor, and is perfect for crudités and vegetables for salads. All you do is bring a pot of water to a boil, plunge the vegetables into the water, and cook until the color comes out and they are just barely tender, usually 30 seconds for green beans, 2 minutes for carrots. Using a spider or slotted spoon, transfer the vegetables immediately to a large bowl of ice water. Cool completely, drain, and if necessary dry before continuing with the recipe.

Greek Green Beans with Tomatoes

I love when the Greek Orthodox churches throughout the South hold their Greek festivals. They're always a good time, with better-than-average food, dancing, and camaraderie, and I recommend that you seek them out in your community. I first experienced these beans at a Greek festival in Richmond, Virginia, and decided then that they were too good not to serve at my house with a whole host of red meats and fish. They're fun and easy.

Serves 8 or more

1 Heat 3 tablespoons of the olive oil in a large pot (a Dutch oven works well) over medium-high heat. When the oil begins to shimmer, throw in the onions and cook for 2–3 minutes. Add the garlic and cook until fragrant, about 1 minute.

2 Add both types of beans and the herbs, tossing to distribute them in the pan. Pour in the tomatoes and their juice. Break up the tomatoes with a spoon. Bring the mixture just to a boil, reduce heat to low, and cover and simmer for 1½ hours. Stir often, but don't add water unless absolutely necessary to keep the beans from sticking to the bottom of the pot.

3 Remove from heat. Season with salt and pepper. Pour the beans into a large serving dish and sprinkle with the pine nuts and feta cheese. Drizzle with the remaining olive oil and serve immediately.

¼ cup olive oil, divided (Greek is nice)

1 cup chopped onions

2 garlic cloves, minced

1 pound green beans, trimmed

1 pound pole beans or Italian beans, trimmed and halved

1 teaspoon oregano leaves

⅛ teaspoon chopped rosemary

1 15-ounce can whole tomatoes

Kosher salt and freshly ground black pepper

¼ cup toasted pine nuts

¼ cup crumbled feta cheese

Slow-Braised Green Beans

Serves 4–6

For most of my childhood, this was the only way I thought green beans could be prepared. I do this recipe once or twice a year just for the nostalgia. The first time I tried to serve my daughter a crisp cooked green bean, I thought she was going to leave home. Fortunately, they are simple to do: The prep work is easy, and then it's just a matter of being patient.

¼ pound smoky slab bacon cut into small dice

1 cup roughly chopped onions

1 pound green beans, trimmed

8 cups homemade or low-sodium chicken broth

1 Spread the bacon chunks in 1 layer on the bottom of a 5-quart Dutch oven over medium-low heat. Slowly cook the bacon. Depending on your bacon, it could take 10–15 minutes. When the fat is about halfway rendered, add the onions, stirring to coat them well. Cook for about 5 minutes, then add the green beans and pour in the chicken broth. Cover and cook over low heat for 2 hours or until the beans are limp and full of pork flavor. Serve immediately.

Aunt Myrtle's Snap Beans

I was well into my teens before I ever heard the words "green beans." Where I come from and to my relatives, those long green things were "snap beans" because that's the way they sounded when you broke them in half. Aunt Myrtle would show up with these snap beans at family reunions and holidays. She told me once that it was a good way to use up any tiny bits of country ham left around the hock. After her death, her sister revealed to me that Aunt Myrtle added a little yellow mustard. Next to Mom's slow-braised snap beans, this is my favorite green bean dish. Try it with roast chicken or some good pork chops.

Serves 4–6

1 Heat the bacon fat in a 3-quart saucepan over medium heat. Add the ham and onions, and cook for 6–8 minutes or until lightly colored. Stir the mixture as you think about it. Throw the beans into the pot and pour in the broth. Bring to a boil, reduce heat, and simmer vigorously for 15–20 minutes or until the beans are tender.

2 Whisk the flour in a bowl with the water and mustard. When the beans are almost done, whisk in a small ladle of the broth. Add the flour mixture to the pan and stir constantly for 3–5 minutes as the broth thickens. Cook for an additional 5 minutes or until the beans are almost glazed. Season with several grindings of pepper and salt, though you probably won't need to add salt because of the saltiness of the ham. Serve immediately.

1 tablespoon bacon fat

2 or 3 biscuit-size slices cured country ham, finely chopped

4 green onions, white and green parts, chopped (spring onions are particularly good)

1½ pounds green beans, trimmed and snapped in two

2 cups homemade or low-sodium chicken broth

2 tablespoons all-purpose flour

2 tablespoons cold water

1 tablespoon prepared yellow mustard

Freshly ground black pepper and kosher salt

Summer Green Beans

Serves 6–8

Only make this dish in the height of the summer when the tomatoes are full-flavored and the green beans are dewy fresh.

Water

1½ pounds green beans, trimmed

½ cup finely chopped onions

6 medium tomatoes, cut into 6 wedges each

4 garlic cloves

1 teaspoon kosher salt

Crumbled cooked bacon (optional)

1 Fill a 3-quart saucepan about half full of water. Bring to a boil over high heat. Reduce heat to low and add the green beans, onions, tomatoes, garlic, and salt. Simmer slowly until the green beans are crisp-tender and the tomatoes have softened, no more than 10 minutes. Strain the mixture, top with bacon, if desired, and serve immediately.

Haricots Verts with Chive Blossom Dressing

I love chive blossoms and don't let a-one go to waste from my garden. This creamy mix adds spunk to these baby green beans. You will have more dressing than you need, so use the extra on grilled fish, poached shrimp, or just a plain old salad.

Serves 4–6

1 In a medium bowl, blend the mayonnaise, the buttermilk, the sour cream, 2 dashes of pepper sauce, 2 dashes of Worcestershire sauce, and the thyme with a generous pinch of salt and several grindings of pepper. Fold in the chive blossoms and refrigerate for an hour so that the flavors will meld.

2 When ready to serve, heat the oil in a large skillet over medium heat. When the oil shimmers, throw in the green beans and quickly cook them for 2–3 minutes. Remove to a serving platter and top with 2–3 tablespoons or more of the dressing. Serve immediately or at room temperature.

¾ cup good-quality mayonnaise

½ cup buttermilk

1 tablespoon sour cream

Hot pepper sauce

Worcestershire sauce

2 sprigs thyme, leaves stripped and minced

Kosher salt and freshly ground black pepper

10–12 open chive blossoms, leaves picked

1 tablespoon olive oil

1 pound haricots verts, blanched for 2 minutes

Fred's Famous Baked Beans

Serves 8–10 or more

This is one of my most requested recipes. Once you try it, you'll understand. This recipe started in Houston, Texas. Martha Sanderson's daughter was in my Indian Princess tribe, and she sent these beans for an overnight campout. Martha thought it amusing that I demanded the recipe. I've printed it in my "Weekend Gourmet" column, and readers love it, writing to me in panic when they misplace the recipe. Martha now says that they are "Fred's Beans." You'll be the hit of your next cookout with these beans, and leftovers are great for several days. The quality of the sausage highly affects this recipe. Try to get locally made country breakfast sausage.

3 32-ounce cans pork and
    beans, drained and rinsed

2 pounds country sausage,
    browned and crumbled

2 medium onions, sliced

1 cup light brown sugar

1 cup dark corn syrup

4 tablespoons prepared
    yellow mustard

1 tablespoon dry mustard

2 teaspoons Worcestershire
    sauce

1 Preheat your oven to 350 degrees.

2 Pour the pork and beans into the largest baking dish you have. I tend to cook these beans in disposable aluminum lasagna pans. Add the sausage and onions and stir. Pour in the remaining ingredients and mix thoroughly. Bake for 1–1½ hours until the beans are not very soupy. These baked beans are better if you cook them the day before you plan to serve them. A quick 30-minute reheat is all you need. Serve hot or at room temperature.

"I Wasn't Cute Enough" Baked Beans

Mike Mills is a champion of barbecue, with the trophies to prove it. He's also served his ribs to many presidents, including Bill Clinton. I've called Mike a friend for many years, all of which I spent trying to get this recipe out of him. It turns out that a few of our female friends already had the recipe. When I asked Mike, "How come they got it but you made me jump through hoops to get it?," he looked at me calmly, smirked, and said, "They were cuter."

Serves 10–12

1 Preheat your oven to 350 degrees.

2 In a large bowl, combine all the ingredients except the beans and bacon. Stir until there are no lumps. Pour in the beans and gently mix with your hands. If you overmix, the skins will burst and the beans will become mushy.

3 Pour the bean mixture into a 9 × 13-inch baking dish and top with the bacon.

4 Cover with foil and bake for 45 minutes. Uncover and bake for another 15 minutes or until bubbly. Serve hot or at room temperature.

2 tablespoons prepared yellow mustard

3 cups ketchup

1 cup finely chopped onions

1 green bell pepper, finely chopped

1½ cups light brown sugar, packed

½ cup sorghum molasses

1½ tablespoons of your favorite barbecue rub

1 28-ounce can pork and beans, drained and rinsed

1 19-ounce can red kidney beans, drained and rinsed

1 15-ounce can chili beans, drained and rinsed

1 15-ounce can butterbeans or giant/large lima beans, drained and rinsed

1 15-ounce can black beans or pinto beans, drained and rinsed

6 slices uncooked bacon

Mama's Baked Bean Casserole

Like the variations on potato salad, I think you need 3 awesome but different baked bean recipes to get you through the summer holidays and tailgating season. When I was at North Carolina State, Mom and Dad would come up for many of the football games. Mother would provide a tailgate for my suitemates and our dates, and Dad would supply the Jack Daniels. We all raved about these beans. The recipe unfortunately was lost, but with a little kitchen experimentation, an exact replica was reborn.

Serves 8–10

1 Preheat your oven to 350 degrees.
2 Combine all the ingredients in a large bowl. Pour into a large baking dish, cover with foil, and bake for 1 hour. Uncover and bake for an additional 20 minutes or until the beans have thickened. Serve hot or at room temperature.

1 pound ground beef, browned and drained

1 large onion, chopped

1 green bell pepper, chopped

3 16-ounce cans pork and beans, drained and rinsed

½ cup light brown sugar, packed

½ cup ketchup

1 teaspoon Worcestershire sauce

1 teaspoon prepared yellow mustard

GLORIOUS GRAINS—THE WAY A YANKEE BECOMES A SOUTHERNER

Grits, Cornmeal, Flour, & Rice

Since the Civil War, the South has attracted folks from around the country as well as around the world. After Reconstruction, textile mills moved in to be closer to their raw materials; one hundred years later, technology and pharmaceuticals began bringing folks. For the most part, the blending and bonding of cultures have been a good thing. When the IBMers first invaded North Carolina's Research Triangle Park, a few things were just too foreign for them to eat. Grits was the major culprit.

I believe that people born outside the South can call themselves southerners* (with the asterisk) after they meet the following standards: they must have lived here for at least twenty years, and they must have learned to enjoy grits, to make a perfect biscuit, and to use a cast-iron skillet for cornbread. I don't think this is too much to ask.

No matter what magazines north of the Mason-Dixon Line decree, you cannot make a "southern" biscuit using hard wheat flour. White Lily has been the gold standard for many years, especially when it was milled in Knoxville, Tennessee. Southern Biscuit Flour is a product of a family-owned mill in Newton, North Carolina.

My mother and most of my kin swore by Red Band, which was gobbled up by a major conglomerate and then unceremoniously discontinued. Regional brands of flour, cornmeal, and grits have long been important to those of us born and raised in the heartland of heaven. I try to support local mills whenever I can. Makers of regional brands often take extra care and are more concerned with quality. Search your neighborhood or check out the Internet. There are some great products out there for you to try.

Southerners are divided about the correct method of making biscuits and cornbread. I am a devotee of all styles. Biscuits can be rolled and cut, beaten, or pinched. I have to confess that I was probably in my twenties before I had cornbread the way most people think of it. After Dad had his heart attack, it seems like cornbread and biscuits went away, but my mother did make a quick concoction of fine cornmeal and a little salt mixed with water and plopped into a quarter inch of hot fat. Those, hushpuppies, and corn sticks constituted my "cornbread" consumption. I started making cast-iron cornbread with my sausage and apple stuffing, and I noticed that a lot of it was being stuffed into me instead of into the bird. From there I started playing with different ingredients and different ways to make cornbread. The only standing southern rule is no sugar.

I love grits—white ones, yellow ones, coarse-ground, and even polenta. I've come a long way since my first bowl of grits, consumed when I was six at a Howard Johnson's restaurant somewhere near Jacksonville, Florida, as we were on our way to a family vacation at Daytona Beach. I know now that those were instant grits, but they began my fascination with how grits could go from a country breakfast to the most urban of dinner parties. One of my favorite meals to this day is fried apples, grits, and sausage gravy with home-made biscuits. If I were on death row, that might be my last meal.

I'm so delighted to see a renewed interest in grits—the grinds that are available, the heirloom products, the heirloom corns being ground into grits. There is no longer any need to eat bad grits. When I look into my pantry, I have a difficult time choosing which grits to use that day. It's a won-derful reversal for such a humble food.

I never thought rice was particularly special until I joined the Southern Foodways Alliance.

It was from that group that I learned of regional rice growers and brands like Carolina Gold. The alliance also taught me that rice could do more than just soak up the gravy from Mama's stewed beef. When I first ventured into Charleston and became aware of the lowcountry's red rice, I became an instant fan. I begged for recipes and combined bits and pieces from various sources into the red rice recipe in this book (page 253).

I guess what I'm trying to say, in a very long-winded way, is that the South's grain-based products are to be celebrated for their diversity and for helping to keep the region's spirit alive. When my father was a kid, a homemade biscuit was an inexpensive pleasure. I don't know what folks in Appalachia or in North Alabama would have eaten with their pinto beans if they hadn't had cornbread. The late Bill Neal, of Crook's Corner in Chapel Hill, North Carolina, made grits a national phenomenon by doing what lowcountry folk had been doing for centuries—serving them with shrimp.

It's all good, and we should take pride in it. That's why you'll be a southerner when you glory in the foods that come from the grains of the South.

True Southern Biscuits

Makes 12 1-inch biscuits

Thanks to the Southern Foodways Alliance and Belinda Ellis, I now can make great biscuits. Belinda, who has been a baking consultant for some of the top southern flours, perfected this method when she was working with White Lily. It's very simple and gives you no excuse for not making biscuits more often.

Vegetable cooking spray

2 cups self-rising soft wheat flour (measured exactly!), such as White Lily or Southern Biscuit Flour

¼ cup solid shortening, butter, or lard

⅔–¾ cup buttermilk (plain milk will do in a pinch)

1 Preheat your oven to 500 degrees.

2 Line a baking sheet with a piece of parchment paper or coat with vegetable spray. Belinda seems to think the parchment paper gives you a better bottom on your biscuit.

3 Place the flour in a large mixing bowl and add the shortening. Using your fingers or a pastry cutter, quickly blend until the mixture resembles coarse crumbs, but not too small. Stir in just enough buttermilk that there is no dry flour. The dough will be sticky. Lightly flour a cutting board or countertop, pour out the dough, and then fold the dough in thirds like you would a letter before putting it in an envelope. Then fold the dough in half, forming a ball and keeping the seam side down. Roll out ½ inch thick. Flour a biscuit cutter and cut out 12 biscuits. Do not twist the cutter. Place the biscuits 1 inch apart on the baking sheet and bake for 8–10 minutes or until the tops are golden brown and the sides look dry.

Belinda's Sweet Potato Biscuits

When Belinda Ellis (or as I like to call her, the Flour Queen) hands you a recipe, you know it's going to be good. This one is no exception. Use these delectable morsels at any meal or make small ones and stuff them with country ham for cocktail parties.

Makes 10–12

1 In a large bowl, combine the flour, brown sugar, baking powder, and cinnamon. Cut the butter into pieces and scatter on top of the flour. Work the butter into the flour with your fingers, a fork, or a pastry cutter until the mixture forms pea-sized crumbs.

2 Mash enough sweet potatoes to measure ¾ cup. Stir the sweet potatoes into the flour only enough to moisten the flour and get the dough to hold together. Lightly flour a cutting board or countertop and turn out the dough. Gently knead 2–3 times.

3 Preheat your oven to 400 degrees.

4 Place a Silpat or parchment paper on a baking sheet.

5 Pat the dough out ½ inch thick. Flour a 2-inch biscuit cutter, cut out as many biscuits as possible, and place them on the prepared baking sheet with their sides touching. (If you want crisp biscuits, place them close together but not touching.) Gather any remaining dough, pat out again, and continue to cut until you can no longer get a 2-inch biscuit. Bake for 10–12 minutes or until the tops are brown.

6 Stir together the orange zest, butter, and honey. Serve with the biscuits either hot or at room temperature.

1 cup self-rising soft wheat flour

1 tablespoon light brown sugar, packed

½ teaspoon baking powder

⅛ teaspoon ground cinnamon

4 tablespoons unsalted butter

1 large cooked sweet potato, peeled and flesh removed, or 1 15½-ounce can of sweet potatoes, drained

Grated zest of 1 orange

8 tablespoons butter, softened

3 tablespoons honey

Flaky Butter Biscuits

Makes 12

When I was a kid and we would visit Dad's family in rural Johnston County, North Carolina, I just loved the biscuits my Aunt Myra Jean would make. They were so flaky, you could peel the layers off. I guess I was about ten when I finally asked if they were homemade. She laughed and said, "Of course!" Well, I found out later that they were those flaky biscuits that came in the tube. Yes, she made them at home, but not from scratch.

I always wanted to do a flaky, from-scratch biscuit. Most of my attempts failed. And then Charlotte chef and pastry instructor Peter Reinhart showed me the way. Not your grandmother's biscuits, but they are awesome.

---

1 cup heavy cream

2 tablespoons distilled white vinegar

1¾ cup self-rising soft wheat flour

1 tablespoon granulated sugar

8 tablespoons very cold unsalted butter

1 Preheat your oven to 500 degrees.

2 Line a baking sheet with parchment paper.

3 Mix the cream with the vinegar in a bowl. Set aside for about 10 minutes. It's normal for the cream to curdle a bit.

4 In a separate bowl, stir together the flour and sugar. Using a cheese grater, grate the butter over the flour. Toss the butter throughout the flour using a wooden spoon. Add the cream mixture and stir until all of the flour is moist. The dough should come together in a ball but not be wet. Turn the dough out onto a lightly floured cutting board or countertop. Flour your hands or a rolling pin and pat or roll the dough to about ⅛ inch thick. Fold the dough into thirds like you're folding a letter to put it in an envelope. Turn the dough and again roll or pat to ⅛ inch thick. Repeat the fold, each time turning the dough, a total of four times. After the last turn, roll the dough into a square ⅛–¼ inch thick. Cut the dough into 2-inch squares. (A pizza cutter is perfect for this.) Place the squares, edges touching, on the baking sheet and bake for 15 minutes or until the tops are golden brown. Serve hot.

Flaky Butter Biscuits and Spicy Tomato Jam (page 51)

Cheese Garlic Biscuits

Makes 12

Who doesn't love a cheese biscuit? People flock to Red Lobster just to eat theirs. This recipe is quite similar, and I've taken a shortcut with the baking mix. These biscuits are good any time but go particularly well with soups and make an interesting variation with sausage gravy.

2 cups buttermilk baking mix (I like Formula L)

⅔ cup milk or buttermilk

½ cup shredded cheddar cheese

4 tablespoons unsalted butter, melted

½ teaspoon minced garlic or ¼ teaspoon garlic powder

1 Preheat your oven to 450 degrees.

2 In a large bowl, stir together the baking mix, milk, and cheese until a soft dough begins to form. Then beat vigorously for 30 seconds.

3 Drop the dough by spoonfuls onto an ungreased baking sheet. Bake until golden brown, 8–10 minutes.

4 In a small bowl, mix together the butter and garlic. Remove the biscuits from the oven and brush this mixture generously over the tops. Serve immediately.

Black-and-Blue Biscuits

If you're tired of garlic bread with your steak, then you need to try this recipe. The biscuits are bold and definitely hold up to a thick New York strip. The combination of rosemary and blue cheese is almost ethereal. Don't be concerned that the cheese oozes out of the biscuit. What it lacks in beauty, it more than makes up for in flavor.

Makes 8–10

1 Preheat your oven to 450 degrees.

2 Line a baking sheet with parchment paper.

3 Pour the flour into a large bowl. Work 4 tablespoons of the butter and the bacon fat into the flour with a pastry cutter or your fingers until the mixture forms pea-sized crumbs. Stir in the blue cheese. Pour in the milk, stirring until the dough is just moist. Turn the dough onto a floured cutting board or countertop. Flour your hands and knead the dough 3 times. Roll or pat to ½ inch thick. With a 2-inch biscuit cutter, cut as many biscuits as you can, reworking the dough when necessary. Place the biscuits about ½ inch apart on the baking sheet. Bake for 10–12 minutes or until the tops are golden brown.

4 While the biscuits are baking, heat 2 tablespoons of the butter, the garlic, and the rosemary in a small saucepan over medium heat until the ingredients melt together. When the biscuits are done, remove the rosemary and then brush the butter mixture over the tops of the biscuits. Serve immediately.

2 cups self-rising soft wheat flour

6 tablespoons chilled unsalted butter, divided

2 tablespoons chilled bacon fat

½ cup crumbled blue cheese

1 cup whole milk

2 garlic cloves, minced

1 sprig rosemary

Linda's Macaroni and Cheese

Serves 4–6

The time: Christmas 2006. The place: my dining room. The event: the best mac and cheese I've ever put in my mouth. I had invited my backdoor neighbor, Linda Johnson, and her husband, Barry, to join us for Christmas dinner. Linda insisted on bringing something. I'm glad she overrode my protests, because what she brought was a marvelous macaroni and cheese. I guess like every parent, I had had so much of the blue box mac and cheese that I had really lost my taste for it. I had played around with some upscale versions, but none came as close to pure comfort as Linda's recipe. The amazing thing about this homemade mac and cheese is that the kids will eat it, too. I think the reason that it appeals to everyone is the combination of cheeses and the brilliance of adding a little Velveeta. My nephew, Hunter Tilley, refuses to come eat with me unless I serve this mac and cheese.

Unsalted butter to grease the casserole

Water

1 pound elbow macaroni

9 tablespoons unsalted butter, divided

1 cup shredded Muenster cheese

1 cup shredded mild cheddar cheese

1 cup shredded sharp cheddar cheese

1 cup shredded Monterey Jack cheese

2 cups half-and-half

8 ounces Velveeta, cut into small cubes

2 large eggs, lightly beaten

¼ teaspoon seasoned salt

Freshly ground black pepper

1 Preheat your oven to 350 degrees.

2 Butter a 2½-quart deep casserole dish.

3 Fill a 4-quart or larger pot about half full of water and bring to a boil over high heat. Cook the macaroni until just tender, usually about 7 minutes. Do not overcook, as it will cook further in the oven. Drain the pasta and return to the pot.

4 Melt 8 tablespoons of the butter. Stir into the macaroni. In a large bowl, blend together the shredded cheeses. Pour the half-and-half into the pot with the macaroni and add 2 cups of the shredded cheese, the Velveeta, and the eggs. Sprinkle in the salt and 5–6 grindings of pepper. Stir to combine. Pour the macaroni mixture into the prepared casserole and sprinkle with the remaining cheese and dot with the remaining butter.

5 Bake the casserole for about 35 minutes, until it's bubbling around the edges and just slightly browned on top. Serve hot.

Laura's Spicy Rice Casserole

My daughter likes for me occasionally to eat healthy, and actually, I usually do. She brought this recipe over one night for dinner, and healthy or not, I love it.

Serves 8–10

1 Preheat your oven to 375 degrees.

2 Pour the rice into a 9 × 13-inch baking dish. Bring the broth to a simmer in a 1-quart saucepan. Stir the hot broth into the rice along with the squash, red peppers, onions, and salt. Cover with foil and bake for 45 minutes. Uncover and continue baking until the rice is tender and most of the liquid is absorbed, usually 35–45 minutes more.

3 Whisk the milk and flour in a small saucepan over medium heat until bubbling and thickened, 3–4 minutes. Reduce heat to low, add 1½ cups of the Pepper Jack cheese, and stir until the cheese is melted.

4 Heat the olive oil in a large skillet over medium heat. Add the turkey sausage, breaking apart with a spoon, and cook until the sausage is done and has taken on some color, usually about 10 minutes. Stir the sausage into the cheese sauce and then pour the mixture over the rice. Scatter the cream cheese and then the pickled jalapeños over the casserole. Sprinkle the remaining cheese over the top. Bake for about 30 minutes until everything is hot and bubbly, the cheeses are melted, and the casserole is just a bit brown on top. Serve immediately.

1½ cups long-grain brown rice

3 cups homemade or low-sodium chicken broth

4 cups diced zucchini and/or summer squash

1 red bell pepper, chopped

1 cup chopped onions

¾ teaspoon kosher salt

1½ cups lowfat milk

3 tablespoons all-purpose flour

2 cups shredded Pepper Jack cheese, divided

2 teaspoons extra-virgin olive oil

8 ounces turkey sausage, casings removed

4 ounces reduced-fat cream cheese, cut into small pieces

¼ cup chopped pickled jalapeños

Wild Rice Pilaf

Serves 4–6

Cooking rice pilaf is one of the first things you learn in culinary school. And quite frankly, it's also one that a lot of us forget. Cooking rice in this manner increases its nuttiness and keeps the grains separate. I had stopped making rice pilaf until my son-in-law suggested a few tweaks. I love this dish. It's fabulous for parties, goes great with turkey and other poultry, and holds its own with grilled pork chops. I know there's rice you can make in ninety seconds, but this is much more flavorful.

2 tablespoons unsalted butter

1/2 cup finely diced onions

1 celery stalk, cut into small dice

1 carrot, peeled and cut into small dice

3 garlic cloves, minced

1 cup wild and white rice blend

4 sprigs thyme, leaves stripped and chopped

1 1/2 cups homemade or low-sodium chicken broth

Kosher salt and finely ground black pepper

1/2 cup toasted almond slivers (optional)

1 Melt the butter in a 3-quart saucepan over medium heat. When the butter foams, throw in the onions, celery, carrots, and garlic. Cook for 5–6 minutes until the vegetables are slightly tender. Stir in the rice and thyme. Cook, stirring, for another 3 minutes. Pour in the broth, increase heat, and bring to a boil. Cover and reduce heat to low. Simmer for about 20 minutes or until the water is absorbed. Season with salt and pepper and stir in the almonds, if desired. Serve immediately.

Woman's Club Browned Rice

Serves 6

My mother-in-law introduced me to this recipe, and when I raved about it and asked for the ingredients, she told me to go look it up in the Raleigh Woman's Club Cookbook. Sure enough, there it was, and a version of it appears in almost every community cookbook. I make no apologies for the ingredients. I have tried doing it differently and cannot replicate this casserole's incredible flavor. Serve this with any kind of beef, from prime rib to a lowly chuck roast. It marries incredibly well with those foods. You talk about a umami bomb (that's that new fifth taste), here it is. The rumor is that this dish freezes well, but there's never been enough left at my house to test this theory.

1 Preheat your oven to 350 degrees.

2 Add all the ingredients to a 2-quart baking dish. Stir until well combined. Bake for 1 hour, stirring every 15–20 minutes, until the rice is tender and the liquid has reduced. Serve hot or at room temperature.

1 cup uncooked long-grain rice

1 10½-ounce can French onion soup

1 3-ounce can mushrooms, drained

1 10½-ounce can beef consommé

6 tablespoons unsalted butter, melted

Southern Green Rice

Serves 8–10

Look through any community cookbook, and you'll find a variation or four of green rice. Green rice was a Sunday-dinner kind of thing and is not seen very much anymore. I think that's a shame, and I routinely surprise people with this rice with an upscale twist.

Vegetable cooking spray

¼ cup canola or olive oil

3 large eggs, lightly beaten

1 cup milk

½ cup finely chopped onions

½ cup finely chopped green bell peppers

1 cup coarsely chopped flat-leaf parsley

2 garlic cloves, minced

Kosher salt and freshly ground black pepper

2 cups cooked white rice

1½ cups crumbled goat cheese

1 Preheat your oven to 350 degrees.

2 Spray a 9 × 13-inch baking dish with vegetable spray.

3 In a medium bowl, combine the oil, eggs, and milk. Stir in the onions, green peppers, parsley, and garlic and a generous pinch of salt and several grindings of pepper. Stir in the rice and cheese. Pour the mixture into the prepared casserole dish. Bake for 40 minutes or until bubbly and hot. Serve hot or at room temperature.

Special Dirty Rice

Dirty rice is a specialty of the Louisiana and Mississippi Deltas. The chicken livers and gizzards give it its earthy notes and dirty color. Jim Villas, a fellow North Carolinian and my mentor, shared this recipe. I am forever in his debt, not only for his long-ago help when I was a new food writer but also for his ongoing friendship.

Serves 6

1 Heat the sausage in a large sauté pan or cast-iron skillet over medium heat, breaking up the sausage with a wooden spoon. Cook for about 10 minutes or until no pink remains. Remove with a slotted spoon and drain on paper towels. Measure out 3 tablespoons of the rendered fat, discard the rest, and return the fat and the sausage to the skillet. Add the onions, celery, green peppers, and garlic and cook, stirring, for 3–4 minutes, until the vegetables have softened just a little. Add the butter, livers, gizzards, thyme, and oregano and a generous pinch of salt and several grindings of pepper. Stir to combine and continue cooking, stirring frequently, until the meats are cooked through, usually 10–12 minutes. Add the broth and continue cooking for 6–8 minutes. Stir in the rice, reduce heat to low, cover, and cook until the rice has absorbed the liquid and is tender, 15–20 minutes. Serve immediately.

VARIATION For great lowcountry red rice, remove the livers and gizzards and reduce the amount of broth to 2 cups. Add a 28-ounce can of diced tomatoes along with the broth. You can also substitute diced smoked link sausage for the country sausage. Remember, every great cook in the lowcountry has a variation on red rice.

½ pound bulk country sausage

1 cup finely chopped onions

2 celery stalks, finely chopped

½ cup finely chopped green bell peppers

1 garlic clove, finely chopped

4 tablespoons unsalted butter

½ pound chicken livers, membranes removed

½ pound chicken gizzards, membranes removed

½ teaspoon dried thyme

½ teaspoon dried oregano

Kosher salt and freshly ground black pepper

2½ cups homemade or low-sodium chicken broth

1½ cups long-grain rice, like Carolina Gold

Arancini with Smoked Mozzarella and Tomatoes

Serves 6–8

Italians use everything, including leftover risotto. The trick we can learn from them is to use those leftovers in a really thrilling way. Enter the arancini—basically fried risotto balls that can be stuffed with just about anything. These are so good that it's almost worth making risotto just to do the arancini.

½ cup smoked mozzarella cheese, cut into small pieces

½ cup oil-packed sun-dried tomatoes, drained and finely chopped

4 cups cooked risotto

Flour

Oil for frying

Marinara sauce (optional)

1 Mix the cheese and the tomatoes in a large bowl and chill until ready to use.

2 Wet your hands and flatten 3 tablespoons of the cooked risotto into a disc. Place 2 teaspoons of the cheese and tomatoes in the center and fold the rice around the filling to form a ball. Repeat until all the ingredients are used.

3 Pour some flour into a pie plate or casserole dish, about 1 inch deep. Roll each ball in the flour to coat. Leave the balls in the flour until they are ready to be fried.

4 Place a 3-quart saucepan over medium heat and fill with about 3 inches of oil. Heat the oil to 350 degrees. Fry the balls for 2½ minutes or until golden. Serve immediately or at room temperature with marinara sauce, if desired.

Southern Panzanella

The Italians think nothing should go to waste, and a simple panzanella salad was their way of dealing with day-old bread. In my humble opinion, this is worth allowing bread to become day-old. I've southernized this recipe by using cornbread. I think you'll find the twist delicious.

Serves 6–8

1 Preheat your oven to 350 degrees.

2 Lightly grease the baking sheet. Place the cornbread cubes on the baking sheet and bake for about 4 minutes. Turn the cornbread and bake for another 4 minutes or so. Remove from the oven.

3 In a large bowl (a wooden salad bowl works nicely), toss together the onions, tomatoes, and basil. Add the vinegar and olive oil and toss again. Add the cornbread cubes and gently toss to combine. Season with salt and pepper.

Unsalted butter to grease the baking sheet

4 cups cubed day-old cornbread

1 cup thinly sliced red onions

1 cup halved cherry tomatoes such as Sun Gold or Supersweet 100s

3 cups seeded and diced heirloom tomatoes, preferably a mixture

12 large basil leaves, cut into a chiffonade

3 tablespoons red wine vinegar

3 tablespoons fruity extra-virgin olive oil (Sicilian olive oil works well)

Kosher salt and freshly ground black pepper

North Carolina–Style Hushpuppies

Makes 3 dozen

It would be a sin to have a fish fry or a pig picking without hushpuppies. Yes, I know, there are plenty of hushpuppy mixes out there, but none will replace the ones you make yourself. These puppies are very North Carolina inspired, as opposed to South Carolina's sweeter ones.

3 cups self-rising white cornmeal

1 cup all-purpose flour

1 tablespoon granulated sugar

1 teaspoon baking powder

1 teaspoon granulated garlic

½ teaspoon dried thyme

½ cup finely diced onions (optional)

2¼ cups buttermilk

Canola oil for frying

1 In a large mixing bowl, combine the cornmeal, flour, sugar, baking powder, garlic, and thyme. Stir in the onions, if desired, and buttermilk so that there are no dry ingredient streaks. Let sit at room temperature while you prepare your fryer.

2 You can deep-fat-fry these or pan-fry these. Both methods yield great results. Just make sure your oil is at 350 degrees before you start frying. To deep-fry, fill a 4-quart saucepan ⅓–½ with oil. Pan-fry using a 2- to 3-inch sauté pan or cast-iron skillet filled with about an inch of oil.

3 Drop 1 tablespoon of hushpuppy mix at a time into the oil, being careful not to put too many hushpuppies in at once. Turn the hushpuppies to get them golden brown on both sides. Repeat with the remaining batter, cooking in batches. Each time you take out a batch, place the hushpuppies on paper towels and let the oil return to 350 degrees. Serve hot or at room temperature. Nobody really cares because they're just that good.

Fred's Basic Cheese Grits

To a southerner, several things are important for a successful relationship: One partner has to make great sweet tea, one has to make perfect biscuits, and somebody has to make really good grits. This recipe will take care of the last requirement. You must, *must* use coarse stone-ground grits locally sourced. Everyone has access to a mill that grinds grits, and they will be far better than anything you might find in the grocery store. This recipe makes a lot, so you can refrigerate the leftovers and warm them up gently with a little water the next day.

Serves 4–6

1 Bring the water and milk to a boil in a 3-quart or larger saucepan over medium-high heat. Reduce the temperature slightly and whisk in the grits. Add a generous pinch of salt and several grindings of pepper. Cook, stirring frequently, for 45–60 minutes or until the grits are somewhat tender. Stir in the cheese until well blended. Stir in the butter. Season with a couple of dashes of hot sauce and a squeeze or two of lemon juice. Serve immediately.

4 cups water

1½ cups milk or cream

1 cup yellow stone-ground grits

Kosher salt and freshly ground black pepper

1¼ cups sharp white cheddar cheese, shredded

3 tablespoons (or more) unsalted butter

Hot pepper sauce

A few lemon wedges

Perfect Fried Grits

Serves about 4

I sometimes make Fred's Basic Cheese Grits just so I can make fried grits, but this is also a good way to use leftovers. The fried grits work at breakfast or as a starchy side dish at any meal. You can also cut the cubes small enough to make wonderful croutons for a salad.

1 cup white or yellow stone-ground grits

4 cups water

1½ cups milk

2 large eggs, beaten

1½ cups bread crumbs

½ cup bacon fat or canola oil

1 In a 3-quart saucepan, bring the grits, water, and milk to almost a boil, then reduce heat to a low simmer. Cook, stirring occasionally, until the grits are tender, about 45 minutes. Pour the grits into a loaf pan and let come to room temperature. Refrigerate overnight. Unmold the loaf and cut into ½-inch slices. Dip the slices into the egg and then into the bread crumbs.

2 Melt the bacon fat in a large skillet over medium heat. When the fat is hot, fry the grits for about 3 minutes on each side until golden brown. Serve hot. Leftovers will keep for 3–5 days.

Grits Soufflé

Every self-respecting southerner needs a grits soufflé recipe in his or her arsenal. It makes a fabulous addition to any buffet, whether it be a breakfast or an after-theater supper. Don't let the word "soufflé" scare you—this one is pretty doggoned foolproof.

Serves 6–8

1 Bring the broth and half-and-half to a boil in a 3-quart saucepan over medium-high heat. Add 2 generous pinches of salt and whisk in the grits. Reduce heat to medium low and simmer slowly for 1 hour or until the grits are soft.

2 Place the egg yolks in a medium bowl. Whisk ½ cup of the hot grits into the yolks. Then pour the yolk mixture back into the remaining grits. Fold in the cheese, garlic, and butter, a few grindings of pepper, and the thyme. Let cool slightly.

3 Preheat your oven to 375 degrees.

4 Butter a 2½-quart soufflé dish.

5 In another bowl, whip the egg whites until they form stiff peaks. Fold the whites into the grits and pour everything into the prepared soufflé dish. Place the dish in a large roasting pan and fill with about ½ inch of boiling water. Bake the soufflé for 30–40 minutes or until set. Serve immediately.

NOTE Many people like toppings on soufflés. Here are a few suggestions you might want to consider: caviar, crispy crumbled bacon, caramelized onions and mushrooms, small diced pickles.

3 cups homemade or low-sodium chicken broth

1 cup half-and-half

Kosher salt

1 cup white or yellow stone-ground grits

5 large eggs, separated

1½ cups shredded white cheddar cheese or an artisanal Swiss cheese

4 garlic cloves, finely chopped

4 tablespoons unsalted butter, melted

Freshly ground black pepper

1 tablespoon finely chopped thyme

1 tablespoon butter, softened, to grease the pan

Boiling water

Spicy Hominy and Cheese

Serves 6–8

"Well, if you can have macaroni and cheese, why can't you have hominy and cheese?," asked Raleigh native Karl Knudson. Karl is a champion of the billfish tournament circuit, but more than that, he just loves to fish. I'm usually lucky enough to get some of his catch, which has included rockfish, grouper, and yellowfin and bluefin tuna. Karl is one of the most natural cooks I know, so I view an invitation to his house for dinner as a command performance. Karl recently introduced me to hominy and cheese. Though I'd never considered the idea, it makes perfect sense, taking advantage of a true southern staple that is now used primarily in the Latino community. That's a shame, especially when you dress the hominy up the way Karl does and add a few of my embellishments. You serve this to any kind of group and ask them to guess what it's made of, and you'll laugh at the answers you get, but there won't be any leftovers.

3 tablespoons unsalted butter

2 cups sliced onions

3 tablespoons Wondra flour, cake flour, or other finely milled flour

1½ cups half-and-half

2 cups shredded Pepper Jack cheese

3 ounces smoked mozzarella cheese, cut into ½-inch cubes

3 15½-ounce cans hominy, drained and rinsed

1 cup toasted bread crumbs, preferably homemade

1 Preheat your oven to 400 degrees.

2 Melt the butter in a 3-quart saucepan over medium heat. Toss in the onions, stir, and cook for about 5 minutes until the onions are tender and translucent. Add the flour and cook for 2 minutes longer, stirring constantly. Slowly pour in the half-and-half, stirring to prevent lumps. Stir in the cheeses. Remove from heat and continue to stir until almost smooth.

3 Pour the hominy into a 7 × 11-inch casserole dish. Pour the cheese sauce over the hominy as evenly as you can. Sprinkle with the bread crumbs. Bake for about 25 minutes until the cheese is bubbly and the bread crumbs have browned a bit. Serve hot or at room temperature.

NONSPICY VARIATION At every dinner there is one kid, one parent, or one friend who has a conniption over anything too spicy, so here's a toned-down version that's just as good. Replace the Pepper Jack cheese with mild or sharp cheddar or just about any other cheese you might enjoy. I've also been known to use goat cheese and to substitute blue cheese for the smoked mozzarella. I guess the biggest thing I've learned about hominy is that it's an excellent carrier of flavor.

Family Reunion Cornbread

Serves 4

My two aunts, Janice Thompson and Myrtle Howell, always made sure that I was well fed at family reunions. Aunt Myrtle was known for her pound cakes, and I'm glad to say that I'm in the proud possession of one of her Bundt pans. Aunt Janice prepares some of the best stewed cabbage I've ever had. But they both prepared a special type of cornbread that was unlike anything you might have encountered. As I grew older and more interested in food, I realized that this style originated in areas where you could buy Cattail's very fine, sifted, water-ground cornmeal. So what makes this cornbread different? It's fried, almost in little patties, but not like a hoecake. The result is a crunchy but tender cracker/cornbread that will knock your socks off. It goes great with traditional partners like cabbage or collard greens but can also surprise you by toting pimento cheese or smoked trout roe at a cocktail party, almost like a crunchy blini. It's hard to give exact amounts for this recipe, so you may have to experiment slightly, using a different amount of water in each batch. You want the bread to be about 2 inches across and ¼ inch thick. Each bag of cornmeal will absorb water differently. Pulling off this recipe requires a loose but not runny mixture. It's not hard to do, and the rewards are great.

1 In a medium bowl, combine the cornmeal with enough water to make a slightly loose batter. Stir in the salt.

2 Pour enough oil into a 10-inch cast-iron skillet or sauté pan to come up about ¼ inch. Place over medium heat. If you want a little pork flavor, add a tablespoon of bacon fat to the oil. When the oil begins to shimmer, about 300 degrees, dip a large soup spoon into the mixture and then ease the batter into the hot oil, shaking the mixture off the spoon and drawing the mixture out in the oil. Remember, your goal is a piece of bread about 2 × ¼ inch. If the mixture spreads too much, add some more cornmeal to the mix. If it is stiff and doesn't spread, stir in more water. Don't worry, you'll get the hang of it, and whatever happens, it will be good. Fry the patties for about 2 minutes or until the bottom is golden brown. Turn and brown the other side. Remove and drain on paper towels. Serve hot or at room temperature.

2 cups fine-ground cornmeal

Cold water

1 teaspoon kosher salt

Canola oil for frying

Fancy Cornbread or Cornbread for Yankees

There, I got in my potshot at those born north of the Mason-Dixon Line. A tremendous number of those folks have found out that the South is a pretty good place to live, so we southerners have to condition them into our way of life. Actually, they've done a pretty good job of bringing some of their foodways, like crusty bread, to our tables. When I have transplanted Yankees over, I usually give them a choice of cornbreads, and this is the one that they're the most familiar with. I hate to admit it, but I like this cornbread a lot. It's just different from what I grew up on and from what most of the rest of the South thinks is cornbread.

Serves 6–8

1 Preheat your oven to 425 degrees.

2 Butter the bottom and sides of an 8-inch square baking pan.

3 In a large mixing bowl, whisk together the flour, cornmeal, sugar, salt, and baking powder. In a smaller bowl, beat together the milk and eggs until they foam. Make a well in the middle of the dry ingredients and pour in the egg mixture. Mix until just combined. Don't overmix, and expect the batter to be lumpy. Pour the batter into the prepared pan and bake for 20–25 minutes or until the top is golden brown and a toothpick stuck into the center comes out dry. Let cool slightly and invert onto a plate. Cut into whatever portion sizes you desire. It's better served hot but okay at room temperature.

VARIATION So you want to make corn sticks? Corn sticks are an integral part of the menu at eastern North Carolina's barbecue joints. All you need to do is make this basic cornbread dough and spoon the dough into a corn stick pan (not the one that looks like an ear of corn). You can also put the dough in a pastry bag or a zip-top bag with one corner cut out and pipe your corn sticks onto a sheet pan covered with parchment paper. Bake in a 450-degree oven for 20–25 minutes or until golden brown. Serve as is, or, for the real taste of eastern North Carolina, Deep- or pan-fry them at 375 degrees for 2–3 minutes.

1 tablespoon unsalted butter

1 cup all-purpose flour, preferably soft wheat all-purpose flour

1 cup stone-ground yellow cornmeal

1 tablespoon granulated sugar

2 teaspoons kosher salt

2 teaspoons baking powder

1 cup milk

2 large eggs

Fred's Favorite Cornbread

Serves 6–8

This is my main cornbread recipe. While it may look a lot like recipes that use canned creamed corn, please don't even consider it here. I use frozen creamed corn: John Cope's white creamed corn is the best, and Pictsweet is also good. Both of these brands have small-kernel corn. I'm not fond of the big guy from the valley because his creamed corn has larger and, to my way of thinking, tougher kernels that I find take away from the experience of the cornbread. I also play with this cornbread a lot. I like to top it with caramelized onions or sometimes chopped, cooked bacon; if I'm really feeling wicked, I use both. My son-in-law likes to put chopped jalapeños on top. Follow the recipe the first time, and after that, go ahead and make it your own.

1½ cups self-rising cornmeal mix

1½ teaspoons kosher salt

1 level teaspoon baking powder

2 large eggs, beaten

1 cup sour cream

1½ cups frozen creamed corn, thawed

½ cup unsalted butter, melted

1 tablespoon canola oil

1 Preheat your oven to 450 degrees. Place a 10-inch cast-iron skillet in the oven while it heats.

2 In a large bowl, whisk together the cornmeal mix, salt, and baking powder. In a medium bowl, stir together the eggs, sour cream, corn, and butter. Pour this mixture into the dry ingredients and fold until just combined, with no dry streaks.

3 Remove the skillet from the oven. Add the oil to the skillet, swirling or brushing to cover the bottom and sides. Pour the batter into the skillet. If you are going to use a topping, put it on now. Reduce heat to 375 degrees. Bake for 35–40 minutes or until golden brown. If you're not using a topping, set your oven on broil and broil the cornbread for 1 minute. Remove the cornbread from the oven and allow it to cool slightly. Cut into wedges and serve hot or at room temperature.

Broccoli and Ricotta Cornbread

If you looked on the Internet, you might find a recipe that calls for a boxed cornbread mix and some cottage cheese and think that sounds pretty good. Well, forget that recipe. Make this over-the-top unbelievable cornbread instead.

Serves 6–8

1 Preheat your oven to 450 degrees. Place a 10-inch cast-iron skillet in the oven while it heats.

2 Cook the onions and canola oil in a large sauté pan over medium-low heat until the onions are translucent, about 5 minutes. Sprinkle the brown sugar over the onions and continue cooking until golden brown, about 5–10 minutes more.

3 In a large bowl, combine the cornmeal mix, milk, eggs, ricotta cheese, cheddar cheese, and butter. Stir to combine. Add the onions and broccoli and fold until evenly mixed. Remove the skillet from the oven. Swirl or brush the olive oil to cover the bottom and sides of the pan. Pour the batter into the skillet. Reduce heat to 375 degrees and bake for 35–40 minutes or until golden brown. Let it cool slightly before cutting into wedges. Serve immediately or at room temperature.

2 cups chopped onions

1 tablespoon canola oil

2 tablespoons light brown sugar

2 cups self-rising cornmeal mix

1 cup milk

3 large eggs

1 cup ricotta cheese

1 cup shredded cheddar cheese

½ cup unsalted butter, melted

1 10-ounce package frozen chopped broccoli, prepared according to package instructions, drained, and dried thoroughly

1 tablespoon olive oil

Cornbread, Apple, and Sausage Dressing

Serves 12 or more

This exquisite dressing first started to take shape during my early years of culinary exploration. I decided to cook a goose for Christmas Eve and found a recipe in the *Silver Palate Cookbook* that suggested stuffing the goose with a mixture of sausage and rye, wheat, and French bread. Over the years, that recipe has morphed into this family favorite. Don't save it just for Thanksgiving or Christmas. It's good with all poultry and pork. It reheats beautifully and makes one hell of a lunch. Be sure to cook your cornbread at least 1 day in advance to let it dry out. That way, it will hold up better and have a more pronounced flavor. And no instant cornbread mixes, thank you very much.

2 pounds country sausage with sage (most farm-stand sausages have enough sage)

2 cups coarsely chopped onions

8 tablespoons unsalted butter, divided

3 tart apples, like Granny Smith, cored and cut into chunks

9 cups cornbread, broken into 1-inch chunks

1 tablespoon dried thyme

2 teaspoons dried sage

½ cup coarsely chopped flat-leaf parsley

1½ cups dried sweetened cranberries

Vegetable cooking spray

Turkey or low-sodium chicken broth

1 Break up the sausage in a 12-inch sauté pan over medium heat. As the sausage cooks, continue to crumble it with a wooden spoon. Cook until the sausage is browned, 7–10 minutes. Remove the sausage from the pan, leaving the fat, and place the sausage in a very large mixing bowl.

2 Increase heat to medium high. Add the onions and cook until soft, about 10 minutes. Pour the onions and sausage fat into the bowl with the sausage. Return the pan to the heat and melt 4 tablespoons of the butter. When the butter stops foaming, add the apple. Reduce heat to medium and cook slowly until the apples are slightly soft, about 10 minutes. Add this mixture to the sausage and onions.

3 Add the cornbread a handful at a time to the bowl, mixing after each addition. Stir in the thyme, sage, parsley, and cranberries.

4 Preheat your oven to 400 degrees.

5 Spray a 15 × 17-inch casserole with vegetable spray. Pour the mixture into the casserole. Cut the remaining butter into small pieces and dot the dressing with them. I have been known to use duck fat in place of the butter. Pour 1 cup of broth over the dressing. Cover with foil and bake for 30 minutes. Every 10 minutes, add a little broth and a little butter and stir to keep the dressing moist. Serve hot or at room temperature.

Don't-Be-Afraid Cornmeal Soufflé

Serves 4–6

Don't be frightened because this recipe uses the word "soufflé." Okay, it does have whipped egg whites, which are classic in a soufflé and make the dish delicate. But it's nowhere near as fragile as a classic French soufflé, and some of my family members think it tastes like upscale spoon bread. Miss Edna Lewis, a visiting chef at the well-regarded Fearrington House, halfway between Chapel Hill and Pittsboro, North Carolina, served a dish very similar to this years ago. So don't be afraid, just enjoy this corn goodness.

2 cups buttermilk or whole milk

⅓ cup stone-ground white cornmeal

4 tablespoons unsalted butter, divided

1 teaspoon kosher salt

3 large eggs, preferably farmstand, separated

1 Preheat your oven to 425 degrees.

2 Bring the buttermilk to just below a boil in a medium saucepan over medium-high heat. Slowly whisk in the cornmeal and bring to a full boil. Cook for 5–6 minutes, stirring constantly. Remove from heat and pour the mixture into a large mixing bowl. Stir in 3 tablespoons of the butter and the salt. Cool for 15–20 minutes. Beat the egg yolks in a small bowl and stir them into the cornmeal mixture. Use the remaining butter to coat a 4-cup soufflé or baking dish.

3 Beat the egg whites by hand or with an electric mixer until they begin to form soft peaks. Fold about ⅓ of the whites into the cornmeal mixture. Then add the remaining whites and fold until no white streaks are evident. Pour the batter into the prepared dish, keeping as much air as possible in the egg whites. Bake for 25–30 minutes until the soufflé has risen and the top is a nice golden color. Serve immediately.

Cornbread Dressing

Some folks don't want a bunch of hullaballoo with their dressing, and when I'm roasting chickens or grilling Cornish game hens, I'm one of those folks. This is a more straightforward dressing. The recipe calls for turkey parts, but you can easily substitute other poultry parts.

Serves 6

1. Place the neck and gizzard in a 2-quart saucepan and cover with water by 1 inch. Place over medium heat and simmer for 1 hour. Remove the meat.

2. Melt the butter in a large sauté pan over medium heat. Add the onions, green peppers, and celery and cook for 2–3 minutes. Add the salt, pepper, and poultry seasoning and cook for about 10 minutes longer.

3. Crumble the cornbread into large chunks in a large bowl. Add the vegetables, the chopped eggs, and about half of the turkey liquid. Toss to combine well.

4. Preheat your oven to 350 degrees.

5. Pack the dressing into a 9 × 9-inch pan. Pour another tablespoon or two of the cooking liquid over the top. Bake for 30–40 minutes or until warmed through, adding the reserved cooking stock to keep the dressing moist. Serve hot or at room temperature.

Neck and gizzard of a turkey

Water

8 tablespoons unsalted butter

2 cups chopped onions

1 cup chopped green bell peppers

2 celery stalks, chopped

½ teaspoon kosher salt

½ teaspoon freshly ground black pepper

½ teaspoon poultry seasoning

1 9-inch round of cornbread

2 large hard-boiled eggs, chopped

Mom's Thanksgiving Dressing

Serves 12

My mother and many other cooks from her generation made their dressing for Thanksgiving this way. Now, my mother loves my Cornbread, Apple, and Sausage Dressing (page 266) and insists that I make it every Thanksgiving. But I also make her dressing every year for one reason—it's great on a turkey sandwich. This dressing is thinner, almost like a pudding, allowing you to cut it into squares to serve. My favorite part of Thanksgiving is the day-after turkey sandwich, or as we call it, Thanksgiving on a Roll. This dressing can be cut to fit the bread and holds together much better than any other dressing. I also use this recipe when I'm roasting bone-in chicken breasts. I serve the chicken breast atop a slab of the dressing and smother it in pan gravy. Try this dressing alongside country-style steak too.

1 pound extra-sage country sausage

1 cup chopped onions

2 cups chopped celery

9 cups cornbread, cut into 1-inch cubes

2 teaspoons poultry seasoning

2 teaspoons dried rubbed sage

1/2 teaspoon kosher salt

1/2 teaspoon freshly ground black pepper

2–3 cups homemade or low-sodium chicken or turkey broth

1 14 1/2-ounce can cream of chicken soup

1 large egg, lightly beaten

1 Break the sausage into small pieces and heat in a large skillet over medium-low heat. While the sausage cooks, crumble it even more. Cook until no longer pink, about 15 minutes. Remove the sausage to a large mixing bowl, leaving the fat.

2 Reduce heat to medium and add the onions and celery to the skillet. Cook until both are soft, 10–12 minutes. Pour this mixture into the sausage.

3 Add handfuls of the cornbread to the bowl, stirring after each addition. Toss in the poultry seasoning, sage, salt, and pepper. Stir until well combined. By this time, the cornbread should have broken down considerably. Add 2 cups of the chicken broth, soup, and egg. Stir until moist.

4 Preheat your oven to 400 degrees.

5 Pack the dressing into either a 15 × 17 or a 9 × 13-inch baking dish. Bake for 30 minutes or until browned and hot. Serve hot or at room temperature.

Fred's Favorite Oyster Dressing

As much as I like my Cornbread, Apple, and Sausage Dressing (page 266), I usually balance it out with an oyster dressing during oyster season. Just make sure you know who's eating with you. Even though the oysters are fairly well hidden in this dressing, you need to be up-front about the bivalve's presence. This may sound crazy, but I really like this dressing with a pork roast or instead of potatoes with a pot roast. Of course, it's absolutely wonderful with a turkey, duck, or chicken.

Serves 6–8

1 Preheat your oven to 350 degrees.

2 In a large mixing bowl, coarsely crumble the cornbread and toss with the bread crumbs. Add all the remaining ingredients except the oysters, broth, and vegetable spray. Toss so that everything is well blended. Add the oysters and fold until they're well distributed. Pour about ¼ cup of the oyster liquid and 2 cups of the chicken broth over the mixture. Fold to combine so that all the ingredients are moist.

3 Spray a 4-quart baking dish with vegetable spray. Pack the mixture into the baking dish. Bake for 15 minutes and then pour some of the remaining broth over the dressing. Continue to bake for another 20–25 minutes until the sides of the dressing are golden brown. Remove and serve hot or at room temperature.

1 9-inch round cornbread (add an extra ¼ cup granulated sugar to your standard mix)

1 cup bread crumbs

3 cups chopped onions

2 cups chopped celery

1 cup chopped green bell peppers

4 green onions, white and green parts, chopped

½ cup melted bacon fat

½ cup chopped flat-leaf parsley

1 teaspoon poultry seasoning

1 teaspoon paprika

¼ teaspoon crushed red pepper flakes

Kosher salt and freshly ground black pepper

1½ pints fresh oysters, drained, liquid reserved (I use standard-size oysters; if some are large, cut them in half)

2–3 cups homemade or low-sodium chicken broth

Vegetable cooking spray

Farro Risotto

I wish I had discovered this ingenious grain earlier in life. I most enjoy farro as a risotto, where its nuttiness and texture seem to peak.

Serves 8–10

1 Melt the butter in a 4-quart saucepan or Dutch oven over medium heat. Add the pancetta and cook until crisp. Remove the pancetta from the pan, leaving the fat.

2 Throw in the onions and cook for 2–3 minutes. Add the celery and carrots and cook for 3–4 minutes more. Add the garlic and cook for another 1–2 minutes. Pour in the farro, stirring so that the grains are coated. Cook for a couple of minutes until a nutty aroma is released. Pour in the white wine and cook until almost completely evaporated, about 3 minutes.

3 Heat the broth in another saucepan over low heat. Add the broth ½ cup at a time, stirring until each addition has almost evaporated. Continue until the farro is tender, usually about 20 minutes. Stir in the cream cheese and allow to melt. Add the parsley and then season with salt, pepper, and a squeeze of lemon. Just like regular risotto, farro risotto waits for no one—serve immediately.

NOTE This dish reheats nicely using additional chicken broth.

2 tablespoons unsalted butter

6 slices pancetta

½ cup diced onions

3 celery stalks, cut into small dice

2 carrots, peeled and cut into small dice

4 garlic cloves, finely chopped

12 ounces uncooked farro

⅓ cup dry white wine

5 cups (or more) homemade or low-sodium chicken broth

3 ounces cream cheese

½ cup chopped flat-leaf parsley

Kosher salt and freshly ground black pepper

A few lemon wedges

Spring Grain Salad with Tahini Dressing

Serves 8–10

Both quinoa and wheat berries are old grains that have found new taste buds. If you're not familiar with these grains, you should be. They are filling and good for you. This is a perfect spring salad that accents the asparagus and green onions.

¼ cup tahini

Finely grated zest of 1 lemon

¼ cup finely chopped cilantro

6 sprigs dill, finely chopped

2 teaspoons granulated sugar

1 tablespoon soy sauce

2 cups cooked quinoa (14 ounces dry weight)

2 cups cooked wheat berries (14 ounces dry weight)

12 asparagus, grilled and cut on the bias

8 green onions, grilled and sliced

Kosher salt and freshly ground black pepper

2 tablespoons mint leaves, finely chopped

1 In a large mixing bowl, stir together the tahini, lemon zest, cilantro, dill, sugar, and soy sauce. Add the quinoa and wheat berries to the bowl and toss to combine. Stir in the asparagus and green onions. Season with salt and pepper. Just before serving, sprinkle the top of the salad with mint. Serve warm or at room temperature.

Wheat Berries with Butternut Squash and Cranberries

This is a very up-to-date twist on fall holiday cooking. This mixture of flavors—sweet, earthy, and tart—sits well alongside a turkey, ham, or goose. It's also perfect when a vegetarian is at your table.

Serves 8–10

1 Preheat your oven to 375 degrees.

2 Add the squash, cranberries, onions, and garlic to a roasting pan. Drizzle with the olive oil and generously sprinkle with salt. Toss the ingredients to coat well with the oil and roast in the oven until the squash is easily pierced with a knife, 25–30 minutes.

3 In a large mixing bowl, fluff the wheat berries with a fork. Stir in the roasted vegetables, followed by the dill, preserves, and orange zest. Serve, topped with the chopped pecans, immediately or at room temperature.

2 pounds peeled and diced butternut squash

1 10- to 12-ounce bag fresh or frozen cranberries

2 cups chopped red onions

3 garlic cloves, minced

2 tablespoons olive oil

Kosher salt

2 cups cooked wheat berries

1 tablespoon minced dill

¼ cup pineapple preserves

Grated zest of 1 orange

1 cup chopped pecans

Quinoa and Scallion Southern "Pancake"

Makes 15–18 5-inch cakes

I absolutely adore going to an Asian restaurant and getting great scallion pancakes. I got this recipe by being a smart aleck, and the fortunate result was a texturally awesome pancake with a really cool, savory flavor. I know that using a mix is cheating a bit here, but it makes this recipe come together quick enough for a Wednesday night dinner.

2 cups seven-grain or whole-grain pancake mix

⅓ cup stone-ground cornmeal

½ cup cooked quinoa

4 green onions, thinly sliced

½ cup buttermilk

1½ cups water

Kosher salt and finely ground black pepper (optional)

At least 4 tablespoons unsalted butter

Spicy Tomato Jam (page 51) or tomato chutney

1 Mix together the pancake mix, cornmeal, and quinoa in a large bowl. Throw in the green onions, buttermilk, and water. Stir until just combined, like you would any other pancake batter. Add a generous pinch of salt and several grindings of pepper, if desired. Let the batter sit at room temperature for 10–15 minutes.

2 Melt 1 tablespoon of the butter in a large nonstick skillet or on a griddle over medium heat. Fill a ¼-cup measure with the batter and pour it into the hot pan. Repeat with as many pancakes as you can comfortably fit on your cooking surface. Just like with a regular pancake, when the top begins to bubble (usually after about 3–4 minutes), it's time to flip. Cook for a couple minutes more on the other side. If desired, place the finished pancakes on a rack over a sheet pan and keep warm in a 200-degree oven. Serve immediately with the tomato jam.

FROM FALL TO SPRING, THEIR SPECIAL TREATS

While the vegetables of fall, winter, and spring don't always get the publicity and hype of high-summer vegetables, they are no less worthy of our time and attention. In the South, we're fortunate that our summer vegetable growing season lasts into September. Toward the end of that month and into October, when the cold arrives, we start to get winter squash, pumpkins, apples, and citrus, all of them intense in their own special ways. And then, about March, after we've had a few tempting 70 degree days in February, the special tastes of spring begin to show up. Asparagus seems to point the way toward the new seasons to come.

Yet another confession: I was in my twenties before I had winter squash. My mother didn't prepare it. I still remember my first taste of fresh asparagus, too—blanched, quickly sautéed, and crisp-tender. It was a revelation. When you're brought up on awful, mushy, strange-tasting canned asparagus, you discover fresh and wonder where it's been all your life. Chanterelle and morel mushrooms bring the deep woods and a hint of mystery to your taste buds. The fall, winter, and spring can be wonderful times to be an eater.

Broiled Texas Red Grapefruit

Serves 4

Growing up, we would have broiled grapefruit for breakfast. But I enjoy having these alongside fish, shellfish, and pork as much as eggs and bacon.

2 ruby red grapefruit

4 tablespoons light brown sugar

1 Preheat your broiler.

2 Slice the grapefruit in half and if desired, use a grapefruit knife to loosen the segments. Place the grapefruit in a baking dish and sprinkle 1 tablespoon of the sugar over each half. Broil for about 8 minutes, checking after 4 minutes. You want the sugar to caramelize but not burn. Serve immediately.

Chanterelles and Eggs

My son-in-law the chef convinced me to try this recipe when I was trying to figure out what to do with chanterelle mushrooms. A chanterelle by itself is an unbelievable side dish, and you can use just the mushroom portion of this recipe. When combined with eggs and served with a steak—a very Portuguese-style meal—decadence has arrived.

Serves 6–8

1 Melt 2 tablespoons of the butter in a large sauté pan over medium heat. When the butter foams, add the shallots and garlic and cook for about 2 minutes. Throw in the chanterelles and cook until they are browned on every side, 5–6 minutes. Remove the pan from the heat.

2 In a nonstick skillet, melt the remaining butter. Pour in the eggs and scramble to a soft consistency. Scrape the mushrooms into the eggs. Stir in the chives and transfer everything to a serving platter. Crown the eggs and mushrooms with the crème fraîche. Serve immediately.

NOTE You can eat this for breakfast or brunch, but try it at least once with a good grilled steak.

6 tablespoons unsalted butter, divided

1 small shallot, finely chopped

1 garlic clove, minced

2 large fresh chanterelles, pulled apart

1 dozen large eggs, preferably farmstand, beaten

¼ cup thinly sliced chives

½ cup crème fraîche or sour cream

Fried Plantains with Latino Salt

Serves 6

The interesting sweetness of plantains makes it the perfect companion to savory foods. Sure, you can save these for when you're cooking Cuban, but you should also try them with grilled chicken or slow-roasted pork. The salt will make slightly more than you need. Keep it in an airtight container and use it to season other vegetables and proteins.

Canola oil for frying

6 very ripe plantains (look for black peels), peeled and cut into ½-inch slices

¼ cup kosher salt

1 tablespoon ground cumin

¼ teaspoon cayenne pepper

¼ teaspoon dry mustard

¼ teaspoon ground coriander

½ teaspoon ancho chili powder

½ teaspoon smoked paprika

1 Place a large sauté pan with 3-inch sides over medium heat. Pour in oil to a depth of 1 inch. When the oil reaches 350 degrees, ease in the plantain slices. Cook until lightly browned around the edges, about 8 minutes. Remove the plantains and place on a sheet pan to cool, reserving the oil.

2 Mix the remaining ingredients in a small bowl.

3 Give each plantain slice a little mash with the palm of your hand. Return the oil to 350 degrees and fry the plantains until crispy, 2–3 minutes. Remove and drain on paper towels. Sprinkle with the salt. Serve immediately.

Curried Acorn Squash

Winter squash are just now beginning to get some respect. This recipe is easy to put together yet classy enough for even a holiday table.

Serves 8

1 Preheat your oven to 400 degrees.

2 Place each squash half cut side up on a 10 × 15-inch baking pan. Sprinkle with ¼ teaspoon of the salt and ⅛ teaspoon of the pepper. Turn cut side down. Add enough water to the pan so that it reaches ¼ inch up the sides of the squash. Bake uncovered for 30 minutes or until fork-tender.

3 In a small bowl, combine the preserves, butter, and curry powder. Add the remaining salt and pepper. When the squash are done, remove the pan from the oven. Turn the squash cut sides up. Spoon 1 tablespoon of the apricot mixture into the cavity of each squash. Brush the remaining mixture on the cut edges. Return to the oven and bake for 15 minutes or until a nice glaze has formed. Serve immediately.

4 medium acorn squash, cut in half crosswise and seeded

½ teaspoon kosher salt, divided

¼ teaspoon freshly ground black pepper, divided

Water

½ cup apricot preserves

4 tablespoons unsalted butter, melted

1½ teaspoons curry powder

Virginia's Roasted Acorn Squash

This is another simple yet awesome recipe that Virginia Bagby shared with me. It's probably my favorite way of preparing acorn squash, and the presentation is impressive, but the work—well, just keep how simple this recipe is to yourself.

Serves 4

1 Cut the bottom of each squash half so that it sits level. Place the squash, cut side down, in a microwavable baking dish. Add enough water to come up about ½ inch on the sides of the squash.

2 Microwave on high for 8 minutes.

3 Preheat your broiler.

4 In a small bowl, combine the butter, brown sugar, cinnamon, and nutmeg. Turn the squash cut side up. Equally divide the raisins and pecans among the squash and sprinkle with the butter mixture. Broil for 2–4 minutes or until the squash flesh is lightly browned. Serve immediately.

2 small acorn squash, cut in half around the equator and seeded

Water

4 tablespoons unsalted butter

1 tablespoon light brown sugar

⅛ teaspoon cinnamon

⅛ teaspoon freshly grated nutmeg

¼ cup raisins

¼ cup pecan pieces

Candied Butternut Squash

Serves 4–6

Perfect fall flavors—earthiness from the squash and sweetness from the rest of the ingredients. Winter squash have deep flavors but are very accepting of other essences.

8 tablespoons unsalted butter

½ cup light brown sugar, packed

½ cup water

¼ teaspoon ground cinnamon

6 cups cubed butternut squash, blanched until just fork-tender, about 10 minutes

1 Melt the butter and brown sugar in a large sauté pan over medium heat, stirring to mix. Add the water and cinnamon, followed by the blanched squash. Reduce heat, cover, and simmer for 10 minutes. Uncover, stir, and cook for an additional 5 minutes until the squash are glazed. Serve hot or at room temperature.

Slow-Roasted Pumpkin

Most folks overlook pumpkin as a vegetable, and so did I until my first trip to Italy. There, slow-roasted pumpkin is a fall menu standard.

Serves 6

1 Preheat your oven to 250 degrees.

2 Coat the pumpkin slices with the olive oil and a good sprinkling of salt and pepper. Place on parchment paper on a baking sheet and roast for 3 hours, until softened but still a bit firm. When the pumpkin has cooled enough to handle, cut off the peel and dice the flesh.

3 Melt the butter in a large sauté pan over medium heat. When the butter stops foaming, add the leeks and sauté until limp, 3–4 minutes. Add the pancetta, ginger, and garlic and sauté until soft, 2–3 minutes. Carefully add the wine and cook a couple of minutes longer. Add the pumpkin and toss. Cook for about 5 minutes. Add the cream, if desired, and cook for a minute longer. Serve hot.

1 small pie pumpkin, sliced and seeds removed

2 tablespoons olive oil

Kosher salt and freshly ground black pepper

2 tablespoons unsalted butter

2 cups thinly sliced leeks

Two ¼-inch pieces pancetta or slab bacon cut into very small cubes

1 tablespoon ginger, peeled and minced

2 garlic cloves, minced

¼ cup white wine

2 tablespoons heavy cream (optional)

Roasted Delicata Squash

Serves 8

Delicata squash is a smallish oblong winter squash that is being planted by a growing number of farmers. If you can't find delicata, don't panic—an acorn squash will work just as well, and actually, I probably use acorn squash more for this recipe anyway. This is an extremely good dish to have around the holidays because it will satisfy a vegetarian's taste for the season but is also popular with meat eaters.

2 tablespoons unsalted butter, divided

2 delicata squash or 1 medium acorn squash, sliced in half, seeded, and cut into 24 wedges

Kosher salt and freshly ground black pepper

6 tablespoons pomegranate juice

2 tablespoons balsamic vinegar

1 tablespoon red wine vinegar

7–8 tablespoons fruity extra-virgin olive oil

½ cup pine nuts, toasted

Pomegranate seeds (optional)

1 Melt 2 teaspoons of the butter in a large sauté pan over medium-high heat. When the butter foams, add about 8 of the squash wedges. Cook until slightly browned on both sides, 7–8 minutes. Remove the squash wedges to a rimmed baking sheet. Repeat with the remaining butter and squash. Sprinkle the squash with a generous pinch or two of salt and several grindings of pepper. The squash may sit at this point for up to 6 hours at room temperature before cooking.

2 Preheat your oven to 450 degrees.

3 Bake the squash for about 20 minutes until tender.

4 Whisk together the pomegranate juice and vinegars in a small bowl. Slowly whisk in the olive oil. Season with salt and pepper.

5 Place the squash in a large bowl. Rewhisk the dressing and pour over the squash. Toss until each squash wedge is nicely coated. Sprinkle with the pine nuts and garnish with pomegranate seeds, if desired. Serve immediately or at room temperature, making sure to include a little of the dressing from the bottom of the bowl with each serving.

Parmesan-Crusted Edamame

Serves 4

Here is a soybean by another name. Fresh edamame can be treated like any of our southern peas and beans. They do well when combined with a little pork and onions, and I think they truly stand tall when very little is done to them. Here I dress them up with a good Parmesan cheese and roast them, adding depth and a salty pleasure. This recipe always surprises friends and family, and there's never any left.

2 cups edamame, thawed
   if frozen

1 cup finely grated Parmesan
   cheese

¼ teaspoon ground cayenne
   pepper

Grated zest of ½ lemon

1 Preheat your oven to 400 degrees.

2 Toss together all of the ingredients. Line a baking sheet with a Silpat, parchment paper, or nonstick foil. Spread the ingredients on the baking sheet and bake for about 15 minutes or until the cheese is browned. Serve immediately.

Fred's Favorite Green Peas

When I was a kid, "Le Sueur" was synonymous with "green peas," and they were not my favorite. Like cooked carrots, I would try to hide the peas under my knife so I could have dessert. It rarely worked. I was probably in my twenties before I ever had a fresh green pea. They've grown on me over the years, and now I look forward to the new crop each spring. This is one of my favorite ways to prepare peas. With mashed potatoes and leg of lamb with mint jelly, let the eating begin!

Serves 4

1 Heat the bacon in a large sauté pan over medium-low heat for 5–7 minutes. Add the onions and stir, scraping the bottom of the pan to get up any bacon residue. Cook the onions until they are translucent, about 3 minutes. Add the peas and stir to coat with the essence of the bacon. Cook for another couple of minutes. Increase the temperature to medium and stir in the chicken broth. Let the broth come to a simmer and then stir in the butter. Add the shredded lettuce and cook until it wilts, about 1 minute. Serve immediately, making sure a spoonful or two of the broth accompanies each serving.

3 strips bacon, cut in strips

1 cup chopped onions

16 ounces fresh or frozen baby green peas

1 cup homemade or low-sodium chicken broth

2 tablespoons unsalted butter

1 cup shredded Boston lettuce leaves

Baby Green Peas with Morels

Two of spring's gifts are little green peas and morel mushrooms. When you put the two together, you wind up with a dish that epitomizes the season.

Serves 4–6

1 Heat 2 tablespoons of the oil in a large skillet over medium heat. When the oil begins to shimmer, add the onions and reduce heat to medium low. Cook for 10–12 minutes or until the onions are tender and caramelized.

2 Add the butter, garlic, and thyme and cook for 4–5 minutes. Add the peas, stirring well.

3 Heat the remaining oil in a large sauté pan over high heat. When the oil shimmers, add the mushrooms and reduce heat to medium. Cook for 3–4 minutes.

4 Pour the mushrooms into the pea mixture. Remove the thyme and discard. Season with salt, pepper, and several squeezes of lemon juice. Serve immediately.

3 tablespoons olive oil, divided

6 ounces cipollini onions, peeled and quartered

2 tablespoons unsalted butter

3 garlic cloves, minced

5 sprigs thyme, tied

1 pound fresh or frozen tiny green peas

2 cups fresh morels

Kosher salt and freshly ground black pepper

A couple of lemon wedges

Currituck May Peas

Serves as many as you need

May peas are a big deal in Currituck, North Carolina. The humus soil and mild coastal climate create excellent growing conditions for these tender, sweet English garden peas. Residents eagerly anticipate that first crop and have a traditional way of preparing the peas. Local folk historian David Cecelski shared this recipe with me. While you may not be able to get Currituck green peas, fresh ones from anywhere work just fine. Old-fashioned cooks boil the peas and potatoes with a little ham or salt pork, which makes the dish the real centerpiece of a dinner.

Fresh May peas and very small fingerling new potatoes, in roughly equal amounts

Water

Flour or flour dumplings, if desired

1 Boil the peas and potatoes with just enough water to cover until the potatoes are tender, about 10 minutes. A few minutes before the potatoes are done, add some flour dumplings (flour, salt, and water or prepared frozen chicken pastry), if desired, and serve. The dumplings will break down enough to make a nice gravy, though many cooks prefer to add a little flour to the broth as a thickener.

Spring Ragout

One of the toughest things for any cook to remember is that when ingredients are at their peak, let their flavor shine through with simple preparation. This recipe does exactly that.

Serves 4–6

1 Melt the butter in a large sauté pan over medium heat. When the butter begins to foam, add the shallots and garlic. Cook, stirring, until the shallots are translucent. Pour in the wine and cook until just a trace of liquid remains in the pan, about 3 minutes. Pour in the chicken broth and cook for an additional 5 minutes. Add the peas, asparagus, carrots, and tarragon. Cook until the vegetables are tender but still crisp, about 5 minutes. Stir in the spinach, tossing until it wilts. Remove from heat and season with salt and pepper. Serve immediately, pouring any remaining liquid over the vegetables.

4 tablespoons unsalted butter

¼ cup finely chopped shallots

3 garlic cloves, finely chopped

½ cup dry white wine

½ cup homemade or low-sodium chicken broth

1 cup baby green peas

1 pound asparagus, trimmed and blanched for 3 minutes

10 baby carrots, blanched for 5 minutes

2 sprigs tarragon, leaves stripped and finely chopped

2 cups baby spinach

Kosher salt and freshly ground black pepper

Asparagus Frites

Serves 6–8

When asparagus are fresh and plentiful, I prepare them any way possible. These asparagus fries are a sneaky way to get asparagus haters' taste buds prepared for all manner of asparagus variations. While this is the basic recipe, feel free to add different herbs and spices to the flour. You can have Cajun frites one night and Italian the next.

2 cups all-purpose flour

3 large eggs, preferably farmstand

3 tablespoons water

2 cups panko bread crumbs

2 pounds asparagus, woody ends removed

Canola oil for frying

Kosher salt and freshly ground black pepper

A few lemon wedges

Whole-grained mustard

Malt vinegar

1 Set 3 pie plates or 8 × 8-inch baking dishes on the counter in a row. Put the flour in one, whisk together the eggs and water and pour them into the second, and put the panko crumbs in the third.

2 Coat the asparagus in the following order: toss with the flour, roll in the egg, toss with the panko. It's easiest to use one hand for the dry ingredients and one hand for the wet. Place the asparagus on a baking sheet.

3 Fill a large cast-iron skillet about ⅓ full with oil and place over medium heat. When the oil reaches 350 degrees, cook a few asparagus at a time until golden brown, about 3 minutes. Drain on a plate lined with paper towels and season with salt and pepper. Continue until all the asparagus are cooked. Serve hot with lemon wedges, mustard, and vinegar.

Asparagus Tarts

Vegetable tarts have an interesting mouth feel that asparagus seems to amplify. You will need a tart pan with a removable bottom for this recipe, but other than that, it's simple. To create a flakier pastry, chill the dough in the tart pan for at least an hour before baking.

Serves 6–8

1 Pour the flour and salt into the bowl of a food processor fitted with a metal blade. Pulse 2 or 3 times to combine. Add the butter and pulse several times until it looks like coarse meal. Add the vinegar and cold water while pulsing the dough. Add just enough water that the pastry holds together when pressed between your fingers.

2 Roll the pastry into a ball on a cutting board or countertop. Using the palm of your hand, press the dough into a circle about 6 inches in diameter. Wrap with plastic wrap and refrigerate for at least 2 hours (overnight is better).

3 Remove the dough from the refrigerator and let sit at room temperature for 10 minutes. Roll the dough into a 14-inch round. To get a nice circle, roll the dough in one direction, give it a quarter turn, roll again, and repeat until you have your crust. Lay the crust in an 11-inch tart pan and remove the excess dough. Chill for at least 1 hour.

4 Preheat your oven to 400 degrees.

5 Remove from the refrigerator and prick the pastry randomly with a fork. Cover with parchment paper or nonstick foil and weigh down with dried beans. Bake for 15 minutes. Remove the paper and beans and bake for an additional 12–14 minutes until lightly browned. Remove from the oven and cool.

6 Sprinkle the tart shell with some of the Parmesan cheese. Add the asparagus and the rest of the cheeses. Whisk together the eggs and cream in a large bowl. Add the tarragon, a generous sprinkling of salt, and several grindings of pepper. Pour this mixture over the asparagus and return to the oven. Bake for 25–30 minutes or until the egg mixture no longer jiggles and the top is golden. Cool 15 minutes before serving. Slice into 6 or 8 pieces and serve immediately, though it's also fairly good at room temperature.

2 cups all-purpose flour

1 teaspoon kosher salt

8 tablespoons chilled unsalted butter, cut into small pieces

1 teaspoon distilled white vinegar

4–6 tablespoons ice water

1½ cups grated Parmesan cheese

2 cups chopped asparagus spears, blanched for about 2 minutes

½ cup diced farmer cheese

5 large eggs, preferably farmstand

1 cup heavy cream

1 tablespoon chopped tarragon

Kosher salt and freshly ground black pepper

Fred's Simple Grilled Asparagus

Serves 4–6

Asparagus has become one of my go-to side dishes, especially this ridiculously easy recipe for grilled asparagus. I used to doctor these stalks up with balsamic vinegar, olive oil, and herbs, but when I was working on my book, *Barbecue Nation*, I had some grilled asparagus and other vegetables at a bed-and-breakfast in Asheville, North Carolina, that I thought were the most superb grilled vegetables I had ever had. When I asked what seasonings they used, their reply was one word: "Pam." I've done my asparagus like this ever since, and I honestly believe that you get more of the vegetable flavor with such simplicity.

2 bunches fresh asparagus (about 2 pounds), woody ends removed

Vegetable cooking spray

Kosher salt and freshly ground black pepper

1 Preheat your grill to high.

2 Spread the asparagus out on a rimmed baking sheet. Spray the asparagus with vegetable spray and sprinkle with 2 good pinches of salt and several grindings of pepper. Roll the asparagus around on the pan until all sides are coated.

3 Grill the asparagus in a single layer for 5–8 minutes, using a spatula to roll the asparagus, much like you would a hot dog. When they've picked up some char, they're done. Season as necessary and serve immediately or at room temperature.

"Swamp Cabbage"

Serves 8–10

In parts of Florida, hearts of palm are lovingly referred to as swamp cabbage. There's nothing cabbage tasting about them. If you live outside of Florida, your only choice may be canned or frozen hearts of palm. Luckily, I have relatives in Florida with access to the stuff, and I demand some every time they make the trip northward. This recipe you'll have to do a little by feel and sight for the number of folks you're feeding if you're not using fresh swamp cabbage. It's extremely good for a fish fry.

1 Place the bacon in a medium skillet and cook slowly over medium-low heat for 5–10 minutes until the bacon is crisp.

2 Place the cabbage, remaining ingredients, and bacon and its fat in an 8-quart stockpot. Fill the pot half full of water and place over high heat. Bring to a boil, reduce heat slightly, and continue to boil for 10–15 minutes until the cabbage is tender and flavorful. Season with salt and pepper. Serve immediately.

3 slices bacon, roughly chopped

2 heads swamp cabbage (or several cans or frozen packages), chopped

½ cup granulated sugar

2 teaspoons thyme leaves

1 tablespoon freshly ground black pepper

1 teaspoon salt

Water

Fred's Fried Apples

Serves 6

Probably one of my favorite suppers on fall and winter Sunday nights is fried apples with grits and sausage gravy. This amalgamation was introduced to me by one of my culinary mentors, Anne Haskins. The combination of those three simple ingredients develops into one of the most comforting meals that I prepare. These are not Cracker Barrel's fried apples, so if you're looking for that kind of sweetness, you probably need to look elsewhere. These apples are only sweet enough to cut and support the other ingredients. To my taste and thinking, they are much better than any restaurant version. My fried apples can also transition to a beautiful side dish with any cut of pork, especially country ham. Come January, you will thank me for this dish.

4 tablespoons unsalted butter

2 tablespoons bacon fat (optional)

8 medium Granny Smith apples, cored and chopped but not peeled

½ cup light brown sugar, packed

½ teaspoon cinnamon

1 Heat the butter in a large sauté pan or cast-iron skillet over medium heat. Just before the butter has completely melted, add the bacon fat, if desired. Stir in the apples, brown sugar, and cinnamon. Continue stirring until the apples are nicely coated and the brown sugar has dissolved, usually about 5 minutes. Continue cooking for 15–20 minutes, stirring occasionally, or until the apples are tender. Serve hot or at room temperature.

Cider-Poached Apples

I believe apples are totally overlooked as a side dish. The sweetness that can develop from an apple is a nice foil to most any savory dish. Don't skip the juniper berries or the star anise. They have a profound effect on the final result.

Serves 4–6

1 Bring all the ingredients except the apples and butter to a boil in a 3-quart saucepan over medium-high heat. Reduce heat and simmer, very slowly, for about 10 minutes, allowing the flavors to meld. Add the apples and place a plate on top of them to keep them in the liquid. Poach the apples for about 15 minutes or until the tip of a knife can be inserted easily. Remove the apples to a serving bowl.

2 Strain the poaching liquid into a 2-quart saucepan and bring to a boil over medium-high heat. Reduce this liquid until it begins to get syrupy and coats the back of a spoon. Whisk in the butter, 1 tablespoon at a time, then pour the sauce over the apples. Serve immediately.

4 cups apple cider, preferably farmstand

2 cinnamon sticks

1 vanilla bean, split and scraped

5 whole allspice

5 black peppercorns

1 star anise

5 juniper berries

Grated zest of $\frac{1}{2}$ lemon

3 Granny Smith apples, peeled, cored, and quartered

3 tablespoons unsalted butter

The Absolute Best Oyster Casserole

Serves 10–12

While some people might think an oyster casserole is a main dish (and this certainly could become one), I would not think of having a Thanksgiving or Christmas meal without an oyster casserole on the side. This recipe is an "it depends" recipe: The amount of butter that you use depends on the amount of oyster liquid that you get. You're looking for about 1½ total cups of liquid. The top of the casserole needs to be heavily peppered, since pepper is the only spice it gets. I always have to keep an eye on the oysters to make sure my daughter and sister don't get into them before I can assemble the dish. Of course, a raw oyster is not a bad thing.

1 quart plus 1 pint shucked oysters with their liquid

1 pound regular Ritz crackers

About 1 cup unsalted butter, melted

Freshly ground black pepper

1 Preheat your oven to 350 degrees.

2 Place the oysters in a colander with a bowl underneath to catch the liquid.

3 Roughly crush the crackers, leaving some large pieces. Sprinkle ⅓ of the crackers in an even layer on the bottom of a 9 × 13-inch baking dish. Layer about half the oysters over the crackers. Repeat, finishing with a layer of crackers.

4 Mix the butter and the oyster liquid to equal 1½ cups. Pour the mixture evenly over the casserole. Sprinkle the casserole with at least 1 tablespoon pepper. You want to literally be able to see the pepper.

5 Bake for 15–20 minutes or until the casserole is a little brown but still moist. Serve hot.

SAUCE ON THE SIDE

From Barbecue to Comeback

Sauces and gravies are an integral part of eating well in the South, especially at my table. Here are a handful of recipes that I use a lot, ones that I feel give you the most bang for your buck. There are several barbecue sauces that will enliven chicken, pork, and beef. Even though I grew up with a Lexington-style "dip," I routinely pull from other regions of the South to vary my grilling and barbecue experiences. A plethora of styles and flavors are represented here—from the Louisiana and Mississippi Deltas, from Memphis, from the Carolina coast, and from places in between. Sauce truly is a side dish in much of southern cooking.

Lexington-Style "Dip"

Makes about 3 cups

Vinegar is king as the base for any North Carolina barbecue sauce. In case you don't know, there's a great divide in North Carolina between Lexington-style barbecue and eastern-style barbecue. The dividing line is somewhere around Greensboro, in the heart of the state's piedmont. From Greensboro west, you find some variation of what is lovingly referred to as "dip." Here's a good starting point. This sauce is almost always used with pork and sometimes serves as the base for Lexington-Style Red Slaw (page 45). My favorite use for the sauce is as a dip for freshly fried pork skins. It's just really, really good.

2 cups apple cider vinegar

½ cup water

½ cup ketchup

2 tablespoons light brown sugar

1 tablespoon hot pepper sauce

2 teaspoons crushed red pepper flakes

2 teaspoons kosher salt

1 teaspoon freshly ground black pepper

1 In a medium bowl, whisk together all the ingredients until the sugar and salt dissolve. Use immediately or refrigerate in an airtight container for up to 6 weeks. Shake well before using.

FRANK BELL While I never had the good fortune of meeting Frank Bell, from what I hear, he was a proud, good old southern boy like most of his World War II generation. After defending this country, he returned home with a Purple Heart, five bronze stars, and one silver star. He helped start several barbecue restaurants around Lexington and became famous for his sauce.

Just a few days before Frank died of cancer, a close friend, Barry Ferguson, asked him for the recipe. It's a lot of a handful of this, and a handful of that, and shakes of this and that. Frank deviated occasionally from his tried-and-true recipe, which he called the "church women's version." The church ladies often scolded him for his drinking habits, but when they needed barbecue sauce for their Wednesday-night meetings, they went to Frank. For forty years, they never knew that Frank was spiking their dip with a right good measure of bourbon.

Left to right:
Slow-Cooked Memphis-Style Barbecue Sauce (page 307);
South Carolina Mustard-Based Barbecue Sauce (page 305);
Lexington-Style "Dip"; Eastern North Carolina Barbecue
Sauce (page 304); East Tennessee–Style Barbecue Sauce
(page 306)

Eastern North Carolina Barbecue Sauce

Makes about 3 cups

In North Carolina, you claim allegiance to either Lexington-style barbecue or barbecue from the eastern part of the state. Lexington-style 'cue uses only pork shoulders; eastern-style cooks up the whole hog. Also, there's no ketchup in eastern-style barbecue sauce. This one will make your lips pucker, but it's sooooo tasty, and I decided long ago that while I grew up on Lexington-style, eastern-style 'cue can be just fine, too.

1½ cups apple cider vinegar

1½ cups distilled white vinegar

1 tablespoon (or more) granulated sugar

1 tablespoon crushed red pepper flakes

1 tablespoon freshly ground black pepper

1 tablespoon kosher salt

1 tablespoon hot pepper sauce, preferably Texas Pete

1 Combine all the ingredients in a medium bowl. Use immediately or store in an airtight container up to 2 months at room temperature.

South Carolina Mustard-Based Barbecue Sauce

You could almost call this South Carolina Lowcountry Barbecue Sauce because it is very common from I-95 to the east and around Columbia. They like a different sauce in the piedmont and upstate areas. Many folks think mustard sauce is weird, but to me it's just another variation in the wonderful world of barbecue.

Makes about 2 cups

1 Combine all the ingredients in a medium saucepan and cook over medium heat, stirring, until the sugar dissolves. Remove from heat and let cool. Use immediately or refrigerate in an airtight container for 3–4 weeks.

1½ cups yellow mustard, like French's

½ cup light brown sugar, packed

½ cup tomato paste

5 tablespoons apple cider vinegar

1 tablespoon Worcestershire sauce

½ teaspoon cayenne pepper

½ teaspoon granulated garlic

½ teaspoon freshly ground black pepper

East Tennessee–Style Barbecue Sauce

Makes about 3½ cups

Belinda Ellis, who hails from near Knoxville, Tennessee, challenged North Carolina barbecue at a Southern Foodways Alliance meeting. I took up the challenge—mostly because it gave me a really good excuse to eat more barbecue. What I found as Belinda ushered me around East Tennessee barbecue joints was a 'cue that's very similar to Lexington-style barbecue. They do cut their meat in slightly larger chunks, but the biggest difference is that ketchup is a major part of the Tennessee sauce. It still has the characteristic Carolina vinegar bite. You heard it from this North Carolina boy's lips: This is darned good stuff. Use this sauce not only for smoked pork but also on ribs and chicken. It ain't bad on a brisket, either. You'll find lots of uses.

1 cup ketchup

1 8-ounce can tomato sauce

1 cup light brown sugar, packed

1 cup apple cider vinegar

1 tablespoon Worcestershire sauce

1 tablespoon paprika

1½ teaspoons onion salt

1 teaspoon dry mustard

1–2 teaspoons hot pepper sauce

1 Combine all the ingredients in a medium saucepan and heat over low heat, stirring until the sugar melts and everything is well blended. Let simmer about 10 minutes. Remove from heat. Use immediately or refrigerate in an airtight container for up to 2 weeks.

Slow-Cooked Memphis-Style Barbecue Sauce

I love going to Memphis, not for any of the Elvis stuff but to eat my way through the barbecue joints in the city and its environs. My friend Melissa Peterson, publisher of *Edible Memphis*, has pointed me to some great places off the beaten path. Memphis sits at the center of the barbecue universe and pulls from every region. The result is a wonderful sauce that's good on pork and ribs as well as on chicken and hamburgers.

Makes about 4 cups

1 If you have a slow-cooker, just throw all the ingredients in, mix 'em up, and cook on high for 4 hours or so. If not, combine all the ingredients except the lemon juice and Worcestershire sauce in a medium saucepan. Place over medium-high heat and bring to a boil, stirring to dissolve the sugar. Reduce heat to low and simmer for about 1½ hours, stirring occasionally. Add the lemon juice and Worcestershire sauce and cook for an additional 30 minutes. Remove from heat and let cool. Use immediately or refrigerate in an airtight container for up to 3 weeks.

24 ounces ketchup

1½ cups water

½ cup apple cider vinegar

⅓ cup light brown sugar, packed

⅓ cup granulated sugar

2 teaspoons freshly ground black pepper

2 teaspoons granulated onion

2 teaspoons dry mustard

1 tablespoon fresh lemon juice

1 tablespoon Worcestershire sauce

Jezebel Sauce

Makes a little over 1 cup

I had never heard of this stuff until I started hanging out in the Mississippi Delta, where Jezebel Sauce is a sacred thing. They use it like folks here in North Carolina use green pepper jelly—they pour it over a block of cream cheese. I tweaked a few ingredients and found a better use for the sauce. It's marvelous alongside smoked sausages of any kind or duck and quail.

1 Combine all the ingredients in a 1-quart saucepan and place over medium heat. Cook the sauce until it begins to bubble around the edges, 2–3 minutes. Remove from heat and let cool slightly. Serve immediately or refrigerate in a jar for up to 1 month.

½ cup pineapple preserves

½ cup apple jelly

⅓ cup grainy mustard

1 tablespoon prepared horseradish

Fred's Favorite Hot Dog Chili

Serves a bunch and freezes well

I gleaned this recipe from my backdoor neighbor, Linda Johnson, who got it from her dad and from Kyle's mom, combining the two into a great hot dog chili. You can change the heat quotient by adding or lowering the amount of red pepper flakes. Linda likes it spicy and uses almost a tablespoon more red pepper flakes than I do. Either way, it's great chili. And what is a hot dog without great chili?

1½ pounds freshly ground round, preferably grass-fed

1 cup chopped onions

1 16-ounce can tomato paste

1¾ cups water

1½ tablespoons granulated sugar

1 tablespoon chili powder

1 teaspoon crushed red pepper flakes

½ teaspoon dried oregano

½ teaspoon kosher salt

1 Cook the ground beef in a large skillet over medium-high heat until the meat is browned and no pink remains, about 10 minutes, breaking up the clumps as it cooks. Drain the fat and return the beef to the pan.

2 Add the remaining ingredients and stir to combine. Bring to a boil, then reduce heat to low and simmer for 1½ hours, stirring occasionally, until the mixture thickens and reaches the desired consistency. You can add more water while it's cooking if you think it's getting too dry. Serve hot or at room temperature, and freeze any leftovers.

Mississippi Comeback Sauce

With a name like Comeback Sauce, it needs to be pretty good. My first experience with Mississippi's favorite was about ten years ago, when I was researching *Barbecue Nation*. The sauce's name and origin are somewhat clouded, but the Mayflower Restaurant in Jackson, Mississippi, seems to get most of the credit. Some claim that this sauce is a lot like Thousand Island dressing, but Comeback Sauce actually has much more nuance. Southern writer Martha Foose gave me the basic components, and this recipe took shape from there. Like many southern sauces, it's excellent with all things fried, and I routinely use it as a base for deviled eggs. Want to really gild the lily? Use it for a crab, shrimp, and lobster salad.

Makes 2 cups

1 Place all the ingredients in a large bowl and stir until thoroughly combined. Cover and refrigerate for at least 1 hour. Use immediately or refrigerate in an airtight container for up to 4 days.

1 cup good-quality mayonnaise

¼ cup vegetable oil

¼ cup chili sauce, preferably Bennett's

¼ cup ketchup

1 tablespoon Worcestershire sauce

1 teaspoon yellow mustard

1 teaspoon freshly ground black pepper

1 teaspoon hot pepper sauce

¼ teaspoon smoked paprika

½ cup minced onions

2 cloves garlic, minced

1 teaspoon kosher salt

Kyle's Unbelievable Sausage Gravy

Serves 6

I think you have to be in the zone to make great sausage gravy. It takes Zen-like patience and a lot of soul. Kyle Wilkerson's sausage gravy is exceptional. One of my favorite meals on a blustery wintery Sunday night is this sausage gravy, grits, and fried apples. Not only does it stick to your ribs, but it also makes your mouth feel like dancing. So get your Zen on.

1 pound hot country sausage (Kyle likes Neese's, I like Bass, but any high-quality country sausage will work; if you can get some direct from a farmer, then jump on it)

½ cup all-purpose flour

5 cups whole milk

Freshly ground black pepper and kosher salt

1 Break up the sausage into chunks and heat in a large sauté pan or Dutch oven over medium-low heat, continuing to break up the sausage. Be patient here and let the sausage brown slightly, 10–15 minutes. Sprinkle the flour over the sausage and stir until everything is coated. Continue cooking for 3–4 minutes, stirring and scraping the bottom of the pan.

2 Slowly add the milk, a little at a time, stirring constantly. Reduce heat to low and simmer, stirring often. The gravy is done when thickened, usually 4–5 minutes. Stir in several grindings of pepper and season with salt. If the gravy gets too thick, add a little more milk or water. Use on whatever your heart desires. You can refrigerate the gravy and reheat it slowly with a little additional water or milk.

Kyle's Unbelievable Sausage Gravy and Good Fried Green Tomatoes (page 77)

Fred's Classic French Mignonette, and a Variation or Two

Makes about ½ cup

I love oysters and grew up eating them with your basic saltine cracker and cocktail sauce. But the first time I poured a little mignonette over a raw oyster, I was hooked. It's a match made in heaven, with the acidity of the vinegar combining brightly with the brininess of the oyster. I'm including the classic recipe and two variations. One uses tarragon as its base: The herb's slightly anise taste increases the oysters' flavor profile. The final version is based on the Pacific Rim–style flavors you find at San Francisco's Hog Island Oyster Company. I usually make all three variations as well as cocktail sauce when having folks over for fresh oysters either on the half shell or roasted.

½ cup red wine vinegar

2 tablespoons minced shallots

2 teaspoons freshly cracked black pepper

⅛ teaspoon finely chopped thyme

Fresh lemon juice

1 Combine all the ingredients except the lemon juice in a non-reactive bowl. Season with lemon juice. Serve immediately or refrigerate in an airtight container for up to 3 days.

TARRAGON VARIATION Substitute tarragon vinegar for the red wine vinegar and chopped tarragon for the thyme.

PACIFIC RIM–STYLE VARIATION Substitute seasoned rice wine vinegar for the red wine vinegar and a tablespoon of finely chopped cilantro for the thyme. Stir in 1 teaspoon of sugar and a pinch of kosher salt. This variation will only keep for about 1 day.

Fred's Take on What Tartar Sauce Should Be

In my opinion, tartar sauce should be made with quality ingredients but not a heck of a lot of them. A good tartar sauce is a simple thing. It enhances something fried. As a southerner, I have always preferred the taste of a tartar sauce made with sweet pickles. If you're from another part of the country—say, the Northeast or the Midwest—just change the pickle to a chopped dill and the sauce will remind you of home. If you need to get fancy, use red onions instead of yellow ones and cornichons instead of pickles. A few chopped capers will round out your upscale sauce. I use tartar sauce primarily with fried seafood, but it also works with a basket of hushpuppies, and some folks love this sauce with french fries.

Makes about 1½ cups

1 Mix all the ingredients together in a medium bowl. Cover and chill for at least 1 hour. Serve immediately or refrigerate in an airtight container for up to 3 weeks.

1 cup good-quality mayonnaise

½ cup sweet pickles or dill pickles, finely chopped

¼ cup minced onions

2 tablespoons chopped parsley

1 tablespoon sweet or dill pickle juice

A Riff on Rémoulade

Makes about 2½ cups

If you're in New Orleans and eating seafood, rémoulade is bound to be close by. I personally don't think the folks in New Orleans should have all the fun. This sauce is a little brighter than most rémoulades and works well with almost any shellfish, but it's extremely good with pan-fried fish. If you're making the Fried Eggplant with "Étouffée" Sauce (page 83), this sauce goes great with it. This rémoulade is also good for dipping hushpuppies and french fries.

1 cup good-quality mayonnaise

6 tablespoons minced celery

6 tablespoons minced green onions, white and green parts

3 tablespoons finely chopped Italian parsley

3 tablespoons ketchup

3 tablespoons prepared horseradish, drained

2 tablespoons coarse-grained mustard

2 tablespoons Worcestershire sauce

1 tablespoon chopped capers, drained

1 teaspoon minced garlic

1 teaspoon hot pepper sauce

1 teaspoon paprika (smoked paprika works well)

1 teaspoon finely minced anchovy

½ teaspoon kosher salt

1 In a large bowl, mix together all the ingredients. Cover and chill for several hours. Serve immediately or refrigerate in an airtight container for 3–4 days.

Oh-So-French Sauce Gribiche

Sauce gribiche is an old-style French classic based on hard-boiled eggs. The flavor of this sauce improves if you make it a day ahead. It's incredible with poached salmon, but it's also fabulous with Fred's Simple Grilled Asparagus (page 296) and even atop fresh sliced tomatoes. Make it once, and you'll make it many times and find many uses for this complex sauce.

Makes about 2 cups

1 Combine all the ingredients in a large bowl. Cover and refrigerate for at least 3 hours, overnight is better. Serve immediately or refrigerate in an airtight container for 3–4 days.

1 cup good-quality mayonnaise

3 large hard-boiled eggs, finely chopped

Juice of ½ lemon

1 tablespoon capers, rinsed and drained

1 tablespoon chopped cornichons

2 tablespoons chopped shallots, placed in a strainer and rinsed with cold water

1 tablespoon chopped parsley

2 teaspoons chopped chives

1 teaspoon chopped dill

1 teaspoon Dijon mustard

Blanche's Special Sauce

Makes about 1½ cups

Blanche Brown was a hostess at the Dibble Tobacco Company's entertainment cottage at the north end of Myrtle Beach, South Carolina. The beautiful oceanfront house served many a meal—and many a cocktail—to visitors from around the world. Blanche has passed on, and the cottage has been sold, but the memories of her cooking still abound. She greatly influenced me, especially my cooking of things from the sea. She used this sauce on asparagus, salads, boiled eggs, shrimp, and oysters. I use it as a quick down-and-dirty Louis sauce with jumbo lump crabmeat.

1 cup good-quality
    mayonnaise

½ cup chili sauce, preferably
    Bennett's (if not
    using Bennett's, add
    1 tablespoon of finely
    chopped sweet pickle)

2 tablespoons prepared
    horseradish, drained

1 Combine all the ingredients in a large bowl. Cover and chill for at least 1 hour. Serve immediately or refrigerate in an airtight container for 4–5 days.

NOTE To make Oysters Blanche, preheat your oven to 400 degrees. Shuck 24 oysters and reserve the liquid and the bottom shells. Heat the oysters with the liquid, ⅓ cup dry white wine, and 1 tablespoon of butter in a sauté pan over medium heat. Poach the oysters until they just curl at the edges, about 3 minutes. Don't overcook them because they still have to be baked. Place 1 oyster in each reserved shell and place the shells on a rimmed baking sheet. Place a dollop of Blanche's sauce on each oyster. Sprinkle with grated Swiss cheese. Bake until golden brown, 4–5 minutes. Serve immediately.

"Étouffée" Sauce

This sauce is absolutely the best in Fried Eggplant with "Étouffée" Sauce (page 83), but it is too good for just one recipe. Don't hesitate to use this sauce to smother fish, shellfish, or pork chops.

Makes about 4 cups

1 Melt 6 tablespoons of the butter in a 3-quart saucepan. When the butter is foaming, whisk in the flour. Cook for 3–4 minutes, longer if you prefer a nuttier flavor.

2 Melt the remaining butter in a large sauté pan over medium heat and add all of the vegetables. Stir in the creole spice and cook over medium heat until the vegetables are caramelized, about 10 minutes. Pour the veggies into the butter-flour mixture. Increase heat to medium high and slowly add the chicken broth, stirring constantly to keep the mixture from becoming lumpy. Bring to a boil, reduce heat, and simmer for 10–15 minutes or until the sauce has thickened. Season with salt, pepper, and lemon juice as necessary. Serve immediately or refrigerate in an airtight container for up to 1 week.

8 tablespoons unsalted butter or bacon fat, divided

6 tablespoons all-purpose flour

1 cup diced onions

3 celery stalks, cut into small dice

2 carrots, peeled and cut into small dice

4 garlic cloves, finely chopped

¾ cup roasted red bell peppers, finely chopped

6 green onions, thinly sliced

3 tablespoons creole spice blend

3 cups homemade or low-sodium chicken broth

Kosher salt and freshly ground black pepper

A few lemon wedges

Potato @#$%*

Makes enough for about
4 potatoes

This is a wonderful topping for baked potatoes, giving them a warm sweetness that you don't get with just butter and sour cream. It's also good on boiled potatoes and awesome when stirred into mashed potatoes.

4 tablespoons unsalted butter

1 cup chopped onions

½ cup sour cream

Kosher salt and freshly ground black pepper

¼ cup chopped chives

1 Melt the butter in a medium sauté pan over medium heat. Add the onions and cook slowly until they begin to take on some color, 10–15 minutes. You can wait here until the potatoes are done.

2 Reduce heat to low and whisk in the sour cream. Season with salt and pepper. Stir in the chives. Remove from heat and spoon over the baked potatoes.

Graduation Brunch

Your favorite sausage and egg casserole

Michael Rider's Asparagus Salad

Fred's Pickled Shrimp

Breakfast Potato Cakes

Mother's Day

Grilled salmon

Southern Green Rice

Haricots Verts with Chive Blossom Dressing

Pretzel Salad

Cheese Garlic Biscuits

Memorial Day

Hamburgers with your favorite condiments

Southern-Fried Onion Rings

Mama's Baked Bean Casserole

Sweet and Crunchy Broccoli Salad

Great Grilling

Grilled T-bone steaks

Portabella "Pizzas" (for appetizers with drinks)

Creamed Spinach and Pearl Onions

Duck-Fat Home Fries

Grilled Romaine

Fourth of July Blowout

Hot dogs for the kids with Fred's Favorite
    Hot Dog Chili

Barbecued chicken

Linda's Macaroni and Cheese

Rachael Thomas's Deviled Eggs

Tomatoes with Simple Balsamic Vinaigrette

Grilled Corn on the Cob with Avocado Butter

Fish, Fish Everywhere

Fried flounder, shrimp, and scallops

Mom's North Carolina Fish House Slaw

Fred's French Fries

North Carolina–Style Hushpuppies

or

Grilled mahimahi and shrimp kabobs

Summer Bean Ragout

Cheese Garlic Biscuits

Grits Soufflé

Bringing Summer to a Close

Honest bone-in barbecued chicken

Beach Bourbon slush

Butterbean Hummus

Shrimp Ball

Sun Gold Pasta Salad

Virginia Bagby's Tomato Pie

Grilled Corn on the Cob with Avocado Butter

Fred's Southern-Fried Okra

Creating Your Own Pork Palace

Smoked pork shoulder

Classic baby back ribs

Lexington-Style "Dip"

Jean's Potato Salad

Benne Seed Collards with Hot Chili Vinegar

Lexington-Style Red Slaw

Fred's Famous Baked Beans

Fancy Cornbread or Cornbread for Yankees

Belinda's Sweet Potato Biscuits

Tailgating 101

Sunday fried chicken

"I Wasn't Cute Enough" Baked Beans

Mediterranean-Influenced Potato Salad

Oven-Roasted Sunchokes with Warm Bacon
    Vinaigrette

Nick's Stewed Tomatoes

Seared Green Bean Salad

Thanksgiving

A glorious turkey

Fred's Pickled Shrimp

Sweet Potato Guacamole

Cornbread, Apple, and Sausage Dressing

Twice-Baked Sweet Potatoes with Sage,
    Sorghum, and Black Walnuts

Cranberry Conserve

Oven-Roasted Broccoli with Black Truffle Oil

Haricots Verts with Balsamic Onions

Any biscuit or cornbread recipe

A Winter Solstice Cocktail Party

White cosmopolitans and Manhattans

Sweet Potato Guacamole

Lighter-Than-Air Cheese Straws

Au Courant Kale Chips

Apple-Walnut Pâté

Shrimp Ball

Oysters with Pancetta and Garlic Butter

Christmas Day

Cranberry martinis

Oysters on the half shell

Standing rib roast

Mashed Potatoes with Caramelized Onions
    and Fennel

Turnip, Collard, and Leek Gratin with
    Blue Cheese Topping

Frisée Salad with Roasted Shallot and
    Bacon Vinaigrette

Fred's Favorite Brussels Sprouts

Ambrosia

Flaky Butter Biscuits

New Year's Eve Midnight Breakfast

Fred's Fried Apples

Fred's Basic Cheese Grits

Kyle's Unbelievable Sausage Gravy

True Southern Biscuits

Happy New Year

Hog jowl or ham

Good Luck Black-Eyes or The Original
   Hoppin' John

Southern Greens with Hot Bacon Vinaigrette or
   Mama's Collards, with One of My Twists

Broccoli and Ricotta Cornbread

Mashed Turnips and Sweet Potatoes

Easter

Leg of lamb

Sour Cream and Horseradish Red Potatoes

Fred's Favorite Green Peas

Asparagus Frites

Mrs. Haskins's Grapefruit Salad

Lentil "Risotto"

It's Warm Enough for a Deck Party

Wine spritzers

Grilled smoked whole chicken

Sharon's Awesome Artichoke Dip

Fred's Opinion on Pimento Cheese

Grilled Sweet Potato Salad with Orange
   Dressing

Fred's Basic Cheese Grits

Southern Panzanella

Index